Paradise Lost or Gained?
The Literature of Hispanic Exile

Edited by Fernando Alegría
and Jorge Ruffinelli

Arte Publico Press
Houston
Texas
1990

This volume is made possible through a grant from the National Endowment for the Arts, a federal agency.

Arte Publico Press
University of Houston
Houston, Texas 77204-2090

Cover design by Mark Piñón
Original painting by Luis Cruz Azaceta:
"The Journey," Copyright © 1986

Paradise lost or gained: the literature of Hispanic exile / edited by Fernando Alegría and Jorge Ruffinelli.
      p.   cm.
    ISBN 1-55885-024-4
    1. American literature—Hispanic American authors. 2. Spanish American literature—Exiled authors—Translations into English. 3. Hispanic Americans—Literary collections. I. Alegría, Fernando, 1918– . II. Ruffinelli, Jorge.
PS508.H57P37 1991
860'.8–dc20
                                 91-11258

                                         CIP

The paper used in this publication meets the minimum requirements of the American National Standard for Permanence of Paper for Printed Library Materials Z39.48-1984. ∞

Contents

Criticism

Art

Contributors

Cover: Luis Cruz Azaceta, *The Journey*

(1986: acrylic on canvas, 124" × 132")
Color separations courtesy of
Frumkin/Adams Gallery

Ismael Frigerio

The works of Chilean artist Ismael Frigerio present an aesthetic text which transfigures the historical and personal. Through the visual narrative Frigerio pursues images of a shared identity and experience among Latin Americans. In confronting the cultural amnesia of colonization, the artist deconstructs the Latin American myth to reveal genocide, acute violence and extreme suffering in his fragmented narrative.

Emblems such as the boat, the serpent and the torso are located in the context of a recollected vision. The retelling of historic events becomes a painful remembering of a truth forgotten. Yet Frigerio's is not only a collective discourse but the realities of a personal journey of the immigrant reflecting in a new setting in the United States on his past, both mythic and real. Perhaps the distance gives meaning to the need for truth in the representation of a cultural identity. The artist confronts the burden of the past with a language that sets him free.

Ismael Frigerio

Laughing Flames IV

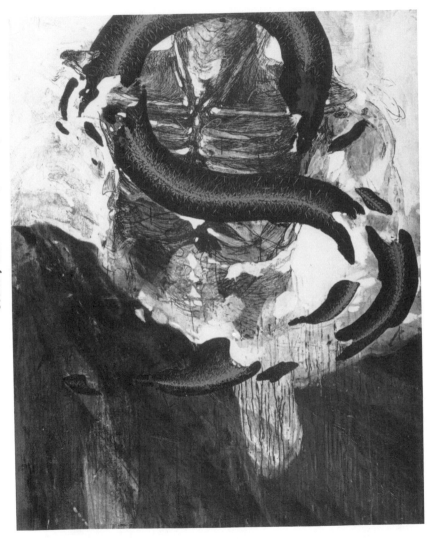

1990: mixed media on canvas, 70" × 52"

Fernando Alegría

Introduction

Ángel Rama:
When Jose Martí appealed to the fishermen and laborers of Tampa for their indispensable support for the cause of Cuban independence, he set up a model of the cooperative effort linking intellectuals and emigrants devoted to a common cultural and political cause which has benefitted from the survival of the national culture abroad as well as from the experience of a non-colonial way of life that is more democratic than that of the homeland. Thus, a process of subtle transculturation has been characteristic not only of the diaspora in general but of the experience of the individual intellectual, subjected to the same unsettling social experiences and abrupt changes as the Mexican day laborer living on the outskirts of Los Angeles, the Colombian peasant settled in Maracaibo or Caracas and the Paraguayan in Buenos Aires.

Julio Cortázar:
I will refer once again to my own personal experience: if my own physical exile is in no way comparable to that of other writers expelled from their countries in recent years, since I left of my own free will and adjusted my life to new realities over the span of more than two decades, my recent cultural exile, on the other hand, which with a single stroke destroyed the bridge uniting me with my fellow countrymen as readers and critics of my books—a bitter blow for one who has always written as an Argentine and loved all that is Argentine—was not for me an altogether negative trauma. I bounced back from the blow with the feeling that the time had come, that the die was cast, and that now it had to be a fight to the finish. The mere thought of the alienating and impoverishing effect which this cultural exile would have upon thousands and thousands of readers who are my fellow countrymen, as well as upon so many other writers whose works are banned in the country, was enough to cause a positive reaction in me, to send me to my typewriter to get on with my work in support of all the intelligent forms of combat. And if those who have closed off my cultural access to my country

think they have thus made my exile complete, they are thoroughly mistaken. They have given me a full-time fellowship, one which will allow me to devote myself more than ever to my work, since my response to this cultural fascism is and always will be to redouble my efforts alongside those who fight for the freedom of my country. Needless to say, I will not thank them for a fellowship of this kind, but I will take full advantage of it and turn the negative value of exile into a positive value with which to fight.

Augusto Roa Bastos:
In ancient times, when the leaders of a community decided to allow an exile to return, they sent him a necklace made of flint, wood or feathers. Thus, in the archaic, mythographic language, 'ring' and 'return' were synonymous. The ring became the sign of the outcast's spiritual perfection, an emblem of hierarchical dignity on a par with that of the chief or shaman. In a strict 'prelogical' logic, this act was in keeping with the principles of good government in the cultural economy of the group.

The exile brought new knowledge back with him. On the soles of his feet he brought the dust of unknown lands; in his eyes, visions of other skies; his double body—in its invisible and visible aspects— and his triple soul bore wisdom acquired through the suffering of 'having wandered for an eternity through the limbo of the dead.' Banishment, then, was perceived as a kind of death, and return as a resurrection. Today, in some of our indigenous communities this ancestral rite is still practiced. A ring of feathers of migratory birds will unite the two universes of life and death, presence and absence, bestowing upon the returning outcast the aura of the wise and just man.

In Paraguay, however, a mestizo *country par excellence—whose aboriginal language, the true popular and national language of Paraguayans predominates as in no other American country—the ring would have to be synonymous with the impossibility of return. In the symbolic language of the Paraguayan exile, the ring could only be the sign of condemnation without cause, of a vile and vilifying punishment: he will wear it throughout his life like a hangman's noose, and the stigma will reach his descendants, born in ostracism and condemned, moreover, to statelessness. For he who believes he has two countries has none.*

Fernando Alegría:
When I left my homeland on September 23, 1973, there was no time to go out on the balcony and look at the white mountain range,

the dovelike image of the Virgin on the San Cristóbal Hill, the dusty treetops of the Parque Forestal; to sigh and silently wonder what fate held in store for me. One had to leave quickly, quietly, without looking back, wrapped in a scarf, if possible without showing one's face.

So I did what everybody does: I told my story, using the minor keys and matter-of-fact tone of a man who, having survived an earthquake, sips his drink, neither complaining nor protesting very much, just talking. The first months of numbness, pain and depression passed. I realized that a new phase of exile was beginning, that from now on there would be other periods, all different, each with its own anxieties, all shattering and overwhelming, and that I would be changing too, passing from one crisis to the next until I reached the moment of truth, unique and definitive—the day on which I would either stop being an exile and return home, or unavoidable, with sadness and resignation, become an immigrant.

It seems to me that only an exile who intends to return has a true exile's consciousness. There is no exile without the intention to go back. For this reason, those who feel most keenly the uprootedness of exile are the workers who will never 'adapt' to their situation, who will live for years, perhaps all their lives, with their bags packed, awaiting the moment of return.

The moment of truth seems to have arrived. What is our writer to do when the emotional charge of the defeat doesn't work any more and diatribe no longer finds an echo? Learn the lesson? We will not forget it: making our individual, parochial voices heard and understood in exile always means suppressing sentimentality, editing out the easy lament and beginning to speak firmly. Hemingway tells in the memoirs of exile of his lost generation that when he didn't know how to start the daily routine of his task as a writer, lacking words but full of some formless feeling that needed expression, he would write 'one true sentence' and after the rest would flow like a river. One true sentence. Yes. Never a filler, nor a rhetorical flourish, no matter how successful they might be with our friends: simply a sentence that plainly tells the situation that at this moment keeps us going, or not; the recognition of our distance as well as of the solidarity that renews us at each step; the memory of some defeat that is becoming blurred; and the vision of a morning, not far off, that will surprise us at the day's task finally writing something else, something true, for example: 'the return has begun' or 'the dictatorship has fallen'.[1]

Introduction

There are many reasons to characterize this collection of writings on the experience of exile of Hispanic peoples as unique, even memorable. The most obvious: it represents the course of a dramatic history which has unfolded throughout the 20th century, concerning not only Latin America but Spain as well. It leaves a mark on our epoch, a shadow and a light on events that have registered heroes and martyrs, tyrants and henchmen. It unites Hispanic peoples across borders, from the tragic Spain of the Civil War to the "dirty wars" of Central and South America. It indirectly involves our Portuguese-speaking brothers and sisters, for in the legendary heart of holy wars, of marches and countermarches and apocalyptic destruction, an allusion to a common political destiny can be detected.

This is a chronicle of exile which does not always result from war, but often from the journeying of races and nationalities, a fleeing which protects the future of a language or the inheritance of a culture before the massive attack of multinational technocracies.

Where have voices been gathered before that tell of the pilgrimage of a Puerto Rican to the alienated heart of Manhattan, or testimonies bearing witness to the landings of rafts and life-jackets on the disaffected shores of Miami? Salvadoreans, Colombians, Peruvians, Chileans, Argentines, Paraguayans, all give testimony in these pages which seem to echo the voices of Darío and Martí on the threshold of Manifest Destiny. Yet there are no proclamations or denunciations in this volume, but instead voices of nostalgic reflection, of evocations and secret wishes, visions of return and the anticipation of a fate discerned in the noise of battle as well as in the joy of solidarity.

These voices, which narrate, or remember, or invent so as to grieve and dream, are no longer those of soloists but of a vast choir which resounds through the years searching for the mysterious signs of a great lost highway.

Perhaps the biggest surprise in these narrations from the diaspora of exile is provided by the narrator's point of view. In general, the dramas are underscored by a carnival-like tone, proving once again that the shortest line between victim and victimizer in times of tyranny is, and will continue to be, a sense of humor. What dictatorship can withstand satire and the belly laugh that suddenly rock its pedestal of ashes? Throughout the century these stories have left high-flying streaks of epic-comedy: *Reasons of State, The Autumn of the Patriarch, The Novel of Peron*, are classical examples.

It is no surprising, then, to notice in this anthology the continuation of the sharp and penetrating mode of expression which is found in stories like "Garage-Sale People," "Tres Dolores Distintos y Un Sólo Amor No Más," "South," "Steppes." To the staccato of these soliloquies, contrast the muted tone of nostalgia in "El Regreso." These are the counterpoints of exile: a polyphony of voices that in the vastness of their wanderings never stop "making roads," as Antonio Machado says in his memorable poem.

On the other hand, the poetry of exile appears tentative, like the look of a distracted or worried traveler who cannot focus with precision, and attempts with turmoil and uncertainty to construct definitions of absence through likenesses that don't always match. The nostalgia of exile feeds on an incongruously ecstatic vision of metaphors and images which do not propose to hit the mark, and which, in their flight, leave a wake of emotion with a trace of Cesar Vallejo's exclamations of despair. These are the writings of young women who suddenly see the faces of their mothers as they look at their daughters of exile. Evoking Gabriela Mistral, someone speaks of "strangeries," of landing on beaches which have lost their islands, of arrival in towns long time disappeared, of finding relatives stretched out in fields between wooden crosses and sad little paper flags.

This is a type of poetry that seeks its levels by enumerations; catalogues of things invented by the train of exile as it traverses the plains we see and feel, but do not recognize. "I Miss Spain" is an anguished hymn which has continued to echo from mountain to mountain. Yet what we find in this collection is rather the smoke that spells out messages from the peaks and the gorges; the sound of drums whose alphabet is lost in the wind of the *cordilleras*.

The essays, in turn, weave other kinds of discourse on the same loom of memory, absence, identity and reencounter. As in all large families, these essays are not equals, but rather they have a common air, a resemblance to one another that relates them. Exile is lived and transcribed in stories and poems; a moment comes, however, when one must assume a reflective and intellectual distance with regard to the experiences one has lived. It is a matter of extracting stories in other modes of the discourse.

An interesting aspect of these essays is the remarkable coincidences which they exhibit despite their differences of style. We are not referring here to their obvious thematic commonality, the fact that "exile" is always at their core.

A number of essays attempt to reconstruct a life experience; they are more documentary than pieces of erudition and criticism.

They coincide, thus, in their narration of the return from the return. To explain: one of the most traumatic experiences which an exile undergoes is the "return" to the native land. After years of longing, bags constantly packed, without ever having a place to call home, the dream one day comes true. But later, when this experience is finally written down, it is because the exile has gone back once again to the land of exile. These testimonies which enrich our psychological perspectives on the question of emigration are only half the truth. The other half has not yet been written: its expression awaits those who will return for good.

There are other significant correspondences. There is the insistence, for example, on the *transformations* resulting from exile—individual changes and collective changes. In one of the epigraphs to this introduction, Angel Rama refers to the "process of subtle transculturation" characteristic of the diaspora. As painful as it is, exile has in its favor the phenomenon of the encounter between different cultures, and the opportunity for fertile interchanges. In another epigraph, Julio Cortazar speaks of the need to "turn the negative value of exile into a positive value with which to fight." Survival, therefore, not only depends on these transformations; it impels their acceptance.

Some of the essays gathered here are themselves examples of the process of change. Others are studies of different sorts of transformations. That of the disguise, for instance: the identity assumed by the filmmaker Miguel Littin, when he clandestinely enters Chile. It is he, but for reasons of security he cannot be himself. This disguise is a metaphor for a more profound change: without a doubt, the Littin before the coup is not the same as the one who returns after it.

Another transformation is what we see in the characters of Donoso; when they return, their values, even their moral fabric, have changed. There is yet another, very basic one for many exiles. It consists in the not being able "to go home," even if they do so physically. As on many other occasions, the poetry of Neruda is apt here: "We, who were then, are no longer the same."

Whether one studies literary texts, or takes on the discourse in first person to relate one's own experience, what these narrations underscore are human situations. And every situation can be told dramatically, lyrically, or satirically, even if pain unquestionably predominates, that "permanent pain" which is mentioned in one of the pieces.

In these essays we read of imaginary panoramas and cultural Meccas—Paris, for example, which for several generations was the

"Latin American intellectual's object of desire." Allusion is made to the "secret homelands" which all exiles carry within them; to constant insecurity, that feeling of not belonging fully anywhere.

Sometimes it is a matter of massive migrations, occurring slowly over the course of a century, and at other times of sudden exile resulting from the coup d'etats and political repression. But always, in every instance, what is spoken of are jarrings of the soul. Upheavals of cultural identity. Countries as neighborhoods, neighborhoods as countries, in the big cities of an empire like New York or Los Angeles. Destroying, strengthening, or rebuilding the values of the individual, the family and the community. A hopeful search for a new space and a new time.

Exile no longer has borders. It has become part of a century which closes the gates and throws away the key: time forgets as it becomes absorbed in spinning out its crossroads.

[1]In "Literature and Exile," *Review* 30 (September 1981, New York): 10–23, translations by Pamela Pye, John Incledon, Peter Egelston, and Kathleen McNerney.

Guillermo A. Reyes

Patroklos

On opening night, after three hours and ten minutes of a transvestite version of *Anna Karenina*, the house went dark. It left the audience in that brief suspenseful moment typical of unsuccessful plays in which the playgoers awaken and wonder if the performance is indeed over.

A sigh of relief arose from the weary crowd of thirty-five as the lights came up. The actors rushed out one at a time to take their bows, grinning and furrowing their faces with an expression resembling a plea for love. None was forthcoming. The applause was a gesture of politeness, with an occasional yelp which sounded lascivious and rehearsed and suggested that somebody in the audience was on intimate terms with one of the actors and would have applauded anything.

The house lights went up and the patrons reached out for their coats. A few of them, men who wore furs and makeup, remained to demand their money back. "Where's Susana del Fuego?" they wanted to know. Some of them were dressed as Susana herself—not in the slick 50s waitress uniform she wore in a television series, but as the behind-the-scenes Susana who was always bedecked in startling classic evening wear that inspired certain types of men to emulation. "We want Susana!" the men shouted, stomping their heels on the termite-ridden floor of the lobby.

Backstage, a torrent of champagne gushed out of one or two bottles. The post-play party was comprised of the actors, director, playwright, designer, stage hands and box-office people, a crowd limited in numbers by the fact that one of the actors, director, playwright, designer, stage hand and box-office person was all one and the same man, and also the producer, Mr. Patroklos E.

When the vocal patrons started to demand their money back, Patroklos went out with the stems of champagne glasses stuck between his fingers and greeted them with utmost charm. "Girls," he said to the group of temperamental men who did remind him of his friend Susana. "If I know Ms. del Fuego," he said, "she'll show up any time now in very bad shape. Get your cameras ready, pad those shoulders and those tits, and have some champagne, you

16

silly cows!" The men reached out to grab their champagne glasses and let the lively little man serve them faithfully.

Patroklos. Patroklos E. This was in fact the name of the balding Chilean-born gentleman of British descent whose parents had been renowned classical scholars in his native Santiago. Now a Los Angeles resident, Patroklos could be described as a Chilean immigrant of Anglo blood with a funny classic Greek name who spoke English as a second language with an accent that made him, in American eyes, Hispanic. In some circles, he was also known not just as an immigrant but an exile, and in others, not just as a man but a gay man. He functioned as all of these things, and functioned always in a debonair fashion. The rumor went that the cracks in the foundation of the Patroklos Theater were padded with champagne bottles.

The theater was a thirty-five room space in a Hollywood locale that had once been a shoe repair shop. Patroklos Productions had moved in after the death of the Armenian owner whose widow donated hundreds of used shoes to the theater. As a result, the actors in Patroklos' low-budget productions were never lacking a rich variety of foot wear.

Recently, a new owner had bought out the building which included donut shops, hard-rock leather wear, Guatemalan and Tunisian fast-food as well as Patroklos Productions. Fire codes were brought up to a legal level, the building was repainted to a Santa Fe orange glow, a handsome logo was built ("Mid-Hollywood Mini-Mall," it read which made Patroklos joke that he'd become a "minimalist"); and the rent was tripled, with no discount for the arts. At around this same time, Actors' Equity of Los Angeles revamped its Equity-Waiver contracts which had allowed small theaters to put on plays without paying actors. A minimal stipend for actors was now required. This meant that Patroklos couldn't afford to pay himself to act in his own plays.

A fundraiser was announced to take place the same evening Patroklos Productions would premiere Edwards' all-male version of *Anna Karenina*. He played Anna's lover, Count Vronsky, while the role of Anna Karenina went to a retired Russian male ballet dancer who called himself these days Masha Vindictia and who performed exclusively female roles. The special guest that night was scheduled to be the well-known actress, Susana del Fuego, also known as Susanne Richards who had once been a runner-up for Miss Kansas. Ms. del Fuego collaborated for years on Edwards' satires such as "Lawless Lesbians" and "Mrs. Pinochet in Man's Clothing." She then made a successful transition to network television where she landed a role as a regular in the long-running series, "Those Darn Waitresses."

There were various rumors about Ms. del Fuego and Patroklos regarding a romantic liaison that transpired when he'd first arrived in Los Angeles as an exile from the Pinochet regime in the mid-70s. He had been the star of a tawdry radio soap opera and felt very much at home in Hollywood where his accent, however, was his first problem. Susana taught him English with a mid-western drawl, and worked side by side with him for five years establishing Patroklos Productions. The plays failed to attract attention for him, but Susana was promptly rewarded with agent and television contracts. Then came the breakup which took place without any public announcement or even a hint of a dramatic confrontation. Susana married a television producer. None of her former friends, none of the drag queens, and certainly not Patroklos, were invited to the well-publicized nuptials.

But friends do forgive and come together in times of need. That at least is the ideal, and one of Patroklos' hopes. After the financial woes of Patroklos Productions were publicized by the small press, Patroklos received a letter in Susana del Fuego calligraphy. Susana was volunteering her services for a fundraiser. Patroklos promptly announced an opening night show boasting the presence of its prominent ex-star, Susana del Fuego, who would be returning to the theater where she first made her mark in the entertainment industry.

Meanwhile, events in Patroklos' native country became news on American front pages and made it difficult for Patroklos to shield himself from them. General Augusto Pinochet organized a referendum on his rule, expecting to win a simple yes/no vote. Chileans voted against the dictator, and Pinochet was obliged to schedule presidential elections open to all legal political parties. By then thousands of exiles had gone back to Chile to play a role in these elections.

During rehearsals for *Anna Karenina*, Patroklos announced to his actors he had no plans to return to Chile at this point and felt it crucial for him to finish work on his drag version of Tolstoy's work. "A dictator's whims and wishes must not be allowed to intervene in the artistic process," he wrote to the L.A. press which published these comments beneath the announcements of Susana del Fuego's one-night appearance.

Rehearsals went on as scheduled. Rumors circulated about artistic disagreements between Masha, the drag queen who played Anna Karenina, and Patroklos. Masha wanted to know who was the real star of the show, himself or the much ballyhooed one-time appearance of Susana del Fuego who couldn't even pronounce the Spanish name she'd adopted. Patroklos made it clear, politely but firmly, that Susana's appearance meant much more to the theater than Masha's expert queeniness. Masha dropped the issue and concentrated on learning his lines, which he had great difficulty doing these days. Many years before, so the legend went, Masha had suffered a devastating accident at the Bolshoi Ballet in which he had allegedly flown off Nureyev's arms into the audience, breaking a leg, hitting his head on a Soviet official's medals of honor and leaving his memory impaired. "My passion, however," he said during his auditions in the L.A. theater route, "remains intact, and as sweeping as my homeland's history." Masha also claimed, however, that he truly was a woman. This complicated things because he didn't want the show advertised as a drag version of *Anna Karenina*, but as the real thing. Nothing was ever simple in non-profit theater.

On opening night, Susana didn't show up for the performance. Before the show began, Patroklos announced that the special guest had been delayed and would arrive during one of the intermissions. The show went on, and after three and one-half hours of this epic production, Susana had not shown up. After an hour of the post-play festivities, with champagne and caviar, only the more drunkenly guests were left and a few homeless had walked in to join the party.

Susana finally arrived much later, looking both drunk and pregnant, and apologetic about having missed the show.

"This theater's shrunk," she said about the tiny space in the Hollywood area with its tattered seats. The lobby was nothing more than an exit to the parking lot in front. The noise from the lively Tunisian restaurant next door tended to make dialogue inaudible. But the theater hadn't shrunk because it couldn't shrink any further.

She claimed she'd only drank a non-alcoholic beer which had made her as sick as real alcohol. She refused to admit her child was ever exposed to her favorite substances, such as smoke, drink, the blast of caffeine. Plain Susana without substances looked average and mortal. She did look radiant, however. She wore a black chiffon outfit designed to fit her pregnant shape and her face was made up to highlight her blushing fair skin which glowed. She kissed every man and woman, never discriminating towards gender. But when the time came to greet her old pal, rumored ex-lover, and associate, she pulled out an envelope. It wasn't a check. It wasn't a contribution to the theater. It was a personal gift for her Patroklos: a one-way ticket to Santiago, Chile. Silence pervaded through the room as she held the present by the tip of her fingers. Patroklos walked away looking insulted and locked himself in the dressing room. Why had she done it?, some of the queens asked her. Why had she pulled a prank like that on Patroklos, dear old Patroklos who had made it clear he wasn't planning to return to his native country at this point? Why had she chosen to humiliate him in public?

"Because I love the man," she said gleefully. She then signed an autograph on a cheese ball with her eyeliner pen and walked out to her Mercedes parked illegally in front of a water tank on Sunset Boulevard.

The production closed a few weeks later but elaborate plans were announced to the press about staging classics, multiethnic, multisexual versions of *MacBeth* and Greek tragedies translated into English from the Spanish translations published by a prominent family in Santiago.

Contributions didn't pour into the theater as expected. Government funding for the arts had suddenly become a national issue and theaters such as the Patroklos were being reviled for not being mainstream and normal. Patroklos realized that Susana del Fuego, as the only veteran of Patroklos Productions who'd moved on to a successful Hollywood career, was the only person who could singlehandedly save the theater from insolvency with a few measly thousands that couldn't have meant a thing to her. Patroklos made another effort to contact her.

Sober and further along in her pregnancy, Susana met Patroklos at Trumps in West Hollywood where she reserved an out-of-the-way table by the corner farthest from the harpist whose music repelled her. It would be the last time they'd be seen together. Patroklos would emerge from the meeting with a hefty check signed by Susana on a stylized checkbook with her picture in front and her resume on the back. What transpired that afternoon at Trumps between the small theater producer and his ex-leading lady is rumored to have gone as follows:

"I didn't appreciate the way you showed up at the party and humiliated me," said Patroklos after ordering his first round of herbal tea.

Susana lifted her long glass of mineral water, looking nauseous. She clinked her glass as if they'd been drinking cuba libres. "Petrie, my dear," she answered. "You know I want nothing more in this world than your happiness. I always did. I never meant to humiliate you in front of your friends. I am your friend. I bought you an airline ticket because I felt it would mean so much to you to be able to return to Chile and work again for everything you fought for. I know next to nothing about Chile except the fact that people are beginning to return there and rebuild their lives again, and you are one of those people. So darling, cheers! I wish I could order champagne, but I'm entering my sixth month now. Please have one for me."

This answer wasn't good enough for Patroklos E. He didn't believe her sudden concern for him and disdained her tendency to speak brightly in joyous outbreaks of useless chatter. They had barely spoken to each other for five years and there were good reasons for that. They had once proclaimed eternal hatred for each other, as theatrical people are bound to do, not simply out of artistic temperament but out of a need to express true feeling bottled up after a lifetime of artifice. Patroklos wanted to know if she could donate to the theater not a one-way ticket to Santiago, but enough money to pay rent for the next six months which would give him time to plan a profitable season. He failed to mention that he'd never had a profitable season. Susana could have called him on this one but passed on the opportunity.

"But what about Chile?" she asked eagerly, pronouncing the country's name with guarded attention as "Chee-lay." He wouldn't answer her questions about returning to his native country, at least not until his third tea (at about this point he was on his second.) He went on about the theater instead.

"We're celebrating our tenth year of Patroklos Productions in a couple of months," he said. "I would like to be able to announce the solvency of the theater, and since you have a weakness for causes, I think this is right up your alley."

"I would love to donate to the arts," she said. "The Chilean arts, of course. You were a popular radio star back in Santiago, and I don't see why you'd want to remain in Los Angeles, where frankly you're not a luminary among luminaries."

"My standing in the community is about the last thing you, Susana del Fuego, could ever possibly care about." He was spreading caviar onto a wheat cracker with the flair of someone pretending to afford it. The waiter looked impressed and gave him an admiringly condescending look as he whisked by. "There's more callousness in you than meets the eye. I know you too well. The first time I came home with beer breath you sent me a death threat signed by the Chilean secret police. And you probably thought that was funny."

Susana refused to comment on that episode.

"I always admired you, Patroklos, as an artist, and I think getting rid of that little theater is the best thing you can do. The owner wants to build a large mall eventually and he's not exactly looking forward to renewing your lease forever. Theater in Hollywood won't survive redevelopment."

"It will survive if people in the industry would just contribute a lot more, especially when they got their start there."

"Well, you were always stubborn." She pulled out the plane ticket again. This is where the third tea drink was delivered. "You always refused to marry me because you said one day you would return to Chile. I want you to live up to that promise, or that excuse, whatever it was. If you don't, querido, I'll take it very, very personally."

"Come on, Susana, you know I gave you that excuse because I wasn't *out* to myself. I was trying to avoid a very serious issue because I just hate begin too serious about life, especially sex which is the most ridiculous thing on earth."

"You could have married me anyway. We went absurdly well together."

"Look, you got the big-time producer you wanted, and at least he's not gay."

"One of his flaws, you might say. Petrie—"

"Please don't call me that."

"If you don't return, then I'll know you were lying to me all along."

"You already know I was."

"How can a man, especially a gay man, not love an extravagant woman like me?"

"I do," he said. There was silence, but Patroklos looked more than uncomfortable. He felt very much ridiculous, his slippery fingers running through the bald spots in his greying hair. She looked inspired by his revelation. He thought her red lips, pouting as if pointing at him, looked really stupid. "I mean, you were like my kid sister, still are."

"That's the last thing I want to be, a kid sister."

"I mean a close friend."

"Why roll around the sheets with close friends when you can do that with perfect strangers, silly? Oh, Patroklos, why didn't it work? What I wanted more than anything else was your companionship. I could have hired a young stud for sex, if it came to that. You and I went well together. We had a partnership. I started to fall in love with the beauty and poverty of theater."

"Susana del Fuego, poverty is the last thing you'd bring yourself to love."

"I did say 'started to.' But look at me now. They have me playing a common waitress with the right one-liners, and my fans are illiterate. How sad it all is ... just because you refused to take me seriously as a woman. You've pushed me away into the humiliating arena of eternal fame and recession-proof prosperity. You should have the decency to be out of my life and to return to your country where you can continue doing what you did before and be more appreciated for it. I hate to see you working as some clerk in an office where people could never appreciate who you really are." This was in reference to the part-time job as a receptionist for a cat food company he held, not a well-known fact.

Patroklos sat for a while, his hands unsteady. "Susana, I can't return to Chile," he finally said.

"Of course you can, you have no one here who can even spell your name right."

"It's a Greek name, people always had trouble with it. My parents prided themselves with their esoteric knowledge. It's part of who I am ... "

"Wasn't your sister named Minerva?" cried Susana. "I wish somebody had named me after Cressida ... !"

"All right, shut up already. I can't go back, Susana. I'm no longer just an exile. I'm now a resident, not of Chile but of Los Angeles."

"It's a smelly city due for an earthquake soon."

"Exactly. Besides, I wasn't even a Marxist in Chile." He meant that Marxists were more directly affected by the violent military crackdown. He himself had been a middle-of-the-road Christian Democrat working for radio serials, and a closet homosexual. The only reason he'd ended up an exile was that he'd signed a letter with other fellow actors expressing their concern for a colleague who'd been arrested and tortured. He and his other friends were then arrested as well, and told there was no torture in Chile. He refused to withdraw his name from the document, and soon he was on a plane. And to think he, like many other Christian Democrats, had initially supported the military regime. He could no longer make sense of world politics, and decided that Ridiculous Theater, already a vogue in the U.S. in some circles, conveyed exactly the type of meaning for his life he'd been searching for all along. Patroklos had made the transition from hammy radio actor who delivered tears and anguish in the most melodramatic fashion possible to something of an avant-guardist in sexually indiscreet, "ridiculous" circles. He'd also come out of the closet. His Christian Democratic friends weren't impressed, and since he'd never been friends with Marxist exiles, he no longer had any contact with the small Chilean exile community in Los Angeles. "All they do is talk politics," he complained about his compatriots. Patroklos preferred to talk about Lubitsch comedies and attended revivals of 30s films starring Jean Harlow. Chilean exiles organized demonstrations and boycotts and joined other groups to protest U.S. intervention in Latin America. Patroklos gave champagne and caviar parties in his small Hollywood apartment. "I never meant to become an exile," he said, "just as I never meant to become queer. I just want life to be passion and bubbles." The glum serious people of the world wanted a better world, but he couldn't understand how that could be accomplished without glamour and extravagance.

On her part, Susana had convinced herself that his sexuality wouldn't be an obstacle to their relationship. They were roommates in a one-bedroom apartment off Santa Monica boulevard where one could open a window and whistle out for paid companionship. Yet Patroklos who slept on a couch in the living room never brought anyone home. She interpreted this to mean he respected her and her sensibilities. She had decorated the apartment with posters from their productions and pictures of each other on stage. The fact that they never slept together wasn't damaging enough to convince her that this man would never become her husband. She never considered herself naive or romantic. She was under the impression their spiritual/artistic bond would mature into a comfortable, prosperous life together. By the time Hollywood came calling, his attitude toward her had changed. He started leaving her alone at night and was away rehearsing his new plays. She wasn't involved anymore when she started making television appearances. Suddenly the actors in Patroklos' plays were often not actors at all, but drag queens, street people, and other people she considered "unsavory." She also suspected that by then he had "consummated" his longing—that is, that he'd crossed the line between politically coming out and physically doing so. It had taken years for this discreet, conservative, proper man to act upon his desires, and that was about the right time for her to move on, without him. But the longing in her and the resentment she felt lingered even now when she was happily married to someone less charming, but straight.

"I could have made you happy," she finally told him that afternoon. "Women can devote themselves to a relationship, and I don't see you gay men doing that." She realized she could lose her gay following for saying this, but she was already known for saying wretched things, the type the press magnified into a controversy after which she'd tearily apologize. "Why would you insist so much on this lifestyle if you can't even get a decent companion to share your life?"

"We all have bad luck in love, don't we? It doesn't justify going back to the closet."

"And I'm saying fighting for liberty in Chile could mean a lot more to people there. Here people don't even bother to vote, and nobody gives a damn about the theater." She pulled out an article she'd clipped from the paper. It was the story of Chilean theater artists who'd received death threats from right-wing death squads. Instead of leaving the country, they had stayed, publicized the death threats. Theater actors throughout the world had responded on their behalf, and even the actor who played Superman had flown into Santiago to make an appearance.

"You could even go back to fight for gay rights," she said. "You'd be a pioneer. Chile is ripe for idealism, I can just see you there."

"You don't understand," he said. "I'm no longer a real Chilean." He stopped himself, didn't want to say this at all. "I couldn't lead a gay lifestyle in Chile, no matter how many things have changed. This is the place where I became that type of man. I seem to owe this country some sort of allegiance for that, even though a lot of people wouldn't care for my allegiance. I've lost it, I've lost whatever it takes to live in one's native country. Blame it on the gay lifestyle, blame it on the weather. I would miss this life so much, I would feel lost away from my theater, its thirty-five wretched seats, mostly empty and my transvestites and the Tunisian restaurant next door with the best cous-cous on earth. I would miss the poor but hopeful immigrants who always need help and make life seem new and interesting again. Everyone lands here sooner or later, and I feel part of the process now—for better or for worse, I've become an unrepentant Angeleno."

She smiled with that by now notorious insouciant look full of flip malice, tenderness, and insolence. She then pulled out her checkbook and quickly wrote a check, handing it to him inside an envelope that also contained the one-way ticket to Santiago. She insisted that he take both, that he couldn't take one without the other. He stashed both the ticket and the check in his jacket. He got up and looked back at the stately, magnificent Susana, with her expressive face covered by make-up that reddened her cheeks, and intense eyes shaded blue by colored lenses. The artifice was superfluous altogether. It corrupted the simplicity of her beauty, the roughness of a somewhat crooked nose and c-shaped chin that gave the entire face an interesting disbalance that she alone could not accept as beauty. He stood in his battered shoes given him by the dead Armenian shoe repairman. "If it makes a difference," he told her, "you're the only woman I've ever loved."

He left her with her hands over her swollen womb, looking away with a tear carefully lodged and held at the corner of her right eye refusing to fall.

A few days later, Patroklos announced that he had raised sufficient funds to keep the theater solvent for another year. He could afford both the rent and—in compliance with new Equity rules—could pay all his actors a small stipend. He also announced that he would be paying a brief but indefinite visit to his native country. He would leave his theater under the administrative supervision of the Russian ex-ballet dancer/drag queen, Masha Vindictia. A celebration party was announced, both to commemorate the theater's solvency and Patroklos' visit to Chile where he hadn't been in fifteen years.

However, rumors persisted that Patroklos had accepted the one-way ticket to Santiago and hadn't yet bothered to add a return. How long would this "brief, but indefinite" visit be? Patroklos wouldn't answer. The queens quietly watched as Patroklos put up all his belongings for sale, and many of them bought the few things worth buying, a few cooking utensils and leather-bound books in Spanish. The furniture went unsold and left by a dumpster where they had been found. During the party, Patroklos distributed a systematic set of goodbye handshakes. There was no need to get all emotional about it, as he would be back to a better life, he said.

Yet another account of the bon voyage party was that he'd gotten drunk after most partiers left and had gone into an uncharacteristically furious rage. He denounced his friends, and even made "politically incorrect" statements about love between men, and how his gay friends had failed to love him romantically, and that perhaps intimacy between men was a contradiction in terms, that he was tired of searching for a perfect love that wasn't forthcoming and why should he devote his entire life to an art form that had driven him to the edge of poverty and, in American culture, its companion, lovelessness. He claimed the Chilean people would appreciate his talents and love him as he was. He'd return to his radio stardom and work for the rebirth of Chilean democracy and this would mean twenty times more than democracy or gay liberation meant to the superficial queens of Los Angeles who'd never known a real struggle in their lives. Guests had walked out of the party, one by one, calling him a self-hating queen, among many other, less polite things.

He had driven himself to the airport in the early hours of the morning, and he hadn't allowed anyone to come see him off. Weeks went by. No one heard from Patroklos. No one received a postcard or a letter, much less a phone call. But one day, the entire cast of a new Patroklos production—a drag queen version of *Medea* with ballet sequences staged by Masha—had arrived at the theater and found themselves face to face with the well-tanned Patroklos E. himself. He said he'd gotten on a wrong plane headed for Hawaii, and had spent two lovely months there. He had even done rewrites of the new Medea adaptation and was eager to direct it and star as Jason. Masha pulled out the champagne from the many hidden compartments of the Patroklos Theater which made the place so debonair and a good time was had by all.

Patroklos didn't tell any of his colleagues that on his way back from the L.A. airport, he'd taken a detour to the immigration department in downtown L.A. There, he spent the entire morning filling out citizenship papers and given the clerks a bad time asking questions about what type of pen to use and which boxes to leave blank and when the procedures would be complete because he was in such a hurry to become a new citizen.

Not long after Chile held its first presidential election in sixteen years, Patroklos voted for a woman in the race for California governor. His drag Medea was not a success, but he planned a biography of his life which he expected would make him the best known, if only, Chilean homosexual exile but new citizen of Anglo descent with a funny Greek name who spoke his ethnic language with a Hispanic accent. That was the true Patroklos.

Enrique Valdés

Una experiencia literaria

Vengo de un largo y lejano país llamado Chile. Un país al que nuestra Gabriela Mistral definió como un remo, "ancho hacia Antofagasta y aguzado hacia el Sur", y que yo defino como un largo dolor; especialmente en la última década dominada por la presencia de una de las más brutales dictaduras militares de América Latina.

Vengo de Chile. Un país que es varios países a la vez, por la variedad de sus paisajes y de su clima. El gran desierto nortino en los límites de Perú y de Bolivia, una zona central llena de árboles frutales y de tierra generosa para el cultivo de la agricultura y la ganadería. Y el vasto y extenso sur, de viento, nieve y lluvia. Esta es la región de la Trapananda: donde la tierra se despedaza en islas pequeñas e insignificantes, donde sólo vive el canto de los pájaros y los lobos de mar.

He titulado *Trapananda* a mi novela principal por dos motivos. Por ser ése el nombre que los conquistadores dieron a toda esta gran extensión del sur de Chile, que existe desde Puerto Montt hasta el Cabo de Hornos. Y porque yo nací en esta parte del mundo cuando mis padres fueron enviados a la zona para poblarla. Una tierra de pioneros, como el Oeste norteamericano, podríamos decir ahora, donde aún no existen caminos y la vida se hace en un caballo o en una carreta tirada por bueyes. Yo me nutrí de toda esa vida durísima y de esa experiencia extraordinaria. Conocí a los arrieros que demoraban un mes o más caminando en la cordillera, para llegar con un rebaño de animales hasta los puertos dónde alguien pudiera comprarlos por una miseria. Conocí a gente que nunca había visto un automóvil, ni menos un tren, en pleno apogeo de la modernidad. Pues tuve la suerte de salir a estudiar al llamado norte, que es la ciudad de Valdivia —una hermosa ciudad del sur de Chile— donde existe la Universidad más lejana del mundo: la Universidad Austral. La razón por la que tuve que hacer ese viaje de descubrimiento fue que en la región de la Trapananda no había liceos ni colegios secundarios y mis padres querían que al menos yo aprendiera a escribir ... Yo no sé si aprendí —realmente— a escribir. Lo digo con toda seriedad, después de tener tres novelas publicadas y dos pequeños libros de poesía. Ahora comparto la alegría de hablar con ustedes de literatura y le pido excusas por hablar de mi literatura, que es mía en mí, como quería Rubén Darío. Pero pienso que es lo mejor que puede hacer un escritor: dar un testimonio de su trabajo solitario y tratar de encontrar un nuevo sentido a una actividad cada vez menos importante en la vida moderna.

En el desolado panorama de nuestros países subdesarrollados, la vocación literaria está marcada por la incertidumbre. Puedo decir que yo he tenido mucha suerte de tener parte de mi obra publicada en forma digna, aunque haya tenido que comprar una gran parte de mis propios libros al editor, ceder mis derechos a las editoriales, encontrar mis propios suscriptores y romper mil obstáculos, como todo escritor que comienza, hasta hoy día. La mismas dificultades tuvieron Neruda y Darío, que también pagaron por sus primeras ediciones o crearon círculos de suscriptores —sospechosamente— voluntarios.

Me disculpo de hablar de mis libros, porque ellos debieran hablar por sí mismos. Pero no me disculpo por hablar de mi experiencia de escritor en los duros años de la dictadura militar en Chile, a partir de 1973 hasta el presente. Pienso que los escritores somos personajes en extinción, aves en peligro de desaparecer definitivamente del planeta. Creo que lo estoy comprobando ahora en los Estados Unidos, donde cada vez es más difícil conocer a un escritor o saber que alguien se dedica a la labor improductiva de escribir y publicar libros, en un país donde la actividad de un artista es casi siempre marginal. Aunque el sistema nos permita la supervivencia hay un desprecio subterráneo por el escritor, visible en esta sociedad y en esta época. ¿Cuál será entonces nuestra justificación sobre la tierra? El escritor es el guardián de la palabra y del lenguaje. Su deber es mantener viva la conciencia primitiva de la humanidad, la visión primigenia y no contaminada del mundo y de las cosas. El escritor es el creador del mito y de la imagen, dice el poeta Jorge Teillier. Es la posibilidad de mantener la vigencia de los sueños y de las utopías, en un mundo cada día más pragmático, que ve el cielo como un terreno de experimentación espacial y no como el lugar donde puede aprenderse el nombre y la historia de las estrellas. Comencé escribiendo poesía, como muchos. Publiqué mi primer pequeño libro de poemas llamado *Permanencias* en 1968, cuando era estudiante universitario, y casi como una consecuencia de una febril actividad literaria que incluyó la creación de la revista de poesía *Trilce*, y el inicio de la publicación de nuestros libros. Mi último libro *Avisos Luminosos*

(1986), es también poesía, pero nació sentenciado a muerte por la dictadura de mi país. En uno de los múltiples actos de la barbarie cultural en que vivimos en los últimos años, la editorial donde se imprimió el libro fue allanada, destruída y saqueada por fuerzas militares. El día anterior yo había sacado 100 ejemplares para un acto de presentación en las tradicionales Ferias del Libro de Santiago de Chile. Son estos pues, los únicos 100 ejemplares de un libro que nació condenado al silencio y a las salas de "rare books" de las bibliotecas universitarias.

La razón del allanamiento y destrucción de todo el material existente, incluyendo la maquinaria de la editorial, no era una razón literaria, sino política. Se trataba de destruir una fuente de información y de crítica al gobierno, pues la editorial había publicado un libro totalmente en blanco titulado "La Hinteligencia Militar": asi, con una H en la inteligencia. Y un testimonio fotográfico titulado "El pan nuestro de cada día", con elocuentes muestras de la represión, la prepotencia y el abuso institucionalizado de las fuerzas militares.

Puede ser que en el mundo de hoy no existan más de cien lectores de poesía. Y la dictadura me daba la posibilidad de comprobarlo. Aunque existen poemas que recogen experiencias del ámbito político, no es la crítica social el tema predominante de este libro. Es una reflexión interior más que exterior. El testimonio de mi incertidumbre vital, la angustia por nuestra naturaleza efímera, mortal y transitoria.

Quiero dejar testimonio aquí de mi deuda y mi cariño hacia la poesía. Creo que ha sido un digno y necesario ejercicio en el dominio de la palabra y en la elaboración de un estilo donde la precisión del lenguaje tenga una función importante. El lenguaje es mucho más importante que los temas y asuntos tratados. La calidad de los libros tiene este mágico requerimiento del que la buena novela hispanoamericana moderna responde sobradamente con el uso riguroso y pleno del idioma. Y para ello, la poesía es, sin duda, el mejor y más pleno ejercicio.

Vuelvo a la Trapananda para recordar el momento en que pensé por primera vez en ser novelista. Era en Aisén, en el extremo sur de Chile y del mundo. Fue durante unas vacaciones de verano en que hice un viaje a caballo, duarante 10 días por las cordilleras de la región, con los arrieros y peones de mi padre que habían traído los animales hasta la región de Aisén para venderlos. Era gente sencilla, verdadera, sufrida y elemental con la que compartí la vida durante muchos días, durmiendo en medio del bosque, tomando mate, la bebida principal de esa tierra y comiendo un

pedazo de carne de cordero asado al palo, es decir e
de madera natural. En medio de ese paisaje adquirí
vez la certeza de mi vocación, que era más bien un d
compromiso social. Fue una noche en que llovía torrenc.
y nosotros dormíamos debajo de los árboles, cubiertos co
lonas muy gruesas que también se empezaron a llenar de agua.
Desperté a medianoche y me dí cuenta que alguien se movía para
colocar leña en la fogata y mantenerla encendida. Después de un
momento, pude ver también a mi padre, a través de las llamas,
sentado en la raíz de un árbol caído, con la cabeza cubierta con
un cuero completamente mojado, tratando a esas altas horas de la
noche de mantener encendido el fuego silvestre para que no nos
congeláramos de frío.

A partir de esta imagen pensé que algún día tendría que escribir
lo que estaba viendo y viviendo. Mi novela *Ventana al Sur* (1975)
recoge toda esta experiencia personal y familiar, como diversos
episodios fragmentarios de una sola experiencia.

No podía tampoco soslayar el tema del desarraigo, que es el
tema de lo auténtico y lo inauténtico en nuestra vida. Tal vez
habría sido mejor no haber dejado nunca aquel paraíso de inocencia y vida natural que era la Trapananda, ajeno a todo lo que es
la cultura moderna. Y esto que llamamos cultura se parece a un
gran maquillaje que oculta lo realmente valioso: la vida instin-
tiva y natural de los hombre y mujeres humildes, pero mucho más
felices que el hombre llamado culto.

Como quien lanza una moneda a la fuente de los deseos, envié
el manuscrito de *Ventana al Sur* a un concurso nacional y obtuve
el primer premio y el interés de una editorial para publicar la novela. Pero era el año 1975 y el régimen militar había impuesto
la censura en mi país. Tanto la novela como el autor necesitaban
sufrir la humillación de pasar por una oficina del gobierno por una
autorización oficial, antes de ser publicada. El episodio que tuve
que superar es ridículo y cómico, y es la primera vez que me atrevo
a relatarlo públicamente.

Una mañana me llamó el editor para informarme que el libro
no se podía publicar por el uso de palabras groseras, a menos que
yo las sacara del texto. Las palabras objetadas no eran otras que
las que usan los campesinos en las faenas duras de la tierra y del
campo y que, naturalmente, son imposibles de eliminar sin alterar
el espíritu de la novela. Como ocurre siempre en las dictaduras,
la ingrata misión de censurar recae casi siempre en funcionarios
secundarios —una secretaria inculta, o un escritor frustrado que
es peor—, que disimulan la persecución política bajo el pretexto

de la depuración del idioma.

El manuscrito de *Ventana al Sur* me había sido devuelto completamente subrayado con lápiz rojo, no sólo en aquellas expresiones como "mierda" o "huevón", tan frecuentes en nuestro vocabulario diario, sino en frases como "quedar ensartada como picarón", o "andar con el culo para la pared". La única explicación que el alto funcionario militar tuvo la gentileza de entregar al editor de Zig-Zag fue que el gobierno estaba empeñado en la depuración del lenguaje, especialmente entre los estudiantes, pues no les agradaba que anduvieran diciendo palabrotas en las calles ni los buses ... y que esta depuración debía comenzar por el ejemplo de los escritores, pues si estos usaban puras groserías en sus libros, entonces a dónde iríamos a parar en el futuro y etcétera, etcétera. Tuvimos que entrevistarnos con las más altas autoridades de la censura y que era un General que había vivido en la región de la Trapananda, que nos recibió muy fríamente en su oficina de gobierno, mientras una radio ordinaria y a todo volumen, pasaba propaganda comercial, que seguramente también estaba siendo controlada en ese momento. Ni el hecho de que yo fuera el autor del libro, ni el conocimiento que el General tenía de esa región lograron su interés. Casi desesperado, esgrimí mi último argumento: el nombre del otro alto General que firmaba la carta que anunciaba el premio Gabriela Mistral, como Alcalde de la Municipalidad de Santiago. Sólo entonces se dignó a mirarme y con igual desprecio, pero dispuesto a ceder un milímetro, me dijo:

—Déjeme la novela y llame dentro de una semana.

Por supuesto que cuando lo llamé ya habían desaparecido las objeciones. Pero habían logrado lo principal: intimidarme y demostrar el poder omnímodo de un sistema militar, e influir sutilmente en la futura creación, por medio de la autocensura. Si eran capaces de objetar el término "maricón", por supuesto que la palabra "socialismo" o "marxismo" y aún "compañero" —que era de uso corriente entre los militantes de la Unidad Popular—, podía significar no sólo la censura, sino la cárcel.

Quiero decir que no fue nada de fácil hacer literatura, escribir libros o artículos periodísticos, durante la dictadura militar. El hecho que yo hubiera perdido mi trabajo en la Universidad Austral en 1973, me hacía un sospechoso, y algunos colegas de la Orquesta Sinfónica donde trabajaba, no dudaban en decírmelo derechamente. Muchos de ellos eran ex-integrantes de bandas militares y estaban muy satisfechos con el régimen. El hecho de trabajar en la principal orquesta de mi país —como violoncelista— envolvía una gran contradicción, muy difícil de explicar y de en-tender, puesto que fui despedido de la Universidad Austral por presuntos actos "extremistas" y a los tres meses —cuando preparaba mis maletas para salir al exilio— gané por concurso de oposición una de las vacantes en la Orquesta Sinfónica, la misma Orquesta que debía asistir a las ceremonias oficiales del gobierno en el edificio Diego Portales para tocar el Himno Nacional al Presidente, en este caso al Dictador. El extremista de la Universidad Austral era ahora un becerro domesticado o un cobarde, pues estuve muchas veces al lado de Pinochet, invitado a sus celebraciones como músico-lacayo y me asombro de no haber tenido siquiera una idea malévola que justificara el calificativo de extremista que tan generosamente me habían otorgado. Después de esos y de otro tipo de "conciertos", sentía un dolor francamente visceral, un desprecio y un asco por todo —también por mí mismo— que tratábamos de depurar con una buena botella de vino en el Bar Unión de la hermosa calle Nueva York 11, donde nos reuníamos un grupo bastante numeroso de poetas, escritores y músicos frustrados. Como no iba a ser para emborracharse de pura ira y pena, un memorable concierto con música de Wagner —El Preludio de *Los Maestros Cantores*—, que tuvimos que tocar en el galpón de un regimiento, mientras guardias vigilaban el recinto con sus armas al hombro. La fogocidad de Wagner no podía ser más adecuada para la ocasión, pero lo increíble del concierto fue que cuando el Maestro Víctor Tevah —director de los festivales Casals de Puerto Rico—, terminó la ejecución del concierto, uno de los oficiales se levantó del primer asiento que ocupaba junto a su esposa y ordenó a los asistentes que nos cantaran el Himno del Regimiento, a grito limpio y al unísono, en muestra de agradecimiento. No soy un músico excelente, pero pasé quince años de mi vida detrás de un atril de conservatorio tratando de aprender a interpretar a Beethoven o Bach. Otros de mis colegas habían viajado a París, Italia o Moscú para estudiar sus instrumentos. Y terminábamos aquí, en pleno galpón de regimiento, llevando la cultura a nuestros torturadores que algún día podrían usar en un cuarto siniestro de tortura, "la sala de música" —del que un detenido me habló— y que consiste en encerrar al prisionero durante horas, noches y días, en una sala con música a todo volúmen, hasta romper la resistencia de sus nervios y hacerlo hablar.

Creo que es la fea palabra frustración la que nos calza perfectamente a un grupo grande de amigos y escritores que consumimos gran parte del tiempo infeliz de la dictadura en bares y cantinas, discutiendo el mejor modo de hacer literatura o peleándonos unos con otros por no tener dinero para la siguiente botella de vino. No comprendo exactamente lo que pasó, pero salíamos discutiendo de la Sociedad de Escritores con el poeta Alvaro Ruiz, cuando se detuvo ante nosotros un furgón policial y nos tomó por los brazos para empujarnos dentro de un vehículo policial y llevarnos a la comisaría. Yo venía de una grabacíon de un concierto para la televisión, y me había despojado de la corbata, pero me la instalé dentro del furgón pensando en el clasismo militar. No sirvió de nada. Alvaro habló de su padre —un General retirado de la aviación— con iguales resultados: debíamos pasar la noche en un calabozo de la comisaría y salir al otro día, previo pago de una multa. De otro modo íbamos a la cárcel. Nos metieron en una celda sucia, con unos diez detenidos desconocidos, mientras afuera se paseaban las prostitutas, también detenidas durante la noche. Cuando aparecía algún oficial le tratábamos de hablar: que era un integrante de la Orquesta Sinfónica de Chile, que ensayábamos —efectivamente— a una cuadra distante desde el cuartel, que llamen a Víctor Tevah, que nos preste el teléfono para hacer una llamada, una sola, que llamen ellos mismos al escritor Enrique Lafourcade, que es nuestro amigo, que nos conoce y dirá que todo era una broma, que en verdad no veníamos peleando por la calle, que mañana a las nueve tengo una grabación de un concierto para la televisión y que por lo menos necesitaba dormir un poco, por favor ... Pero nada. Nos acomodamos en los rincones de la celda, entre borrachos y gente desconocida, tratando de encontrar una solución razonable a nuestro problema y tratar de dormir, hasta que llegó la amanecida. Una mujer de uniforme se asomó entonces entre las rejas para decir que el que tuviera algún dinero podía pagar una multa y largarse. Yo lo tenía y pedí salir, pues debía ir a cambiarme a casa y volver immediatamente a la TV para la grabación. Y vivía muy lejos del centro de Santiago. Indignado, además con Alvaro Ruiz —a cuya agresividad culpé entonces del incidente— no hice nada por pagar su multa, convencido que lo haría él mismo. Una vez libre, llamé a su casa para avisar que necesitaba ayuda.

Es verdad que, como pude, llegué a mi trabajo. Pero algo muy humillante había vuelto a ocurrir. No sólo se resintió la amistad con Ruiz, si es que alguna vez la hubo, sino que hasta era imposible mirar de frente a mis compañeros de Orquesta —y menos al Director—, mientras grabábamos un programa cultural, directamente desde el cepo.

Creo que de todos los tipos de artistas, el músico-intérprete es el que guarda mayor dósis de frustración en su alma. Yo podía comprobarlo en la agresividad y en la competitividad de mis compañeros que —humillados por el sistema— no podían hacer otra cosa que humillar también en torno de ellos mismos. En cambio mis amigos escritores y yo mismo, optamos por esconder la cabeza y olvidarnos del mundo de porquerías en que nos tocaba vivir. Pasábamos tardes enteras, desde el mediodia hasta la medianoche en La Unión Chica —un bar que estaba frente del famoso Club de La Unión, donde asistía la gente adinerada del comercio y del gobierno—, perdiendo miserablemente un tiempo delicioso, escribiendo en el mismo bar, haciendo proyectos infinitos. A pesar de esta decadencia, los miembros de esta confradía publicábamos libros, colaborábamos en las revistas literarias: *La Gota Pura, La Castaña, Trilce* y *LAR*, entre muchas otras; y obteníamos premios importantes, como el Municipal de Literatura y el Grabriela Mistral.

Pienso que fue mi amigo y maestro Pedro Lastra el que se dio cuenta de que esta situación no podía prolongarse más de diez años sin serias consecuencias y me ofreció la posibilidad de hacer un doctorado en la Universidad de Illinois, donde ahora escribo estas páginas, con alegría y nostalgia, como un pecador arrepentido que trata de encontrar su camino de Damasco, o el de la literatura, que es el mismo. Mientras vivo y estudio acá en Urbana, Illinois, entre grandes sembrados de maíz y la biblioteca de Alejandría al alcance de nuestras manos, recibo las noticias de la muerte del gran Maestro Víctor Tevah, de dos de mis amigos violinistas —René Rodriguez y Mario Prieto—, de dos de mis amigos escritores: Andrés Sabella y el querido y abstemio Enrique Lihn, con quien hicimos un acto de chelo, poesía y teatro para Monsieur Pompier. En cambio, los amigos de La Unión aún gozamos de relativa buena salud (¿hasta cuándo, Señor, hasta cuándo?) y tendremos la alegría de ver el renacimiento de la democracia en nuestro país y escribir entonces ese penúltimo libro que preparábamos durante tanto tiempo en los bares, en la cárcel, entre la miseria y el vasallaje de un pueblo derrotado que, sin embargo, se levantará.

Trapananda (1984) es mi libro más querido, el más premiado en el terreno mismo de la dictadura. Es también el libro más desgarrado en su concepción y hechura estilística. La novela narra dos grandes historias en forma paralela. Una es la historia del destierro que sufre la familia del protagonista en la Trapananda, en el sur de Chile, durante la dictadura del General Carlos Ibáñez del Campo, en el primer cuarto de este siglo. La otra historia es un viaje interminable de dos personajes —Raimundo y Antolín— desde Argentina hasta la Trapananda, a la que nunca llegan, pues terminan perdidos entre el barro la nieve y soñando con encontrar algún día la tierra prometida.

Trapananda es una novela del fracaso. De la soledad y del desencanto. He querido dejar en ella toda la tristeza de una generación que, como la de muchos otros, creyó en un proyecto político y social para nuestra vida y para nuestra historia y fracasó estruendosamente. Y no es la historia de un fracaso político —que eso sería lo de menos—, pues el político siempre se rehace en la acción y la esperanza. Es un fracaso mucho mayor, pues envuelve la vida toda, el arte, la esperanza el amor y la convivencia. Por ello comparto la interpretación de un crítico que ha señalado que todos los personajes de la novela "están marcados por el signo del destierro. Porque destierro es también el de Raimundo y de Antolín en Argentina, el de Andrea en tierras del interior y muy especialmente el de Camilo —el personaje central—, cuando sale de la Trapananda rumbo a la ciudad donde se educará". Pero una novela no es solamente una anécdota que el autor descubre algún buen día de iluminación, como lo es aquí el destierro que sufren los padres del protagonista, Camilo, durante el gobierno de Ibáñez y que forma el primer episodio de la novela. Aquel período de la historia de mi país empezó a interesarme por muchas razones: en primer lugar por razones biográficas, pues mis padres viven aún en la región. Pero también por el parecido de ese gobierno militar con el actual régimen de Pinochet. Y porque ambos gobiernos usaron el territorio de la Trapananda como lugar de destierro y deportación para los políticos que se les oponían o los criticaban. Faltarían otras doscientas páginas para encerrar la totalidad épica de la fundación y colonización de Aisén, con sus legados de vida humana, de tragedias y de aventuras. Pues en verdad, el personaje del padre, Efraín Ramos, en mi novela, es una mezcla del padre real y de un profesor también desterrado, convertido en colono y pionero muy a pesar suyo, es decir a la fuerza. Pero no cometamos el error de confundir la novela con la realidad, pues aunque un escritor tenga su punto de partida en hechos reales, su ambición es muy otra. El personaje de la novela debe ser mucho más amplio y complejo que el personaje real. El novelista trabaja con un enorme arsenal de datos reales e imaginarios, sacados de la biografía, de su imaginación o tomados del ámbito de la cultura literaria y de los libros.

El artista es un ser marginal —dicen nuestros parientes cuando descubren la sospechosa vocación en alguno de sus hijos. Si la familia es la primera en mirarlos con desconfianza, la sociedad francamente los rechaza, como a una peste. Pero de esa marginalidad nace su fuerza, que es transformar la poesía en experiencia vital y con ello tratar de transformar el mundo en que nos toca vivir y en el que nunca podríamos estar totalmente contentos. Si fuéramos tan felices, no sería necesario escribir.

Sin embargo, creo que el arte es una afirmación de la vida, un acto de fe y de esperanza, que ahora me permite compartir con ustedes el mundo misterioso y siempre apasionante de la literatura. Esta íntima afirmación por la vida creo que está consignada en la última página de mi novela, que me servirá también para terminar mis palabras.

Una hoja blanca es un paisaje de la infancia dentro de mí. Tomo mi taza de café y salgo a mirar el territorio blanco de la Trapananda desde una loma. La nieve cubre todos los ramajes; pero los árboles más altos alcanzan a mostrar sus brazos negros sobre la nieve. Parece una hoja blanca en la que uno hubiese pasado muchas horas tratando de recordar, dibujando puntos arbitrarios con un lapiz.

—Yo soy quien debía estar muerto.

—No importa —dice mi madre—. ¡Con que estés vivo me basta!

Flora González Mandri

El Regreso

Para Luz María Mandri, In Memoriam

Un avión que lleva veinticinco personas no vuela tan alto como un avión transatlántico. Lo bueno de eso es que uno está más cerca de la tierra que del cielo y se puede ver muy bien el paisaje. Los cayos de la Florida son impresionantes desde arriba, el puente que los comunica sirve de hilo como para que no se dispersen y se pierdan en el Mar Caribe. Nosotros habíamos salido de Miami después de una espera bastante larga en el aeropuerto. Estábamos en marzo del ochenta y hacía dieciocho años que yo había salido de Cuba. Los nervios de la anticipación me tenían pegada a la ventana grabando en la mente todo lo que veía y lo que sentía. Había un sol brillante ese día y el mar estaba de ese azul verde perfecto del Caribe. Cuando nos acercamos a Cuba pude notar la silueta de cabeza de caimán con la espuma de mar que bañaba las costas. ¡Qué isla más verde! Y era un verde oscuro, no ese verde claro de los bosques de Nueva Inglaterra al que yo me había acostumbrado. Me di cuenta en seguida que recordaba mucho menos de lo que pensaba. Cuando aterrizamos casi corrí hacia el edificio marcado Aeropuerto Internacional José Martí. Me paré un segundo para sacarle una foto y notar que después de haber visitado grandes aeropuertos en todo el mundo, el de La Habana se quedaba bastante chiquito. Antes de entrar al edificio me invadió una incertidumbre inexplicable. Los otros cubanos que ya habían regresado me habían prevenido de todas las reacciones inesperadas que se apoderarían de mí. Busqué la "pecera" que yo había habitado el día que me fui de Cuba y no la encontré.

Nos pusimos en la cola para presentar los pasaportes; yo venía con un grupo de norteamericanos y, al ver los suyos, los aduaneros los dejaron pasar inmediatamente. Cuando me tocó a mí, yo presenté el mío norteamericano.

—¿Usted es cubana?

—Sí, aquí tiene mi pasaporte cubano.

—Espere aquí un momento.

El resto siguió adelante y yo me quedé esperando a otro señor que me iba a hacer una serie de preguntas. A mi izquierda había una señora cubana al lado de su gusano repleto de ropa obviamente para su familia. La apertura durante la presidencia de Carter había visto la llegada de muchos cubanos a Cuba a visitar a su familia y a mostrarles con sus riquezas materiales el éxito del "American Dream". Al cubano le encanta ostentar y ésta no dejó de ser una demostración de lo que se tenía y no se tenía en los Estados Unidos. Muchos cubanos regresaron a Cuba metiéndose en grandes deudas para poder llevarles de todo a los familiares. La señora que estaba a mi lado se veía bastante preocupada pensando que le iban a confiscar parte de lo que había comprado para su familia. Yo también llevaba mi gusano que me había prestado un amigo para poder llevarle cosas a mi tía María Luisa. Lo que más me preocupaba era que llevaba una cámara y una grabadora; en realidad, yo no había planeado el viaje con mucha anticipación y no había habido tiempo para ponerme a comprar cosas para la gente. Yo simplemente cogí de mi ropa y de la de Merci para llevarle a María Luisa y a la niña de Mario.

—¿Y cuál es el propósito de su visita?

—Vengo a ver a mi familia y a conocer a algunos escritores cubanos como Luis Márquez.

Me pidió que abriera la maleta.

—¿Qué trae en este bulto?

—Ropa, algunos libros y una grabadora.

—¿Y para qué esta grabadora?

—Para entrevistar a Luis Márquez, el de las novelas testimoniales.

—¿Trae algo para su familia?

—Sí, ropa para mi familia y la hija de mi primo.

—¿Casi toda ropa de mujer? Bueno.

Las manos me temblaban con ese miedo infundado que me vino a acechar desde un momento anterior donde no había tenido la conciencia de la madurez para sentirlo. Yo estuve todo el tiempo sonriendo y conversando con él pero con mucha desconfianza por dentro.

Fuimos hasta El Vedado en una guagua que estaba reservada para nuestra gira. En ella iríamos por todas partes de La Habana. De allí en adelante empecé a reconocer edificios, calles, y la Universidad de La Habana con su escalinata famosa. Empecé a reconocer cosas que había olvidado, como que las casas estaban pintadas de colores vivos en vez de ser simplemente blancas o grises o de colores oscuros. Empecé a reconocer en La Habana vieja las calles

estrechas y las aceras más estrechas aún. Me enamoré de la Catedral de La Habana y de la plaza acogedora. Sin decírselo a nadie
había temido que la belleza de nuestra capital se quedaría atrás
después de haber visto las grandes capitales europeas. Algunos
cubanos del exilio decían que La Habana estaba hecha un desastre, que las fachadas se estaban cayendo, que no había pintura para
nada. Pero nada de eso disminuyó mi atracción por los barrios antiguos. Incluso me gustó mucho más que el viejo San Juan, todo
maquillado con los dólares norteamericanos para el beneficio de
los turistas.

Por el día teníamos cosas planificadas como una visita al museo
nacional de La Habana, con sus grandes columnas y sus patios y
pasillos coloniales. Lo verde lo invadía todo. Fuimos a una fábrica
de telas donde el aire estaba tan espeso con el algodón que apenas
se podía respirar, también a una escuela rural donde los niños tra-
bajaban en el campo medio día y asistían a clases la otra mitad. En
esa escuela nos quedamos bastante tiempo; los muchachos todos
muy bellos, con sonrisas enormes y una energía increíble, todos
querían hablar con nosotros que veníamos de afuera del país. Nos
hicieron una presentación sobre las actividades diarias, visitamos
las aulas con todos los libros nuevos; había un aula especial para
las ciencias de la que se sentían muy orgullosos. Las maestras eran
sumamente jóvenes, dos en especial tenían dieciocho años y todavía no habían terminado los estudios para maestra. Yo estuve
con una mente inquisidora todo el tiempo que estuve en Cuba.
Cuando los niños presentaron sus actividades en el campo, las
niñas hablaron de una cuota más baja que la de los niños a la
hora de recoger tomates.

—¿Por qué hay una diferencia entre las cuotas?

—Los niños mismos establecen esas cuotas y por lo general
cumplen sus propias expectativas. Las niñas de trece años están
en una edad de desarrollo y no se puede esperar que ellas hagan
la misma tarea. Los varones siempre han recogido más que las
hembras.

Luego le hablé a nuestra guía: —¿Por qué a esa edad ya se les
está inculcando a las niñas que pueden realizar menos cosas que
los varones?

—Las cosas hay que cambiarlas poco a poco, son muchos años
de colonización.

—En otros departamentos como en el entrenamiento militar y
la labor cívica, la mujer participa igual, ¿por qué no en el trabajo?

—Las cosas cambiarán, hay que tener paciencia. Yo me quedé
insatisfecha con sus respuestas. Si van a hacer la Revolución, ¿por

qué no integrar a la mujer cien por cien? Me pareció que todavía había una mentalidad que sostenía que el papel de la mujer era el de procrear y apoyar al hombre en la Revolución. No me parecía que hubiera mucha diferencia entre la mujer rebajada a procrear una familia, y la mujer rebajada a procrear una nación. Pero mi estancia fue muy breve y era difícil ver las cosas objetivamente cuando yo estaba dispuesta a confirmar mis propios prejuicios. Obviamente mi feminismo era demasiado individualista para los cubanos. En ese sentido hablábamos dos lenguas distintas.

Muy pronto después de llegar llamé a mis tíos Paco y Luisa para ir a verlos. Fui a su casa la misma noche de mi llegada. Conseguí un taxi que me llevó a la Víbora. Cuando me acercaba a la casa, empecé a reconocer las calles hasta que llegamos a la esquina de Juan Delgado donde estaba la casa de ellos. Paco me estaba esperando afuera y cuando lo vi quise ir a abrazarlo inmediatamente. Con el entusiasmo de la cosa cogí mi cartera y el bulto con la ropa que les traía y se me quedó la cámara en el carro. Ni me di cuenta que la había dejado. Esa noche conversamos bastante, sentados en la sala en los balances. Me quedé a dormir y a la mañana siguiente me sirvieron un café con leche con galletas que en un tiempo me habría encantado pero resultó difícil tomarme la leche cremada que tanto me gustaba cuando era niña.

Mientras el resto del grupo disfrutaba de actividades de puro turismo, yo me quedaba fuera por estar con Paco y Luisa más tiempo. Con ellos tuve conversaciones largas y tendidas sobre la familia y el tren de vida diario en el país. Los cuentos que ellos me hicieron comprobaron que el espíritu de supervivencia estaba tan candente en Cuba como en el exilio, sólo que los fines de la lucha quedaban a extremos opuestos del arco iris. Paco me contó que al principio de la Revolución había renunciado al puesto que tenía de vendedor en una tipografía que se llamaba Jota Suárez que estaba en la calle Habana 102. Paco se había convertido en carpintero de primera categoría; en el apartamento de arriba, que le había pertenecido a abuela, tenía su taller. Subimos. Para mí fue muy triste subir al sitio donde había pasado tantos momentos lindos con abuela. El apartamento estaba completamente vacío de muebles y lo que había sido el cuarto estaba lleno de aserrín, de madera cortada, etc. Bajamos pronto. Yo quería que Paco me hablara más de ahora, de lo que estaba haciendo con la carpintería.

—Para la carpintería sí que tengo permiso, lo difícil es encontrar los materiales. Hay lo que le llaman la semana del tareco, que la gente bota todo lo que no quiere y el gobierno pasa con unos camiones y recoge todo lo que no sirve, operación tareco. Una vez empezaron a botar muebles porque no tenían manera de arreglarlos. Al lado del cuartel de enfrente, había un montón de muebles que llegaban más arriba de las matas. Un domingo fui por ahí con destornillador y martillo y empecé a desarmar balances y los muebles que estaban buenos, y los cargué todo pa' casa. Yo dije, saco las maderas de aquí, que eran muchas de caoba y así pude reconstruir muchos muebles. Yo reconstruí muchos balances.

Y ahora tengo que poner algo sobre la cuestión de las rejillas. Un día fui a Bauta y alguien descubrió que había un montón de rejillas en un almacén que habían venido de Viet Nam, y como no tenían espacio, las tenían a la intemperie y se habían mojado; y como se mojaron se mancharon, y como que ellos desconocían el caso, creían que esas rejillas ya manchadas no servían y yo empecé a ir a Bauta y empecé a comprar. La primera vez me la vendieron pero cuando fui la segunda vez no me la quisieron vender, porque decían que eso era nada más que para la gente de Bauta. Yo tuve una discusión porque, si eso es un artículo que está por la libre, ¿por qué no me van a vender a mí? Si usted no tiene un cigarro y llega a cualquier establecimiento de La Habana y pide cigarro, se lo venden, porque eso es un artículo por la libre. Así que usted está en un error—tuve una discusión con el administrador de la casa que se dedicaba a reconstruir muebles. Yo me dije, te voy a fastidiar, porque voy a mandar a toda mi familia que está en Bauta a comprar rejilla. Mandé a los amigos y todos a comprar rejilla y acabé con la rejilla que tenían allí. Y así estoy reconstruyendo muebles y poniendo rejillas. Todos los muebles están defondados. Con eso gano mucho dinero.

En nuestra casa de la Víbora que está al lado de la casa de Paco, habíamos dejado dos balancitos que Isa y yo habíamos usado toda la niñez. Y la gente que ahora vivía en la casa los habían dejado afuera porque no se estaban usando. Los balancines estaban metidos en una casita que había hecho papi en el patio para guardar cosas y luego los sacaron y los tenían a la intemperie, y estaban todos desbaratados. Ellos los iban a botar, y Paco les dijo.

—No, no los boten que yo los puedo arreglar.

Las piezas que estaban podridas las botó y las hizo nuevas. Cogió las piezas y reconstruyó los dos, que quedaron como un dije y uno de ellos se lo dio a Blanca, una sobrina, y el otro se quedó en la casa para cuando vinieran visitas de niños. Y ahí estaba el balancito que yo había visto en tantas y tantas fotos a través de mi niñez. Y Paco lo había pulido como una joya.

Un día fuimos a Bauta a visitar a la familia de Luisa. Fuimos en tren. En Bauta la gente me acogió como si me hubieran conocido de toda la vida. La comida fue el acontecimiento del día. Hicieron arroz, vianda, ropa vieja, postre y un cafecito. A mí me impresionó cómo, sabiendo la poca carne que había, me la ofrecieron a mí y querían que comiera mucho. Estaba muy rica pero como yo no sufro de la escasez de carne que hay en Cuba, no como mucha carne, incluso, casi nunca. Me encantó la amabilidad del cubano que siempre se extiende con las visitas, se tenga o no se tenga qué dar. Lo que sí me gustó es que en el patio tenían una mata de toronjas llenita de frutas.

—¿Por qué dejan todas esas toronjas en la mata, no se van a echar a perder?

—Ay hija, en esta casa nadie come toronjas; las regalamos a un hospital. Ellos las vienen a buscar de vez en cuando.

—¿Qué tal si yo me como una? A mí me encantan.

Me la bajaron de la mata y me la comí entera con mucho gusto. En los Estados Unidos yo siempre ando buscando fruta fresca porque me encanta y no la hay por el clima tan horrendo donde yo vivo. En Bauta donde hay toronjas hasta para hacer dulce, ni se las comen frescas ni hacen dulce.

Después de comer me tiré en la cama un rato y la sobrina de Luisa me vino a hablar. Ella y su marido tenían tres hijos y él se ganaba la vida sacando fotos a la gente, incluso me tiraron a mí todo un rollo con Paco y Luisa en el patio para que tuviera un recuerdo de Cuba. Ella empezó a contarme de la odisea que era vivir en Cuba. Cómo se pasaban el día haciendo cola para conseguir la comida, que una vecina avisaba que había papas y todos corrían a hacer cola para comprar papas. Ella estaba harta de que la vida girara en torno a las necesidades básicas. Se veía que estaba loca por la ropa que yo traía puesta. Me dijo que qué bonita mi blusa con tanta tela, aquí había que hacer la ropa un tanto ajustada para ahorrar tela. Yo traía una pulsera de madera india con dibujos de florecitas muy bonito y se pasó todo el tiempo mirándola. Por fin se la regalé; me daba pena y me molestaba un poco que estuvieran tan obsesionados con lo material. Claro que a mí no me faltaba nada. Desde que llegué a Cuba, me di cuenta que no podía pasar desapercibida; la ropa que traía y la forma de desenvolverme eran muy distintas a la mujer cubana de allá. Todo el mundo en esa casa quería irse. Hablé con las niñas y una me dijo que sí que se quería ir y la otra que no, que ella estaba muy contenta en Cuba, que estaba en los pioneros y que si los padres se iban ella se quedaba con la abuela porque ella no tenía ningunas ganas de dejar su país. Lo dijo con mucha convicción.

El próximo día quedamos en vernos de nuevo. Paco dijo que

me acompañaría a la comisaría del Vedado para informar que había perdido mi cámara, si no, me iban a poner una multa bastante grande por haberle dejado la cosa a un familiar. Yo le hablé a un señor en un escritorio que me dijo que tenía que esperar un rato. Cuando entré no dejaron que Paco me acompañara. Estuve hablando con el tipo por mucho tiempo, tratando de convencerlo que yo no le había regalado la cámara a nadie y que me diera un papel con una firma para salir del país. Pero esa tarde no estaban muy ocupados en la comisaría y el tipo halló en mí una forma de entretenimiento. Yo lo veía por la sonrisita que tenía pintada en la cara. Lo que yo decía le tenía sin cuidado y era evidente que no me iba a resolver el problema. La conversación que teníamos era un juego en que yo estaba diciendo la verdad pero todo lo que decía se consideraba como una mentira. En Cuba, como en todo país latino, las cosas funcionan por el disimulo y a muy poca gente se le ocurre decir la verdad. Yo, que siempre he funcionado con la careta de la honestidad, simplemente porque pienso que no me salen bien las mentiras, me sentí muy rara sabiendo que la verdad no era más que otro hilo del tejido que se estaba urdiendo en esa conversación. No tenía ni más ni menos importancia, ni vigencia. En aquel entonces me sentí como un bicho raro en mi propio país, pensando que en el norte mi manera de proceder era mucho más común. El que anduviera con Paco, que sabía cómo funcionar muy bien, me dio coraje para seguir el jueguito y empezar a sentirme menos extraña. Luego pensé que quizás estaba perjudicándolo con todas estas cosas y me sentí mal. Al salir sin el papel firmado pero sabiendo que nadie me lo pediría en el avión, Paco me recibió con su risa de siempre y esperamos un rato la guagua en el sol caliente del mediodía. Yo estaba dispuesta a esperar pero él dijo que estaba harto de las esperas y que mejor nos fuéramos en máquina. De chiripa conseguimos una y me llevó al hotel.

Esa tarde una amiga y yo fuimos a Casa de las Américas. Tuvimos que caminar algo para llegar, y acostumbrada a los climas del norte, el sol cubano me agobiaba un poco, sobre todo cuando se trataba de subir y bajar lomas. Llegamos a la UNEAC primero y a mí de idiota se me ocurre preguntar por Arturo Reyes. El tipo me mira con sorpresa y me dice:

—Usted está confundida, compañera, el escritor que tenemos es Arturo Rodríguez, no Reyes.

Comprendí que Reyes había desaparecido del mapa de La Habana y que había metido la pata hasta más no poder preguntando por él. Yo tenía una correspondencia para otros escritores de parte de mi profesor en la universidad pero era evidente que ya no iba a conseguir nada. La idea era poder tener la oportunidad de conocer al poeta laureado del país pero como es natural estaba inaccesible, ese día era precisamente el día internacional de la mujer y todo el mundo estaba celebrando; sin las mujeres que eran imprescindibles no se podía hacer nada. Yo salí de allí super frustrada, pensando que todo era un complot contra mí y con unos nervios y una rabia encima que no correspondían a la situación. Fuimos hasta Casa de las Américas donde el sobre que yo llevaba para Martínez Recio surtió el efecto de que él saliera a saludarnos. Estuvo muy amable con nosotras, un señor muy fino, guapo, y con una guayabera impecable. El día que nos íbamos a Santiago lo vi en el aeropuerto y me saludó por mi nombre. Me sorprendió mucho que me hubiera recordado. Al despedirse de nosotras en Casa de las Américas dejó instrucciones que nos dieran libros publicados recientemente. Salimos con una pila enorme. Otro día estuvimos en la Biblioteca Nacional. Allí también nos regalaron libros, me encantó el edificio con sus escalinatas y salones de lecturas, todo muy soleado con ventanales enormes y estudiantes con la nariz pegada a los libros. De allí fuimos a varias librerías; yo tenía una lista bastante considerable de cosas que quería conseguir. Me compré una versión muy linda de *La Edad de Oro*, conseguí un librito de una poeta joven que me gustaba mucho, me llevé varias copias de *El Ingenio*, pero no pude conseguir la mitad de las cosas que quería. Me dijeron que mucho de lo que se publicaba se agotaba en seguida y que no se tiraban otras ediciones de las cosas. Me fui conforme con lo que tenía.

Si por el día nos la pasábamos danzando por toda la ciudad, de noche una amiga puertorriqueña se encargaba de que fuéramos a bailar casi diariamente. Poco después de llegar al hotel empezamos a notar a un grupo de hombres jóvenes que andaban por ahí sin hacer nada. Gloria se hizo amiga de uno de ellos y antes de darnos cuenta era nuestro compañero constante. El intercambio era muy simple: él nos llevaba a todas partes y nosotros lo invitábamos a comer y a tomar tragos. Como él había montones. Un día él y yo salimos al Morro a visitar el museo de armas coloniales y a caminar por La Habana. Nos sentamos en frente de la bahía observando el mar. Yo le pregunté qué le parecía la Revolución. Nunca antes habíamos abordado el tema. El me dijo que era músico bailarín y que no tenía mucho trabajo en el momento. Vivía de los turistas. Me dijo que la apertura a los cubanos de afuera, los de la comunidad, había sido algo bueno al principio. La gente joven se entusiasmó porque de repente se empezaron a ver "blue jeans" por todas partes, los parientes llegaban cargados de artículos de consumo. Pero luego empezaron a haber rencillas porque algunos tenían y otros no; la gente empezó a sentirse insatisfecha porque mientras que nadie tenía nada todo estuvo bien; ahora la gente no hacía más que comparar lo que se tenía. Su opinión era que Fidel no estaba seguro de qué es lo que iba a hacer ahora. Claro que la decisión quedó fuera de sus manos porque poco después que yo me fui invadieron la embajada del Perú y el incidente en Mariel hizo que la gente empezara a hacerse preguntas. Si la Revolución funcionaba tan bien, ¿por qué salió tanta gente joven, sobre todo hombres? Todos los muchachos que frecuentaban los hoteles desaparecieron del otro lado del Caribe. Gloria me dijo que nuestro amigo estaba en Nueva York y que la estaba pasando muy bien con su familia. Para Fidel la cosa resultó maravillosa: se deshizo de todo ese grupo de gente insatisfecha y limpió los hospitales mentales y las cárceles.

Las críticas más virulentas que escuché cuando estuve en Cuba fueron por parte de los taxistas. En seguida que se enteraban que era de "la comunidad" me preguntaban que qué pensaba de lo que veía en Cuba. Yo le dije a un señor de unos cincuenta y pico de años que me parecía muy bien que todo el mundo recibiera educación y salud pública gratis. No había terminado de hablar cuando se puso a decir:

—Sí, todo eso está muy bien, pero ¿a qué precio? Yo estoy muy cansado de luchar y de llevar una vida con lo mínimo. Hace tanto tiempo que no me he comido un bistec que se me ha olvidado a qué sabe. Hace tanto tiempo que no celebro las Navidades que es una vergüenza. Dicen que los turrones son baratos allá y que siempre se comen en Navidad, ¿es verdad?

Opté por no montar más en taxi porque me sentía como la receptora de toda la rabia del que estuviera descontento con Fidel. Como yo venía de afuera y por lo visto la pasaba muy bien, sentí todo el resentimiento de los que se quisieron ir y no pudieron. Eso por un lado, y el resentimiento de los que se quedaron porque querían fundar un nuevo país, pero estaban un poco cansados ya de batallar sin poder disfrutar de algunos excesos. Ellos se sintieron defraudados por los que nos fuimos, especialmente nosotros que nos habíamos ido de niños. Nosotros no teníamos ni idea del trabajo que se había efectuado desde el triunfo de la Revolución. Nunca se les ocurrió que a nosotros nos tocó lo mismo en un país extraño. Yo escuchaba y escuchaba. Por el momento no podía procesar ninguna de estas opiniones; las emociones las iba acumulando porque, si no, el tiempo se me iba en pensar, y en los diez días que tenía en Cuba tenía que absorber lo más posible para luego poder llegar a alguna conclusión. Para colmo había venido con un grupo de norteamericanos y no podía compartir con nadie los miedos, las ansiedades y el entusiasmo que se me venían acumulando adentro.

Lo único que me salvaba era que me pasaba las noches caminando por La Habana Vieja y bailando al aire libre. Había un norteamericano que bailaba muy bien y que llegó a ser mi pareja cada vez que salíamos. Una noche nos tocó bailar en un parque cerca de la bahía con una orquesta y un bar muy bien situado bajo unos árboles con hojas descomunales. Las luces de la ciudad se veían reflejadas en el agua, había una brisa que le calmaba los nervios a cualquiera y después de unos tragos de mojitos ya estábamos todos para bailar la noche entera. Cuando salíamos a bailar nos quedábamos hasta las tres o las cuatro. Las guaguas seguían funcionando a esas horas y como nosotros éramos los únicos pasajeros, los cacharros casi volaban por las calles estrechas de la ciudad. En su vuelo parecía que se iban a desintegrar en cualquier momento; todos los tornillos estaban sueltos, avanzábamos con un estruendo de matraca para frenar apenas en las esquinas donde resultaba difícil doblar. Nunca me tocó montar una guagua en horas que todo el mundo salía del trabajo; los cubanos tenían que sufrir el calor y la apretazón. Yo me salvé porque de día íbamos a todas partes en el ómnibus con aire acondicionado. Por la noche era distinto, la velocidad creaba una corriente natural dentro de las guaguas que se precipitaban con gran estruendo por las calles de La Habana Vieja.

Desde que llegué a Cuba traté de conseguir pasaje para ir a Camagüey pero las cosas se dificultaban. A mí me habían advertido antes de salir que tendría que insistir como loca para poder salirme de la gira planificada y visitar a mi gente en la provincia ganadera. Insistieron en que no aceptara que me dijeran que no. Me dijeron que no mil veces. Llamé al aeropuerto constantemente y me decían que hacía varios meses no había vuelos a Camagüey, cosa que dudaba sinceramente, pero el que me lo decía lo afirmaba como para que no lo contradijera. La guía de nuestro grupo se hacía la que no sabía qué hacer. Paco me dijo que para conseguir vuelo había que sentarse en el aeropuerto a esperar. Una vez abuela esperó tres días seguidos antes de poder irse a Camagüey. Yo no disponía de tres días para esa espera.

Llegó el momento para irnos para Santiago y yo todavía no había resuelto nada. En el aeropuerto de La Habana pregunté de nuevo y nada. Me resigné a irme a Santiago y viajar de Santiago a Camagüey en burro si era necesario. En el camino a Santiago le eché un llanto a nuestra guía y ella me prometió que de Santiago podría partir en tren o en guagua. Llegamos a las afueras de Santiago y nos llevaron a un hotel con cabañas y piscina. El calor era mayor allí y nos metimos unos cuantos en el agua para refrescarnos un poco. El lugar estaba desierto. A la mañana siguiente fuimos a la plaza de la ciudad, una verdadera joya de la arquitectura colonial con la casa de Diego Velásquez con sus tinajones, columnas y flores. Quise entrar a ver el interior pero no se permitía. Qué desilusión. Entré a una librería pero no pude concentrarme. Sólo pensaba en que me quedaban cinco días en Cuba y no había visto a mi gente. De allí fuimos al cementerio a ver las tumbas de los próceres incluyendo la de Martí. Allí estaba, blanco, joven, valiente. Pasamos por la tumba de Estrada Palma y no nos detuvimos. Yo pregunté por qué y me dijeron que él había vendido el país a los norteamericanos, cosa cierta, pero la omisión me hizo ver que la historia había cambiado en Cuba. El cementerio me encantó porque estaba lleno de árboles muy frondosos, de allí me traje unas flores que sequé dentro de uno de mis libros y una vaina en forma de corazón de las que caían a montones de un árbol que yo no supe reconocer. Tanta flor y tanta primavera me dio una coriza tremenda. Yo había traído píldoras para eso precisamente pero se las dejé en La Habana a una de las del grupo que se quedó con una angina impresionante. Del cementerio me despedí del grupo y me fui a la estación de guaguas a esperar una que salía a la una para Camagüey. Mientras esperaba fui al baño y me encontré con una señora de un mal humor impresionante. Ella era la encargada de que los baños se mantuvieran lo más limpio posible; parece que su genio surtía efecto porque el sitio estaba impecable. Cuando me tocó mi turno me dijo:

—Cuidado con dejar el inodoro como una porquería. Hoy en día la gente no tiene ningún sentido de higiene. Apúrese. Hay otra gente esperando.

No dejó de hablar hasta que cerré la puerta detrás de mí. En realidad toda Cuba estaba super limpia, en las calles de La Habana no había visto ninguna suciedad. Ahora que estaba en el interior de la isla era lo mismo. Salí a buscar el ómnibus consciente de que sin estar acompañada por la guía tendría una mejor oportunidad de relacionarme con los cubanos. Por fin había conseguido lo que quería. Lo malo del caso era que tenía que regresar de Camagüey al día siguiente por la noche.

El viaje de Santiago a Camagüey en guagua debió haber tardado seis horas por la carretera central. Pero ese día no iba a ser así. Para empezar yo estaba con un cansancio de no dormir lo suficiente por ya casi una semana. Me dormía cada vez que estábamos en el camino pero me despertaba en todas las paradas. En el interior de la isla había una epidemia que estaba matando a los puercos. Decían que la epidemia había sido un proyecto de la CIA para arruinar la economía cubana. Para prevenir que se llevaran los gérmenes de un lado a otro había puntos de registro por todas partes y nos hacían bajar para que pusiéramos los zapatos en una solución de cloroformo de seis por ciento. Yo dudaba de la eficacia del método pero había que cumplir con las paradas. De vez en cuando había que bajar las maletas también y las registraban para estar seguro que nadie estuviera llevando carne de puerco de un sitio a otro. Al salir de cada pueblo la guagua pasaba por dos charcos para limpiar bien las gomas con el cloroformo. Quedaba una peste impresionante en la guagua después de todo el proceso; a mí me lloraban los ojos y me dio sinusitis.

La memoria que tengo de ese viaje fue de dormir un sueño muy pesado y de despertarme no queriendo sentir el olor fuerte del cloroformo. Como nos demoramos tanto en el camino, tuvimos que parar para comer en una estancia en el campo. Había un comedor; yo tenía un poco de hambre pero lo que tenían no me apetecía mucho. Por fin pedí unos vegetales que consistían de unos ajíes verdes fritos en una salsa con bastante grasa y un arroz blanco. No me gustaron mucho pero me quitaron el hambre. Después de comer nos sentamos todos en un patio a esperar a que terminara de comer el chofer. La gente se puso a conversar. En seguida me preguntaron quién era y qué hacía por allí. Les conté que iba a visitar a mi tía en Camagüey y me dejaron tranquila. Yo estaba todavía exhausta. Se pusieron a hablar de los contrabandos o la bolsa negra ya permitida, el mercado alternativo. Contaban que un tipo compró una maleta llena de cepillos de lavar porque ese día los vendían. Los metió en la maleta y se fue a varios pueblos a vender cepillos para ganarse la plata. Como en los otros pueblos no había, los pudo vender a un precio más alto. Yo no entendí si estaba permitido o no hacer lo que él estaba haciendo. El caso es que con estos registros ahora era más difícil mantener los negocios. La gente se divertía haciendo los cuentos y riéndose a costa de los que pasaban los apuros por los registros tratando de explicar que los cepillos se los llevaba a su familia, y el oficial decía que qué familia tan grande tenía y él respondía que sí. Nada, que al fin lo dejaron ir con sus cepillos y sólo tuvo que pasar un breve mal rato. La gente decía que sin ese mercado alternativo no se podía vivir. Yo pensé que qué maravilla que el cubano siguiera siendo el mismo, con un sentido del humor fabuloso, sobre todo en los momentos de dificultad. Ese cuento no difería mucho de los que se escuchaban en Miami cuando la gente pasaba trabajo con el inglés, o con las largas horas de trabajo a salario muy bajo. Sentí que el cubano era el mismo en todas partes y que no importaba lo que fuera, lo tiraba todo al choteo. Ya se estaba haciendo de noche y en el horizonte se podían ver las palmas reales y las montañas que se imponían oscuras frente a un cielo color violeta rosáceo.

Cuando llegamos a Camagüey, me monté en un taxi comunitario que nos llevaría a nuestras respectivas casas. Había tratado de llamar a María Luisa desde casa de Paco en varias ocasiones pero no hubo manera de comunicarse. Cuando me metí en el taxi me di cuenta que era la única mujer, todos los demás eran hombres que me preguntaron en coro cómo es que viajaba sola. Les conté que venía de los Estados Unidos a ver a mi tía. Les pareció impresionante que viajara sola de todas maneras. A mí me pareció raro que se sorprendieran tanto. Yo estaba tan acostumbrada a viajar sola o con mi hija que ya ni lo pensaba. Además estaba muy emocionada de estar en Camagüey y de tener la oportunidad de ver a María Luisa y a Mario. Después de todo Mario era mi primo favorito. Le di al taxista la dirección de la calle Lope Recio. En un abrir y cerrar de ojos ya estábamos enfrente de la casa. Tenía una puerta enorme de caoba con una ventanita pequeña para hablar con la gente. Le pedí al conductor que esperara a que me abrieran la puerta temiendo que la gente ya estuviera dormida o que hubiera salido y me quedara en la calle. El mismo tocó a la puerta y al ver que se abría la ventanita yo salí de la máquina para que me viera María Luisa. La reconocí en seguida. Para mí no había cambiado nada en la memoria, la misma cara, la misma voz callada y lenta.

—¿A quién desea?

—María Luisa, soy yo, Merceditas.

—Merceditas ¿qué?

—Merceditas, la hija de tu hermana Mercedes.

—¡Ay, Dios mío! Pasa, pasa. Por fin salió del espanto de ver a alguien que salía del pasado sin anunciar su llegada. Me abrió la puerta y la máquina se fue.

La pobre María Luisa no sabía dónde meterse del susto que le había dado. En el momento en que yo llegué estaba descongelando el refrigerador que estaba en el comedor de la casa. La casa estaba toda oscura y ella hablando conmigo y diciéndome que tenía que terminar de sacar el hielo del congelador. Traté de ayudarla pero estaba tan nerviosa que dijo que ella mejor lo hacía sola. Se fue un segundo a la cocina para llevarse la olla de agua caliente que había usado para descongelar. Cuando regresó llamó a su amiga para decirle que yo había llegado; Eustacio estaba dormido y Mario había venido a comer pero se acababa de ir. Empezó a preguntarme por todo el mundo y me preguntó si le había traído fotos de toda la familia. Ni se me había ocurrido traer fotos. Por casualidad tenía un montón de fotos de todo el mundo y se las dejé. Ella se puso contentísima. En un momento se me quedó mirando y me dijo que qué raro hablaba. A mí se me cayó el alma a los pies, pues su comentario confirmaba que yo no pertenecía ya más a este mundo. Después de un rato, ya serían las once o más tarde porque me sentía agotada, le dije que por qué no nos acostábamos y podíamos hablar más mañana.

La casa de Lope Recio era la casa de las Barrios, de los nacimientos de Navidad tan detallados. Esa noche yo sólo me di cuenta del comedor donde estaba el refrigerador y una mesa enorme sin sillas. Obviamente no se usaba. La casa era ahora de José Morel, primo de mami, pero él no dormía allí, sólo estaba por el día. Por la noche se iba a casa de su prima. Para ir al baño, que estaba al fondo, tuve que pasar por el pasillo que daba al patio interior; ahora estaba todo cerrado con puertas. Pude ver a Eustacio acostado en una camita con el mosquitero puesto. Cuando regresé al cuarto de enfrente, que era donde dormían María Luisa y la niña de Mario, ella había traído una sábana limpia y nos acostamos las dos en la pequeña cama. El colchón era duro, como de paja. Me cubrí con la sábana y esperé a que regresara María Luisa. Ya acostada me di cuenta de lo alto que eran los techos de la casa. Con el cansancio y el regreso sentí un vértigo que me hizo cerrar los ojos para abrirlos sólo la mañana siguiente. De alguna manera había llegado a mi patria en esa cama y pude descansar por primera vez desde mi llegada. Obviamente no me moví en toda la noche, estaba en la misma esquinita en la que me había acostado.

Por la mañana miré hacia la cuna de la niña y estaba vacía. María Luisa no estaba por ninguna parte. Examiné el cuarto. Una ventana enorme con reja daba a la calle. Enfrente de la ventana estaba la máquina de coser llena de retazos. La cama, la cuna y dos armarios grandes se amontonaban en el cuarto bastante grande. Me levanté y me vestí rápidamente. Los cuartos a la derecha de la casa se comunicaban por grandes puertas. Caminé hacia el fondo de la casa observando los armarios repletos de ropa de dormir con monogramas bordados con esmero, los cajones llenos de libros, las maletas encima de los armarios llenos de no sé qué. Las paredes no se habían pintado en siglos y añadían al sentido de abandono del lugar. Las telarañas colgaban en lo alto de las esquinas, seguras de que nadie las molestaría en ese cielo inalcanzable. Presupuse que todo lo que había en esos cuartos eran prendas de las familias que se habían ido del país dejando baúles de objetos que María Luisa no tocaba. Pensé, ¿cómo es que ella duerme en una cama sin sábanas cuando hay armarios aquí llenos de ropa de cama? Me imaginé que ella con su parsimonia habitual no había sentido la necesidad de usar nada de lo que no le pertenecía. Llegué a la cocina y la encontré vacía salvo por los ratoncitos que corrieron a esconderse. En el traspatio vi a dos ancianas encorvadas, pequeñitas por la edad, el vestido negro cubierto de un delantal gris, las piernas flaquitas, la cabeza atada con pañuelos de colores. La cara arrugada de la que se acercó a mí hacía acentuar una nariz aguileña y unos labios de ciruela por la falta de dientes. Las dos barrían el patio con escobas de paja al son del canto de los gallos que insistían en dar la bienvenida al nuevo día. Mi presencia en la cocina ni las inmutó; barrían sin prestarme atención. Yo era una intrusa en la casa que ellas habían atendido generación tras generación. Vi una canasta llena de tomates y huevos duros. Me comí un huevo y dos tomates que me supieron a cielo, estaban tan dulces.

Regresé a la sala donde encontré a María Luisa limpiando el piso. La niña se había orinado y como no tenía pañales que ponerle se pasaba siguiéndola con un trapeador. Sentí una lástima infinita por la abuela que tenía que cuidar a la nieta sin la ayuda de una mujer joven. Y ¿qué hacía Mario que no colocaba a la niña en una guardería? Calculé que se necesitarían meses para restaurar el orden en esta casa que se había constituido en el baúl de una familia enorme: una familia unida en un tiempo, pero completamente dispersa en la actualidad. Los cuartos con sus armarios atiborrados y las maletas amontonadas marcaban el silencio y la tristeza de una algarabía que antaño llenó los pasillos con alguien que tocaba el piano, los niños gritando y las mujeres atareadas con el cafecito del ir y venir de las visitas. El patio central, ahora abierto, estaba repleto de pequeñas jaulas con canarios que cantaban a coro con las palomas con su runrún perenne. El jardín interior estaba hecho un desastre, las yerbas malas habían invadido los canteros que todavía lucían geranios de varios colores. La fuente central estaba callada.

María Luisa había llamado a medio mundo para avisarles de mi llegada y pronto se llenó la casa con el dime que te diré que hace poco había añorado. Ofelia que me había dado clases de inglés de niña para prepararme para el viaje me regaló un tinajoncito con un bohío dibujado para que no me olvidara de mi tierra. El resto quería saber de Isabel y Alfredo, de mi hermana, de Rosa, de Rosi, de mami y papi. Cada uno se turnó hablando en la grabadora para mandar saludos a los de allá, que no escribían pero que siempre pensaban en ellos, que uno se ponía muy vago, y además con todos los problemas que tenemos, que para escribir de cosas desagradables no vale la pena, pero sinceramente hablamos mucho de ustedes, eso es de corazón.

Eugenia dio noticia de la gente joven, de Mariana, la hija de Antonio y el esposo que están viniendo a dormir conmigo porque ellos se casaron y allá no hay espacio y por las noches me acompañan. Mariana está en estado, muy trabajadora y competente. Aida el otro día hablaba de ti, de Isabel. Ella quiere mucho a Isabel. La pobre no anda muy bien, se fue a casa de Adelaida que se la llevó por dos meses a estar con ella porque está muy nerviosa. Le tiene miedo a la cocina, no quería comer, está muy desganada. Los deseos de ella, sinceramente son irse con Maricarmen, de irnos las dos, pero eso no es tan fácil, hay muchos trámites que llenar y económicamente nosotros en estos momentos no podemos movernos. Aida lo que recibe son sesenta pesos y yo hice una gestión de la pensión de mamá hace dos años y no me han contestado; entonces nosotras estamos con presupuestos muy reducidos, y por ahora es difícil que podamos ir, pero bueno, nadie sabe si la vida y Dios nos ayuda. Mi carácter igual, yo trato de sobreponerme, todos los días paso por casa de Adelaida porque si no voy se pone nerviosa y vengo pa'casa y voy pa'llá y le doy vuelta a la casa. La suegra de Raquel vino de los Estados Unidos y nos dijo que Maricarmen está en la mejor disposición de ayudarnos. Vamos a ver si podemos resolver aquí de algunas situaciones que tenemos y podemos irnos.

Todavía me encuentro capacitada para trabajar, y yo creo que me abriría paso; en toda mi vida en cualquier lado siempre me he abierto paso. Ese es mi carácter porque a mí no me importa trabajar en cualquier cosa. Vamos a ver si Dios nos ayuda. Mucho cariño y muy agradecida por el regalito que nos mandó que nos vino muy bien. Llegó uno de esos días que uno piensa que no sabe por dónde resolver y vino así caído del cielo, así que muchos cariños a todos, vamos a ver si nos podemos unir allá, que yo sé que ese sería el deseo de mamá, que ya el día catorce cumple dos años de muerta y nosotros le mandamos a decir una misa y quiero que ese día también pidan ustedes por ella, y le manden a decir una misa en nombre mío y de Aida. Cariños a todos, a tu hermana, y también a Rosa, que la recuerdo mucho, de todos me acuerdo. Estoy un poquito nerviosa, porque figúrense, me parece como si los tuviera delante y eso me pone, vaya, me pone mal. Si te es posible quiero pedirte un favor que le digas a Maricarmen, que si es posible le mande unas medicinas a Aida, que está muy nerviosa, alguna medicina para los estados depresivos que es lo que ella tiene, unas vitaminas porque está muy delgadita, esas inyecciones que le mandaron una vez, hidroxil, que le estuvieron muy bien pa'la cuestión de las manos que se le entiesan y el brazo que lo tiene muy mal.

Eugenia habló largo y tendido y después habló María Luisa: Aquí estamos bien, lo vamos pasando bien. Recibí un regalito, que me vino bien, y aquí está la nieta, que está muy graciosa pero luchando con ella. El trabajo sobra, pero ahí vamos pasando. Le damos muchos cariños a todos. Recibí carta de Isabel, dos cartas recibí, tarjeta de Merceditas, de Isabelita y de Mercedes, pero que no contesto porque tengo muy poco tiempo, siempre estoy corriendo, pero ya recibirán noticias de nosotros por Merceditas y les contará cómo estamos. Muchos cariños y muchos abrazos a todos y que vengan algunos, que vengan pronto. Hablaron también Ofelia, María Isabel Morel, Ramón, que si pasan por New Jersey que saluden a la familia de allá. Eustacio dijo: Aquí estamos pasándolo, ya usted sabe, como es el mambo, perdone la palabra. Que estén todos bien de salud, que es lo principal, es lo que a ustedes les deseo. En eso llegó Mario y nos abrazamos. Me dijo que qué prima tan guapa tenía; yo lo encontré muy bien a él también.

Después de un rato se fue la gente y nos quedamos un grupito pequeño. Yo le di a Mario y a María Luisa alguna ropa que les había traído. Todo les pareció fantástico, a mí me entró no sé qué cosa al no poder quedarme y ayudarlos a echar pa'lante. Era evidente que en esa casa se necesitaba mucho más un par de manos que otro vestido o unos jabones para lavar la ropa. Lástima que no le traje pantalones de trabajo a Mario, traía unos puestos que estaban rezurcidos con parches que tenían huecos también. Andaba con unas botas de trabajo gruesas pero sin medias y sin cordones. Por lo menos le había traído medias. A María Luisa le dejé mucha de la ropa que yo había traído para mí; me dio mucha lástima no llevarle más ropa a la niña. El trajecito que le llevé le quedó un poco chiquito porque estaba muy gordita. Decían que tomaba mucha leche y que no andaba mucho con otros niños, porque estaba metida en la casa todo el tiempo con la abuela. Yo le pregunté a Mario que por qué no la ponía en un jardín infantil por lo menos parte del día. Me dijo que se había separado de la mujer y que ella era muy inestable y por eso decidieron que la abuela cuidaría a la niña. En una casa, si no había mujeres que trabajaran, no había muchos beneficios, porque muchas cosas se podían conseguir mediante el carnet de trabajo de la mujer. Todos los beneficios para los niños se dan por parte de la mujer; como la madre de la niña no estaba en un trabajo por mucho tiempo, entonces no podía recibir ningún beneficio. Mario pensaba que a los hombres se les discriminaba un poco en la sociedad cubana, que el hombre trabajador era un cero a la izquierda. Yo pensé que ya era hora que a las mujeres se les concedieran algunos privilegios. A mí me dio lástima por la niña que obviamente necesitaba estar más con gente joven y con otros niños y por María Luisa que ya no estaba para estar corriendo tras una niña de dos años. En fin, esta abuela se veía bastante saludable e incluso se le veía muy bien aunque se quejara de que se estaba poniendo muy vieja.

Salimos al patio a esperar que estuviera la comida. Eustacio se había pasado toda la mañana preparando un banquete. Mario se puso al sol y pude verlo en kodacolor. Lástima que se me hubiera perdido la cámara y no pudiera sacarle una foto para que lo viera toda la familia. Tenía la cara curtida por el sol, los ojos muy pardos con pestañas muy largas. Usaba bigote y las patillas bastante largas; decía que ése era el furor ahora. Se quejaba que estaba un poco calvo, que se le estaba cayendo el pelo.

—Me estoy dejando crecer los bigotes bien largos para echármelos pa' arriba y cubrirme la calva.

Tenía cuarenta años pero aparentaba un poco más. El trabajo a la intemperie lo estaba avejentando prematuramente. Era más o menos de mi estatura, muy delgado y sumamente cariñoso. Cuando me vio me dio un abrazo como para que no se me olvidara más nunca. Me recordó mucho a Isa que también es cariñosa e impulsiva, por algo se llevaban tan bien los dos de niños. María Luisa y Eustacio vivían del retiro de sesenta dólares de él y luego él iba de voluntario a un comedor y siempre le regalaban comida para traer a la casa. Por eso nunca les faltaba nada de comer.

Eustacio nos llamó a comer y nos sentamos en el comedorcito al lado de la cocina. En la casa no había agua corriente y había que buscar cubos de agua del pozo para hacerlo todo. La niña no había querido hablar en la grabadora antes pero ahora yo simplemente puse la grabadora en la mesa mientras comíamos y hablábamos. Entonces se puso a cacarear constantemente. Eustacio preparó arroz, fricasé de pollo, chícharos y café para terminar. A mí me encantaron los chícharos; él comentó que de eso se vivía hoy en día, que esa era la comida cubana. Como yo no los como muy a menudo me supieron a gloria. María Luisa estaba muy nerviosa y no se sentaba, quería servirnos constantemente. Los gallos cantaban desde el traspatio, y la niña cuando vio que nosotros comíamos sin prestarle atención empezó a pedir pan, para luego no comérselo, pero por lo menos estaba participando en el jaleo.

Mario nos habló de su trabajo, que estaba más o menos a dos kilómetros de distancia de la quinta donde empezaba a construir su casita y trabajaba allí hacía quince años. El se graduó de la tecnológica pero como a él no le gusta ser jefe no gana más dinero; a él no le gusta que lo manden y tampoco le gusta mandar a los otros. En la jefatura se busca enemistades, y tiene cincuenta problemas, cincuenta rollos.

—Yo también hubiera podido estar de maestro, pero no sé si yo hubiera servido de maestro. La lucha de los muchachos no me gusta, yo creo que no tengo tabla pa' eso. Y a mí siempre me ha gustado la mecánica, ahora estoy en la parte eléctrica, me mudé pa' hí, es más limpio y más cómodo. Y en definitiva estoy ganando lo mismo, cambié de oficio, de los motores, a lo eléctrico. También estoy metido en lo de la televisión, armar la parte del chasis.

—¿Por qué no me hablas de esa quinta donde vives ahora?

—La quinta en realidad es la mitad de una quinta, cien metros de largo, por veinte de frente, la casa está muy mala y ahora pienso hacer un chalecito poco a poco cuando vaya consiguiendo los materiales. Ahora mismo ya tengo las placas para el techo, estoy construyendo con prefabricado y después que tenga la casa vendrá la grúa y le pondré el techo.

Los domingos se dedicaba a las matas en el patio. Tenía plátanos manzanos, varias matas, y había que darles condición. Entonces María Luisa iba a estar un tiempo en la quinta y un tiempo acá en la casa de Lope Recio. Mario dijo que se sorprendió muchísimo cuando lo llamé a la fábrica porque yo había dicho mi nombre y no sabía si yo era su prima o su tía (en los Estados Unidos las dos llevamos el apellido de papi).

—No pude salir del trabajo antes porque con la zafra hay un trabajo violento. Vamos a ver hasta cuándo podemos estirar el tiempo.

—Qué lástima que no te puedas quedar a comer, dijo María Luisa. Ana va a venir a comer y ella se hubiera puesto muy contenta de verte.

Se pusieron a revisar los acontecimientos de la noche anterior, recontando la sorpresa de María Luisa que está corta de vista, y no me reconoció, que no estaba preparada para tal llegada, que qué empuje tenía yo que me fui pa' los Estados Unidos sola, y venir aquí a Cuba, sola, vaya, hay que tener valor, no creas tú, las mujeres aquí no son tan echás pa'lante. El no pensó nunca que iba a volver a vernos a ninguno de nosotros, María Luisa repitió que ahora sí tenía esperanza de volver a ver a la gente de allá. Ella dijo que iba a cuidarse pa' ver si podía ir a Miami.

Eustacio trajo el café y se puso a hablar de su trabajo.

—¿Cuántos años piensas tú que yo tengo?

—No tengo la menor idea.

—Ochenta y uno, pero trabajo muy duro todavía en el comedor. La vida en Cuba es dura, pero aquí no se pasa hambre. Claro que no hay la abundancia que había antes, pero aquí no se ha muerto nadie de hambre. La gente se ve gorda, los muchachos se pasan el día entero comiendo helado. Todo el mundo gana, y hay bastante dinero. La gente come mucho en la calle. La gente que son jefes, ingenieros, ganan mucho dinero. Mario trabaja el sábado media jornada, como todo el mundo, pero en la fábrica se reunieron un día y decidieron que era mejor trabajar todo el día un sábado y el otro no. Así no hay que levantarse tan temprano y uno puede contar con dos días de vez en cuando para ir a la playa y divertirse.

Me preguntaron cómo había encontrado a Camagüey, que estaba muy grande, que había muchos más repartos, que la universidad estaba ahora en Máximo Gómez y que ahora iban a inaugurar un ingenio nuevo. Yo había visto muy poco de Camagüey. Si me hubiera quedado un poco más de tiempo hubiera podido haber visto la casa de Vista Hermosa, que María Luisa decía que tenía unos cocoteros enormes ahora, que casi no había cambiado nada excepto las matas. En la mañana, poco después de haberme despertado, tenía que ir a la estación de ómnibus a conseguir pasaje para el viaje de regreso. Me dijeron que si no lo conseguía en la mañana que no iba a poder viajar de regreso a Santiago. Yo estaba un poco preocupada con lo del pasaje. María Luisa me dijo que para ir en guagua nos demoraríamos toda la mañana. Yo le dije que tenía que regresar en el ómnibus de la una y que lo mejor sería llamar una máquina. Ella llamó y le dijeron que no había nada en ese momento, yo le dije que me dejara llamar a mí. Llamé y les dije que era cubana de la comunidad y en seguida me dijeron que la máquina pasaría en unos minutos. Arreglamos a la niña en un dos por tres y nos fuimos juntas a la estación. Repetí lo de la comunidad y me dieron el pasaje de inmediato, la máquina nos esperó y regresamos a la casa. Pero en el camino no reconocí nada. Cuando ya era hora de irme, la despedida con María Luisa fue bastante triste. Agarré mi bulto vacío y me lo puse al hombro. Mario tenía una motocicleta pequeña y me iba a llevar a la guagua. Montada detrás de él, yo iba muy ligerita, pasando por las calles de mi infancia. Reconocí la plaza Agramonte que ahora me pareció de dimensiones minúsculas; había jugado tanto allí de niña.

Llegamos temprano a la estación y comprendí que era el momento de la despedida. Empecé a llorar. Mario muy cariñoso me dijo que no llorara, por favor. Le pregunté que de veras cómo estaba María Luisa, que si le podía dejar mi cartera, cualquier cosa. El me dijo que no, que ella no necesitaba cartera porque nunca salía. Estuvimos hablando un rato, luego le dije que se fuera, que regresara al trabajo, que yo estaba hecha un desastre y que no hacía más que llorar. El se quedó hasta que se fue la guagua y pude verlo cuando se iba en su motocicleta. Empecé a llorar sin control, me habían advertido que cuando empezara a llorar no iba a poder parar por un largo rato. Una muchacha sentada a mi lado trató de consolarme preguntándome por qué lloraba. Yo se lo expliqué y entendió. Sentí que tenía derecho de llorar todo lo que quisiera. Me puse a escribir mis reacciones del día increíble que había pasado en Camagüey y a observar el lindo paisaje cubano. Camagüey era una provincia llana pero muy rica en agricultura. La caña se veía de un verde tierno en el horizonte; también me impresionaban las palmas sobre todo reunidas en palmares.

El ómnibus llevaba una radio y podía escuchar la música cubana que tocaban y alguna norteamericana. En vez de anuncios tenían consejos de cómo criar a los hijos, hasta lecciones de historia y de semántica: se dice poetisa, no poeta, para las mujeres. El anuncio de la cadena me llegó a ser muy conocido: Radio Progeso, Cadena Libre, La Habana, Cuba, Primer Territorio Libre de América. Después de unas horas de viaje subió un manicero vendiendo maní azucarado, qué rico. Mucho más tarde hicimos una parada y la chica que iba sentada a mi lado bajó y regresó con dos barquillas del helado para ver si así dejaba de llorar. Su gesto tan generoso casi que me hizo llorar más pero me tranquilicé para complacerla.

El viaje de regreso a Santiago no fue tan largo como el otro. No hubo paradas y como no necesitaba dormir pude disfrutar del paisaje. Casi todo Oriente estaba cultivado de frutas, los campos se veían muy lindos, como jardines a la inglesa aparcelados con las montañas de fondo. Cuando llegué a Santiago ya era la hora de la comida. Cogí un taxi para que me llevara al motel y el tipo empezó a hacerme preguntas. Esta vez era un hombre de mi edad, maestro de escuela, que manejaba la máquina para aumentar sus entradas. En seguida empecé a sentir en él el resentimiento de alguien que hubiera querido tener la libertad de movimiento que yo tenía. Me dijo que para mí era muy fácil favorecer la Revolución, cuando podía ir y venir a mi gusto, que no tenía que trabajar dos puestos, que él y su mujer eran los dos maestros y que no ganaban lo suficiente para vestir a los muchachos que ya estaban bastante grandes y que un par de pantalones costaba cuarenta pesos y que a esa edad ya no se conformaban con sólo un par. El se creía que yo era rica, que si tenía dinero para viajar a Cuba tendría que estar bien. Por supuesto todo era relativo, era verdad que mi situación estaba mucho mejor que la de él pero yo también empecé a resentir el hecho que ahora tendría que darle más dinero de lo que se merecía por el corto viaje de la estación al hotel. Después de la experiencia de Camagüey estaba super sensible; ya había sobrepasado los límites de la objetividad que pude mantener en La Habana. Me sentí culpable por haberme ido, claro que la decisión no había sido mía. Tuve que empezar a preguntarme si yo me hubiera ido si hubiera sido mayor de edad. Ni en ese momento ni mucho más tarde pude contestar esa pregunta. Ya que el destino de uno cambia, no hay regreso, sólo nuevas opciones. Llegué al hotel y la gente estaba comiendo. De allí todo el mundo se iba a una presentación especialmente para nosotros de un comité de defensa de la revolución. Yo estaba renuente a ir porque me sentía deshecha. Me senté a la mesa con una de las personas con quién más confianza tenía y empecé a contarles el desconsuelo que sentía después de estar con mi familia. Para empezar, la visita fue muy corta. Los encontré a todos muy bien pero faltos de la unión familiar que habíamos conocido antes. Además una culpabilidad genuina de no poder quedarme con ellos y llenar ese vacío familiar se apoderó de mí.

El resto del grupo me convenció que no podía quedarme sola y que mejor que viniera a pasarla bien un rato. Toda una cuadra se había reunido para hablarnos del trabajo de la Revolución a nivel popular. Los representates principales hablaron de los deberes de todos en la cuadra: había que hacer guardia por la noche, había que visitar a los recién casados, a las nuevas madres, había que mantener las calles limpias, etc. Los niños recitaron y cantaron canciones patrióticas; se podía sentir en el aire un espíritu de comunidad. Yo en ese momento me sentía muy sola en los Estados Unidos porque estaba batallando por terminar la disertación y en esos momentos lo que me estaba ayudando era aferrarme al individualismo que dice que si uno trabaja con miras al futuro las cosas se realizarán. Una buena dosis de apoyo comunal me vino de maravilla. La soledad del trabajo en casa me había hecho olvidar la posibilidad de compartir las penas. El viaje a Cuba resultaba tan difícil porque nunca hubo un momento en que una acción o un sentimiento no repercutiera con preguntas incontestables y con la intensidad de una visita demasiado breve. En esta cuadra llena de gente bailando y con los brazos abiertos sentía el cariño acogedor que tanto me faltaba en la tierra de las grandes oportunidades. Mi viaje al interior me había devuelto la Cuba de mi infancia, sin aprensiones ni necesidades de justificarme.

De regreso a La Habana tuve la suerte de dar una vuelta por el malecón de despedida. Era un día gris y no había nadie caminando. El viento hacía que las olas sobrepasaran la pared que nos separaba del mar y nos mojamos varias veces. La cosa empezó a ponerse fea. Las nubes negras avanzaban con furia y el viento se puso mucho más recio. Empezó a llover a cántaros y fuimos a refugiarnos en un edificio. Un muchacho sin camisa y sin zapatos se apareció corriendo como por encanto y enfrentó a las olas que ahora inundaban la acera. Empezó a bailar y a dar saltos frente al mar pensando que estaba a solas. Se me quedó en la mente la figura hierática del muchacho con los brazos en alto y la cabeza baja como un cóndor anclado en la tierra y retando la fuerza del viento y la marea.

Al día siguiente nos íbamos de Cuba y yo empecé a pensar que no me quería ir. Cuando llegamos al aeropuerto esa mañana me saqué una foto al lado de una palma real pequeñita que hay allí. En el aeropuerto compré unos afiches muy lindos que con el nerviosismo de la salida dejé enrollados en un asiento. La espera no fue muy larga. Hacía un calor de esos sofocantes sin brisa. Estaba aturdida por las experiencias de los días del regreso y no sentía nada en particular. Me fijé en las sala de espera que en mi última salida me había causado tanta ansiedad. No se parecía en nada a la que llevaba en el recuerdo, esa pecera de cristal que había de determinar mi vida por tantos años. Igual que la primera vez que salí de Cuba, no recuerdo la salida. Como la primera vez, salí con un gusano de tela que esta vez estaba lleno de libros y no de ropa. El gusanito dentro se había convertido en mariposa, todavía volando por encima de las cosas para entenderlas mejor. Pero la distancia y el olvido del punto de vista aéreo no facilitan las respuestas, sólo engendran más preguntas. Habría que regresar otra vez para sumergirme inconscientemente como un pececito tropical en las aguas de lo cubano. Temo que esas quimeras no se darán nunca.

Pablo La Rosa

Steppes

To be or not to be a soldier, that was a question. To become a green marine or to escape in a yellow submarine. To drop acid with Tim or to drop the bomb on Ho Chi Minh. To burn your draft card in the park or to burn Viet Cong with napalm. To search and destroy gooks in rice paddies or to research books in libraries. But to question or not to question: That was, is, and forever shall be the question.

It was the best of times, it was the worst of times. Yesterday life wasn't such an easy game to play, but oh how I long for yesterday. Oh where, where have all the flower children gone, long time ago. Where, oh why have you gone Abbie Hoffman, yesterday. It all went so suddenly, a state of mind jolted and gone away.

Forgive me, but I cannot help the way I am, the way I look at things through a glass darkly no matter how bright the sun; nothing escapes the enzymes of my acid tongue, the corrosive juices of my gut reactions. The main reason my wife left me was my gloom and doom attitude, as she put it, the way I criticized everything from the President's foreign policy to her penchant for ruining hose on a daily basis. In another age, in another society I may have served a purpose, but no one wants to be awakened from their upscale dreams, to be warned of the possible derailment of their smooth-running bourgeois express.

Among all the distinguished and tenured minds of a prestigious university the one that influenced mine most belonged to an obscure custodian from the Russian steppes. His name was not Vladimir, but in order to protect the privacy of his widow and for a more expedient, literary reason I shall refer to him as Vladimir.

We exchanged our first words one fall evening in the fourth floor men's room of _____ Hall, the Humanities building of a major midwestern university where I was a graduate student in Comparative Literature and he, a night janitor. At first I resisted his overtures to conversation. I had a fellowship to do research, and his visits to the small office I shared with two ever-absent, ever-stoned fellows detracted from my duties. But after a few of his narratives I looked forward to the time he'd finish his chores on the fourth floor and join me for coffee. The stories he told from the Old World cut through the language barrier like an archetypal double edge. In those days his mind was still sharp, though quickly deteriorating from a nightly pint of vodka chased by however much Thunderbird it took to anesthetize it. An unpolished Nabokov, he was able to mock in broken English the inconsistencies of his adopted fatherland with crude but pulverizing observations. To those who may not follow the Nabokov analogy, may I suggest stripping *Lolita* of sex in your next reading. You might discover that instead of a tempting tale of tardy tenderness, as one no doubt older reviewer with fantasies of his own interprets the work, it is one of the most acid reactions to the American Way ever expressed in writing.

To repeat myself, I was a doctoral candidate in Comparative Literature. My dissertation, left unfinished like so many projects from the sixties, dealt with a Cuban movement of absurdist fiction that preceded the post-Castro social realism. It was the artistic freedom unleashed by the revolution that made this movement possible, and though this had nothing to do with literary research, I was very much interested in the subject and wanted to understand why within two years the revolution was denying the freedom to write "defeatist and reactionary" literature. Vladimir provided me with an insight. Revolutions, to paraphrase him, do not exist beyond the spontaneous struggle that overthrows the established order, and the new intelligentsia takes itself too seriously to allow the possibility that life may be meaningless. Vladimir should know. He had survived several upheavals, including *the* Revolution.

At the time I was waging my own struggle for having requested a third student deferral. There was absolutely no way I could rationalize my worth to society as an apprentice literary critic any longer. I despised most of my professors and had come to agree with Governor Wallace that the majority of academes use briefcases to brownbag their peanut butter sandwiches. I had sunk to such a low level of self-esteem that I defaced my Master of Arts diploma by inserting an apostrophe between the letters of the preposition and then connecting the f to the Arts with a hyphen.

Yet I was reluctant to give up the academic life. I sensed that those of us fortunate to be on campus during the late sixties were in the midst of a Golden Age that would not be replicated in our lifetime. It was romantic to be alive, it was a period of great expectations and experimentation, hardly any of the latter empirical. Lyndon Johnson had decreed the American Pie to be of Texas proportions, and enough of his Great Society bribe eluded the bureaucracy to end up in unlikely hands. Our campus was, consequently, full of extraordinary characters whose least interest lay in scholarly pursuit. One could walk into a beer joint any evening and find someone plotting the Great American novel or ways to dismantle the very structure that made his idleness possible. *Ubi sunt*, I'd like to know, the Marxist radicals and the black militants, the jazz musicians who jammed at the Gaslight every Wednesday night, the promising poets who won the English Department contests. Oh where, where have all the flower children gone, long time passing. When nostalgia drives me to a college campus on a rainy fall afternoon and I confirm that America's obsession with plasticity, so poignantly symbolized by the neon sign in *Lolita*, is now manifested by the love of video games, I am painfully reminded of one of Vladimir's last lucid statements: "A movement fermented by the boredom of excess materialism instead of hunger—he said with characteristic pessimism—will not be a revolution but simply a revolt."

There were other reasons why I hadn't severed my ties to academia. The university was a refuge from a society unwilling to fully admit a refugee who showed too much otherness. I carried a card that certified me as an alien, by definition "one excluded from some group, an outsider." The adjective connotation given by the same dictionary, "repugnant," succinctly expresses how one is perceived by the general public. Forced into solitude at an age when most of my peers engaged in mutual masturbation, I discovered literature.

The proud recipient of a fellowship, I entered graduate school armed with a fervent belief in the power of the word to reveal deeper realities, be these personal or universal, and to transform mankind for the better. Since I believed that literature was valid only as an activity that shed light on the human condition, I found myself rebelling from the very first lecture against the trend to dehumanize it, to make of it no more than a linguistic exercise with no meaning beyond the text. I was disturbed to the point of incoherence whenever one of those shallow critics minimized the importance of the author, asserting that the artist was a tool that served the grand scheme of language instead of the opposite. They were like the Cuban officials who demanded that writers serve the scheme of their "revolution." They were jealous of the creator, so they systematically researched and destroyed.

The friendship between Vladimir and me deepened into affection as Indian summer decayed into fall. My peers didn't understand the relationship, for on the surface we didn't have much in common. He was a good thirty-five years older than I, we were from opposite ends of the world, he liked to drink and I preferred to smoke dope. But the fact we were immigrants superseded all other considerations. We discovered in each other a deep-rooted fear of not belonging and a profound longing for our homelands, which with all their imperfections we remembered as Paradise.

Wanting to know more about the Russian character, I had checked out a collection of stories by Chekhov. One story in particular caught my attention. Appropriately titled "In Exile," it juxtaposed the characters of an old man who had given up all hope in life and a young man who desperately clung to ideals no matter how hopeless they appeared. I was somewhat troubled by the parallels I saw between the fictional construct and our situation. Like the young Tartar, I still nurtured hopes of returning home someday, but Vladimir, like the old man condemned to row the barge eternally across the river, had lost hope of ever setting foot on the motherland again, a realization that filled his pale blue eyes with a glaze of sorrow. And like the old man in the story, the palliative for his infinite sadness was alcohol.

I didn't suspect how strong his dependence was until Vladimir invited me to dinner for the first time in October. Anticipating a tasty meal, something I didn't enjoy often as a bachelor, I treated myself to a reefer as I traversed the autumn-emblazoned campus. My appetite rose to a crispness that matched the late afternoon's air, and I stopped to buy a bottle of Ruffino Chianti at a liquor store located just outside university proper. I was feeling pretty good when Vladimir answered the doorbell, but he was in higher spirits. He greeted me effusively and introduced me to his wife Elga as if I were a beloved nephew back from a long journey. We sat down to a neatly prepared table covered with a variety of dark breads, cheeses, crisp vegetables, and herring. In no time Vladimir and I polished off a fifth of Smirnoff. I watered mine down, but he drank it straight in small, frequent sips. At six o'clock he turned on the TV to the Lawrence Welk show. He asked Elga to dance and I watched them waltz elegantly around the small living room, lost in their memories. The polka number brought them back to reality and they grabbed me by the arms. We stomped to Myron's accordion noisily, arms locked in a circle.

The physical activity aroused our appetite. Elga joined us in drinking the Chianti with the main dish, a hearty, well-stocked stew. This was followed by cake and Turkish-style coffee; the resulting high demanded more vodka. Elga informed Vladimir there was none left. The festive mood turned sour, Vladimir accusing Elga of hiding his only source of joy. A brief but terse argument ensued in Russian. Finally Elga stood up and went upstairs, I thought for the evening, but within minutes she returned with an open, half-empty bottle she had been stashing. Now he'd have to do without vodka tomorrow, she reminded him, because liquor stores were shut on Sundays in America.

Elga disappeared. I was saddened by the episode and asked Vladimir if he minded I smoke; *I* needed my palliative. He said he didn't mind, but I felt compelled to explain I was thinking of smoking marijuana, not tobacco. He replied he didn't care; young men had a right to smoke reindeer dung if they were so inclined. I lit up, he sipped, and soon we were taking turns telling each other about one childhood in great expanses of snow and another in seas of sugarcane. We described simple games we had played with friends, recalled how life seemed solidly entrenched along immutable paths until suddenly, two revolutions derailed history. At some point the conversation became monologues, one in Russian and one in Spanish, and although neither spoke the other's language we understood perfectly what each was saying, and when we finished speaking we wept.

Towards the end of October I received the first registered letter ever sent me. Although the manner of delivery was very personal, the envelope contained a form letter drafted by an impersonal narrator and addressed to an abstract implied reader. But the implications were quite clear. The draft board was making it easy for me to sever my umbilical cord to academia. The National Defense fellow was to become part of the national defense. The members of the board could see through my transcript riddled with B's that my heart wasn't in the paper chase, and they were sparing me the anxiety of writing a dissertation. The members of the board may have been common folks, but they were no dummies. They knew a bogus dissertation when they saw one. They were not as easily persuaded as Congress, who had voted to spend billions blindly for the Humanities in the name of National Defense.

For the first time in my life, the possibility of going to war was real. Until then the idea of war had been, like the idea of death itself, a fascinating topic to consider from the comfort of a reading chair or the safety of the imagination. As a boy I had often pretended to be an American soldier in World War II, specially when I accompanied my father and his cronies on hunting forays to the

Zapata swamps. While the hunters massacred hundreds of sitting ducks basking in the winter tropical warmth, I emptied my pellet rifle on imaginary Japs hiding in the bush. Later, as a teenager full of patriotic fervor trying to measure up to a grandfather who had fought alongside the Rough Riders in the Spanish War, I had gone as far as signing up for what turned out to be the Bay of Pigs invasion. Fortunately for me then, my father, the staunch anti-Communist, made sure my name was honorably deleted from the list of volunteers and put me away in a private school, well protected from the Cuban zealots who ruled Miami.

There was so much literature, great literature, inspired by the folly and grandeur of war that as a student of *belles lettres* harboring ambitions of *producing* literature, I could not help but wonder if war might not be a necessary evil for the formation of character, indeed a prerequisite to full manhood. The example of Hemingway alone sufficed. Moreover, was my generation's reluctance to fight an "immortal war" disguised cowardice, as the hawks claimed? For whatever dark reason lurking in my subconscious, I had decided not to resist the draft board's ruling.

When Vladimir dropped by the office at the customary hour that evening, I showed him the letter and explained the contents. Seeing he was confused, I joked about going to fight the Communists in Vietnam so that we both could go back home. But he didn't see the humor. Vladimir's blue eyes turned inward. He was gone an eternity, and when he came back the fire in his pupils told me he'd been in hell.

Vladimir's visits now had one purpose, and one purpose only: To convince me that war was the most horrible thing in life, and that I should do whatever was necessary to avoid being drafted. Not that I had many options. To claim conscientious objector status would have been ludicrous for someone who hadn't set foot in church for ten years and who was proud of his agnosticism. There was a chance I'd fail the physical, but I'd been a competitive swimmer and still worked out two or three hours a week to relieve tension. Leaving the country was totally out of the question. To gain political asylum in the U.S., I had given up my Cuban passport and what few rights went with it to Immigration; without a passport, I couldn't even cross the border to Tijuana.

Vladimir's nightly pleading began to have an effect on my outlook. His descriptions of the horrors he had witnessed during World War II were much more graphic than the bloody footage we saw every night on Walter Cronkite, though I had started to watch those clips with different eyes, too. I began to keep track of the casualties and to figure the odds of my being one. Every day, or so it seemed, the chances improved.

I decided to tell no one else about the impending physical, not even my family. It had been scheduled for the first week of December. If I passed it, I could finish the semester, spend Christmas at home, and report to the induction center for assignment after New Year's.

What I remember most about the physical is the final lineup to check for hernias, the rape at the end of eight hours of torture. Two rows of about one hundred men each faced off. We were told to drop our pants. A doctor and an assistant began the inspection. First you were ordered to bend over, grab your buttocks, and expose your anus. After checking for hemorrhoids, the doctor squeezed your scrotum and asked you to cough. This grotesque procedure could mean the difference between life and death, between life in a wheelchair and freedom.

If I had any doubts about going to war after Vladimir's impassioned pleas, they were shredded by the demeaning battery of tests administered by abusive, arrogant officers. I surprised myself at how very consciously I objected to their authority. I didn't believe a word they said, and above all, I didn't want to put my life at their mercy.

One lucky fellow was found to have a hernia, but it wasn't I.

The institution where I was committed after being found mentally incompetent to stand trial for arson was located clear across the state from the town where the university was, three hundred miles to the west. When Vladimir and Elga came to visit me, they kept remarking how much the landscape reminded them of the steppes. It was late winter, and beyond the hospital fences the winter wheat was beginning to push through the snow.

We had a happy reunion. Elga had baked me a batch of cookies, and she had brought some nice tea that we brewed in the kitchen. Since it was Saturday, they insisted on watching Lawrence Welk. We even danced to the polka to the cheers of my fellow mates who were in the rec room.

My friends had to catch the lone bus going east at eight, so it was a short visit. We hugged and kissed Russian style, and they promised to come back in the summer when the wheat was ripe.

Just as they were leaving, Elga reached inside her purse and handed me a sealed envelope. I waited until I went to bed before opening it, expecting to find a note and a little cash to spend at the hospital store. Instead I found a hand-written confession, signed by Vladimir and witnessed by Elga, admitting it was he, not I, who had started the fire in the Dean's office of the humanities building. I was to turn it in to the police at the end of the war or after Vladimir died, whichever came first.

It was a true confession, but I burned it and threw the ashes out into the night.

Juan Armando Epple

Garage Sale People

I'm going for a spin, he said, and before I could ask him where he was heading, he had the car in reverse and was backing out over the daffodils he himself transplanted when we moved from Springfield. The daffodils suffer whenever he's angry or confused about one of the assignments they give him to write; he starts enthusiastically but then drops them saying he can't find the right tone.

My daddy's typewriter is like my mom's sewing machine that she bought at a garage sale; it works okay for a while and then breaks down. My mom says when he writes nonstsop for an hour it's because he's answering a letter from one of his friends, those ten-page epistles they like to send to each other. And when he writes for a few minutes and then there's a long silence in his room it's becuase he's thinking over some problem, ... like homework Miss Greenfield gives us? ... and we know at any minute he'll come downstairs and cruise through the kitchen uncovering the pots on the stove or head straight out to the yard to water his tomatoes, saying it helps him concentrate.

"I bet your papa wanted to watch the news and you changed the channel on him," I said to Marisol who had settled in front of the TV with a package of cookies and Def Leppard records scattered around her, glued to one of those music programs where singers change scenes every verse.

"No, he told me he had to write some letters. Besides, the only program he likes is the news at 7. I went in to ask him why he didn't write Granny too and let's get her here finally, even if it's just for a visit. That's when he jumped up from his chair and pumm ... was gone. You think he went to the Post Office?"

Since I don't understand anything about American football, much less baseball, and it's even harder for me to understand English in the movies (it's like speaking while you chew potatoes, Marta says, trying to imitate a phrase), the only way I can deal with Marisol's questions is to get out on the streets to warm up my muscles. Even this metaphor doesn't fit, because everytime I catch

69

myself in a mirror, it confirms that I'm gaining several pounds a year, and my first gray hairs have already arrived. It's the most interesting age for a man, Marta says, at the same time she runs her finger along my incipient double chin. Besides, every time I decide to go running I find myself competing with hundreds of athletes all wearing their Nikes, and convinced that Eugene is the running capital of the world and every one of them—even the modest— truly believing they can win the NY marathon. So I finally opted for the classical wheelchair of this country, even if only to imagine that we are discovering new routes, gliding through these rigorously laid-out streets with traffic lights and patrolmen regulating my exercise, swearing loyalty to this car which was so shiny at the beginning and now moves by jerks, like a Pinto with the flu.

When I was learning to drive and Chinaman (Chinaman was from Antofagasta and even he didn't know why he had the nickname) taught me a few basic maintenance tips like checking the pressure in tires, changing the oil and putting antifreeze in the radiator, I thought it would be a good idea to get myself some of those tools he carries in the trunk of his convertible (this is a real convertible, my friend, he exudes, flashing a sleeve over the canvas top ... from the good old days, you can even turn it into a bed should the occasion arise), so I stopped once at one of those little signs that say "Garage Sale," looking for extra equipment for the car. Bit by bit my curiosity became an obsession as I discovered that garage sales are small family markets gringos set up in their garages or on their lawns, where they put out second hand and even some new things, acquired on their tourist safaris no doubt or at those irresistible sales in the big department stores, stuff they accumulate until their boundless desire for new things forces them to offer it all up for a few bucks to make room for new purchases. My first few times out I got carried away by enthusiasm, enthusiasm for the variety of objects set out on little tables or casually placed on the picture post card lawns. I started bringing home unexpected trophies; Marta's reactions went from compassion to concern: a plow from the era of the gas engine (the farm in the South we had to sell in a hurry to get out of the country in time), prints, fishing lures, picture frames, a new Mexican *guayabera* shirt which I wore even in mid-winter, not so much to imagine how life would have been in that country had our visas arrived in time but mainly to relive the goodbyes in the Bomba Bar, jot down addresses, go over the coded language we would use to communicate with one another, and gringo Hoefler looking warily at the chairs—every day one more was empty—his mind made up to remain till the last for some secret ancestral reason, and now a toast to the "Scourge of Puebla," a pair of imitation Colt 45s made out of tin, like those idealized in the westerns written by Marcial Lafuente Estefania who turned out to be a Spaniard who never left his own country, earning his living writing stories of the Far West which he diagrammed with the help of a map taken from *National Geographic*, Frankie Avalon or Cinco Latinos records, and those best sellers so passé people have to throw them in a box in hopes that someone will cart them off free, help yourself. I put a halt to my casual purchases one day when, coming home with a terrific mannikin worthy of a place in my office, there was Marta in the midst of putting our own junk away in the garage, trying to make some room: "If you keep up this sport of yours, I'd appreciate it if you would bring home something a little more useful. I asked you a long time ago to get me some canning jars, or a vacuum cleaner that works since you don't want to buy a new one."

In our years away from Chile we had to change countries twice (in some countries to get a resident's visa you need to have a work contract first; in others you have to have the residency in order to get a job, and then there are other countries where they don't want us even as tourists) and once in the United States we had lived in more than five states before we finally got something more or less permanent in Eugene. Oregon drew us immediately, like a secret force, because it looks so amazingly like the South of Chile. Our moves had us packing and unpacking, selling or giving away what little furniture we acquired, crating and uncrating Dario's books, because there's one thing for sure—a woman can say goodbye to her vacuum, the pots and even the china, but Mr. Big's books have to be put in the coziest part of the truck. We'll buy it all new there, dearie, don't worry. Then we had to send our new address to family and to the friends for whom we still existed, take Marisol's vaccination certificate and school records to yet another school; she didn't even know what to put anymore in the "country of origin" section. She ended up writing MARISOL (which guaranteed her a spot in the geography class), and even planning a little garden spot in the backyard to put in some cilantro and basil. For sure, these proud exiles are always ready to travel, "looking for New Horizons," but wherever they go they keep longing for the *empanadas* and *humitas* Granny used to fix for them. When he got into these garage sales it didn't bother me too much because it seemed harmless entertainment, but when he began to sing praises in front of these "Persian markets" as he called them in front of other Chileans, I had to rein him in. Hilda told me confidentially that people were not calling us "the Persians."

In school nobody knows where Chile is, so they call me Hispanic or Latin sometimes. One time I told the English teacher that it was a beautiful country with a lot of mountains and fruit trees, and she smiled and said how true, she had wonderful memories of a trip to Acapulco. Maybe they don't know where it is because it's so small on the map, kind of like a string bean, and that's why so many Chileans have had to go abroad to live. What I don't get is, if it's so small, how come everything there is so big. Any time Chileans get together at my house—everywhere we've lived there's a group of Chileans who call each other every day and get together to eat—they create a country I don't think exists on any map. The watermelons there are bigger and sweeter than the ones at Safeway, grapes are the size of plums there, Mt. Hood doesn't come up to the ankle of Aconcagua, there's nothing like a stew of *congrio*, which must be an enormous fish like a shark but tasty, the wine they sell here tastes like sweet ink or the beer tastes like piss, and there is no comparison between bread baked in the South and that plastic stuff they sell here. One day they got together to discuss something about passports and to look at a list Uncle Romilio brought, inventing surnames that began with the letter "L" (like Lunatic, Limpid, Lolosaurus, Lucifer, Laborious, Lanco, Liberator and so on). We kids began to draw. I drew a mountain range and went to show it to my Papa. He looked at it a long time, then he became serious, and corrected my mountain range, saying it was much taller and more difficult to cross. He didn't see that I had also drawn an airplane. That afternoon he criticized everything my aunts and uncles were saying—we have to call all grownups from Chile aunt and uncle—saying that *empanadas* are originally from Chile and the *cueca* is a dance brought to Chile from Africa. Finally our visitors had had enough and left, and one of the uncles shouted at my papa that the only thing clear was that we considered ourselves Persians now.

Marisol had put us on the spot again with her innocent logic, just that sunny day with raspberry pie, when I said something about the flour they sell at the supermarkets and she spoke up to say that if Granny knows how to make better pies, why don't we go to Chile to see her? Dario stood up and walked to the kitchen, Does anyone want more coffee?, giving me that "You brought it up, you answer her" look. But at this point in exile it's hard to explain to a girl who grew up in this country what it means to have an L on your passport—I mean, we don't even know what the "L" stands for— so I tried to explain that airfares were out of sight these days, that Papa had been trying to save money but we barely have enough for one ticket and it's not fair for just one of us to go back to Chile, right? I don't know if I convinced her, but she ate an extra piece of pie, played with her napkin a bit, then announced that she was reserving the television until 12.

I closed myself up in my office, but in a while she came up, lifting my papers as if interested in what I write and then looking out the window. She proposed: why don't we invite Granny to spend the summer with us? It's just one ticket, right? and this girl for whom we have spent years painting a country filled with specific tastes and odors, fixed and obsessive memories, faces which still seem just around the corner, and above all family presences which grow even as they fade in time, how can we jump up and tell her her grandmother died a few months after we left Chile? I gently mussed her hair and said, "Good idea, Miss, let's see what we can do," and I left.

That day I hit a couple of garage sales not seeking anything in particular, and I stopped at one house to take a look at some gardening tools they had, with prices precisely marked on those little white papers, in hopes of finding a hoe. I was about to go back to the car when I found the old woman, installed on a reclining chair, staring off into a world prior to all Sundays filled with questions and garage sales. At first I thought she was another mannikin, artfully arranged on the chair to show off a blue velvet dress with lace or the box of Hindu prints on her lap. But when I drew closer to inspect some shirts and look at her, I was surprised to see her reach out her hand for the 25-cent souvenir-of-Seville fan, and begin to fan herself energetically with perhaps a bit of coyness.

Seeing me stretch the collar of a shirt, the owner of the house came up with an ear-to-ear smile and the typical supermarket question: "May I help you?" The shirts were practically new, their daughter had gotten married and they had decided to sell off some of their belongings because they were moving to an apartment, he offered. You know, he added, as you get older you need less pace.

Impulsively responding to my dilemmas, I pointed with my finger and asked him:

How much are you charging for that granny over there?

The man stared at me, then quickly disappeared into his house.

I started retreating fast, fearing well-deserved insults which might improve my grasp of the English vernacular, but before I got around the corner I heard him call me, almost sweetly. A blond lady was standing beside him, wiping her hands on an apron.

Putting a friendly hand on my shoulder and dropping his voice at the numbers, he said, "What about five hundred bucks?," like he was making the deal of the year.

Taking my confusion as a bargaining ploy, the woman added, "She's really worth much more. To tell you the truth, we weren't even thinking of selling her."

"And besides, she's completely healthy," her husband interjected. "She's just started to use glasses. A month ago we got her a complete check up and the doctor said she'd live for many more years. In her condition, the doctor predicted ... "—my possible relative was about to let out an approving guffaw, but his wife cut him off with her elbow—"she might outlive us all."

"You really want to sell her?" I asked in perplexity.

"The thing is, the apartment is so small and the only way was to send her to a retirement center, and really, she's so used to family life she just doesn't deserve to end up there. We hadn't imagined that there might be another solution: a young family, full of plans, because you, judging by your accent, must be a Hispanic immigrant, right? You can give her a new opportunity, and in a Latin environment where you value the old ways ..."

"How much can you offer for her?"—the woman went on,— "Besides, we'll give you all her personal effects and you can't imagine how much of value she's accumulated over her lifetime. And we'll throw in some kitchen items because you wouldn't believe what great apple pie she makes, from a secret recipe she inherited from her mother, and she likes to cook with her own pans."

We spent a couple of hours on the deal, and after working out a way to pay, we agreed that I would come back for her in a couple of weeks. A wise decision, because you can't just up and make these changes from one day to the next.

*   *   *

That night during dinner, I noticed that Dario was quieter than usual, and he even drank *mate*, which he practically never does because he says it gives him insomnia. Looking at Marisol who was drawing something on her napkin, he suddenly started proposing a series of changes in the house routine, asking if we still had that cot we bought when Heriberto El Chilote came from California to visit us.

Anticipating the surprise, I casually allowed, "Because we've got to get another bedroom ready. I booked a reservation for Granny today, and she'll be making us a visit in two weeks."

Then I went outside into the backyard because it was still light, and the hills surrounding the Williamette Valley intensified the degrees of green, stretching towards the last golden sparks of the sun. It was like being on Lake Llanquihue once more, smelling the secret rhythms of the seasons, but without being there.

But I also went outside because I wanted to make sure that the beans were climbing up the stakes, that the danger of frost had passed, and that the hoe was really of good quality—that hoe my new Northamerican relatives threw in as an extra.

Translated by R.M. Jackson

A. Pablo Iannone

South

Rather than a poem, it's a little song. Yes. I wrote it many years ago, during one of those cold Northern falls when I used to live almost in Canada and nothingness, and the birds, you know?, had begun to migrate in unending flocks. Did you hear that some go as far as the other tip of the continent? I imagined them crossing the Amazon, going along the Andes, wishing to see the pampas, like me, and I felt nostalgia, and wrote the song. Its title is Sur. Yes. Of course. That's why. Catalina wrote the music for it; but when we broke up we stopped singing it together and the last time she visited us, do you remember she mentioned it? She had lost the music and we had both forgotten it. No. What am I going to write, more poetry? This little song must be the last in the series. Poetry makes me nervous. No. What do you mean translation! Poetry cannot be translated. And as you can imagine, I don't know enough English to get myself into that. But if you understand Spanish! What need is there for me to translate it for you? If you want to, I'll read it to you; but in the mother tongue, man. Besides, this way you'll practice. And especially this song, it would be treason to translate it. Here, it's really as they say: translator, traitor. But why? But why? I have to read it for you to see why. What do you mean it can't be treason? What do you mean it can't be that big of a deal? Of course it is! No, I'm not exaggerating at all! Do you believe that because you have lived with me for three years and some, you already know everything about me and my culture? See what I'm always telling you? You have a little box for everything. But this country is unbelievable! And it must have stuck on you! It stuck when you were a kid. How do I know where!? At school which, no offense, leaves much to desire, or at home, where you people were so many that there was not time to try to understand anyone. I'm telling you again. Take off the blinders, man. Look before talking. And listen. Listen first and see whether I'm exaggerating. And where are you going now? What! I bet you got upset! Look at the expression on your face and you'll see why I'm saying it! And the tone, man. The tone that came upon your voice! Metallic. Businesslike. What rush is there all of a sudden to wash clothes? There you go again. I told you a thousand times that love is not a contract, or the fifty-fifty, or the even Steven. And what proves the "you too, José?" You too, José! You too, José! Which after all isn't true because I don't budget my love like you do, nor do I keep on adding and subtracting to see whether you don't or you too. And I'm telling you because I remember the ... thousand times that it turned out afterwards it was a fact that me too, and I had said it myself, and shit! Of course I'm shouting, not as in this regimented country where good people don't shout and with a calm voice and the economic pressure and the legal trick and the "excuse me" if they sneeze, and no violence, they give it to the Blacks, the Chicanos, and the Puerto Ricans, and to us, the foreigners, the smallest minority, and what is worse, when it concerns me, because my skin isn't brown or black and they believe I must be Italian, "I know you're not one of them" they tell me in a friendly manner, like the guy at the diploma factory that time! What do you mean what do I want to do? There you go again. That you're not like that guy, that calling you a racist is to lie, that I'm more than exaggerating, and that the sneezing thing is only polite after all. Ah! Yeah, sure. I scare you because I get violent and you, visceral racist, because that's the kind of racist you are, you define violence as it suits you and as it turns out, oh surprise, I'm violent and scare you because I raise my voice even though I never touch anyone's hair. And let me tell you, that when you threw yourself on the ground in that parking lot calling the police it was all in your head and it was all your playacting. And you? Of course. How could you be violent if you don't raise your voice like us, undeveloped people, even though with all that calm of yours you stab me in the back as soon as I turn around. Of course, I suppose this doesn't count by definition. But look if you're not a racist: tell me, what language are we speaking? What a coincidence! Even the fights are in English! And why do I always have to use your language? Simply because you, imperialist, need not worry about using mine? In what kind of melting pot are we living? In the one that melts me and shapes me in your image and likeness? What a sneak! Yeah, calm down, calm down. Racist! That's what you are! That's what you are and I'm shouting it all I want! One and a thousand times I'm shouting it and screw the neighbors, who are all that matters to you! What? Oh, that's what you were looking for! Oh yeah, you have a right to respect and either I treat you well or you leave, etc., etc. And I in the meantime can't keep my dignity! But who put the crown on your head? OK! OK, madam! Sorry. OK, Ms! Piantáte if you want to!

There you go again. I know. I heard it a million times. That the slang and please speak to you in Español for export. Yeah, that of the Royal Academy of the Language and monarchic Spain. But God creates them and they get themselves together! Dije "Split! Take off! Go away if you want to!" Of course. As I always told you. See, see you were going to do this in the end? I sang it to you. Or don't you remember? See how in the end you're dropping me? And just like that. As if it were no big deal. What happens is you don't understand. What happens is you're an Anglo. But when are things going to sink into your head? You don't understand, I'm telling you. If you did, you wouldn't be doing what you're doing to me. But don't believe for a moment I'm going to drop on my knees begging you to stay. I also have my dignity even though you never gave a shit about it. If you want to, man, go. It's your decision. It's your decision, carajo, and don't put me in your little universal box again! Yeah, lost perspective, lost perspective. I lost nothing. And you, what you have is the perspective of this damn country where everyone can talk and no one talks about anything worthwhile. Of course they're good people! Who's saying they aren't? But go find greatness around here. You won't even see it in films. It's not the same. There you go with your little universal box again. It's not the same I'm telling you, racist skirt! And don't ask me, that your questions have me fed up! Yeah, sure. First you drive me crazy and then I'm supposed to explain what you don't understand, but staying calm. How can I stay calm, carajo, if I'm from nowhere? The citizen of nothingness. The shit citizen. That's what I am. I'm telling you it's not the same. And quit asking me. I don't know how it is! It's been about fifteen years since I left! How do you want me to know. Yes, I went back a few times, but always in a rush and keeping a low profile so they wouldn't stick it to me. Why, I even used to go back around Christmas partly because they were also busy celebrating and were not likely to come after me as they might have been at other times. The country disappeared from under my feet. I know what it isn't; not what it is. Do you understand me once and for all? You, with your order and understanding only what's utterly clear, and it turns out what's utterly clear is only what could happen here, in this ideal Anglo-Saxon world where you get mugged when you least expect it. But here is not there. Yeah. It's easy to say that. It's easy to announce to the world "I understand that these are different countries with different histories and different values." But that's an abstraction. People there are kinder. They're not as competitive as here, where you have to be on guard all the time.

The same thing again! See how you want to get me screwed and refuse to understand? It's impossible that you can do this again and again and again without realizing it. I didn't say people here are evil. I'm not ungrateful. This country maybe helped me more than my own. And I acknowledge it. And we have much to learn here from the democratic ideals though they sometimes are not practiced much, from science and technology though they mainly use them to fight the Russians. As regards home, pal, don't get confused. Those motherless types you mention are the military, the police, and some other sons of bitches! Most people are not like that! You believe they are because TV has brainwashed you in this great democracy of the North. What? But you really believe que me vas a chamuyar, que la vas a arreglar con parla barata como de costumbre? Sorry Mss I'll make it perfectly clear in *your* English. I said: do you really believe that you'll fix this by giving me lines and cheap speeches as usual? No, pal. No, wretched racist! Ah! And it's me who splits. What do you mean no? Why not? Don't I even have the right to split? Where has the freedom of the anticommunist propaganda gone? What! Is there slavery again in this the land of Washington and Martin Luther King? That you are leaving? Split, if you want to. But if you're going to split, do it soon. Ciao! Good bye, Miss America! Good bye, and don't ever come back. I'm going to read my little song to myself, alone as I ought to, and don't interrupt me. I'm busy.

> Al Sur el destino.
> Al Sur vuelve el tiempo,
> la esperanza anida,
> y todo es afín.

What are you staring at? Did you already pack the suitcase? Yeah, I'll send you everything, don't worry. And I'll pay the rent and whatever you want for the sake of the respect I need and will get only when I'm alone in this house. And listen to what I'm saying, so you see I have a conscience: if you want to stay here until you find an apartment, fine. I will sleep in the other room. I'm stepping aside. No spouse abuse here. I'll even help you find an apartment. Now what? But who can ever understand you? Or is it that after all you want me to go to a hotel? You women are all alike. When I'm leaving, that I should stay, that you're leaving; when I'm staying, that I'm staying and who do I think I am. Do as you please. I'll keep on reading my little song. Listen. Listen to the truth in this guy's soul at least once before you leave.

Pájaros tardíos
cercados de inviernos:
el alma oprimida
y un afán: huír.

Maybe in your confusion you touched the right cord. Maybe I should write poetry again. But of course, who's going to care? If I begin to write poetry lonely like a dog and without any support or anyone who loves me I'll end up in the insane asylum. And you, you won't change! It's pointless to dream. I know you haven't suggested any change in plans and that you'll be "out in no time!" I know. But watch out: don't even think of splitting and leaving that mess of panties and stockings which make the room look as if it had been decorated with banners. I still plan on living here. If you leave everything like that, man you're scratched. And the truth is you are. Because look. You're leaving me simply because I didn't translate that shitty song to you. I'm not saying a thing; but think about it. Because of a shitty song I can translate for you any time. Do as you see fit. Leave if you want to. But don't go around saying I didn't make an effort. Of course I made it! Or are you blind? Look at that! I humiliate myself, I lose my dignity for us, and she doesn't even notice. What do I have to do? Tell me. What do I have to do for things to be good between us? I'm alone. That's what's happening. Estoy solo como un hongo. Not even God would be more alone if He existed with this merry-go-round world which would bore Him and drive Him crazy. I can already see the end. I should have died as a little boy when they took out my appendix. Crazy or dead: this is my future. As my omen-song says:

Final presentido
en dagas de hielo.
Memorias vencidas
y un afán: huír.

I'll translate it for you even if you don't care.

End foreboded
in ice daggers.
Defeated memories
and an urge: to flee.

What a piece of shit! What a piece of shit of a life did I get! It's clear why you're leaving me. Because I'm worth nothing. And you're right to leave. I'm finished. I can't stay, nor go back, nor go on. You can say what you want. Without you, I have nothing left. But what do you care. If you cared you wouldn't leave. Or aren't you leaving? You see? But how can you do this to me? Don't you understand? What happens is that I get down and exaggerate, y me da la viaraza. I go crazy, Sue. Yo no sé. Poetry makes me nervous. Please, Sue. Please. Escucháme. Listen to me. I love you. I beg you. Por favor. Sue. Don't leave me. Sue. No me dejes. Please. Give me another chance.

Louis Marcus Rodríguez

Tres dolores distintos
y un solo amor no más

Cuando te miré, estaba ansioso como un lobo al acecho. Percibí desde el crecer de tus senos a los ojos verdes que parecían ocultar tesoros. (La cintura hubiese podido ser más fina, pero estábamos en Chile y no en Hollywood). Entonces te volviste para buscar un libro, algún papel, cualquier cosa, y pensé: "Lindas ancas de entonaciones orientales. Buen poto, también ..." Te lo digo con toda honestidad.

(Sus piernas eran largas para una chilena, es verdad, con tobillos que los zapatos hacían resaltar). Andabas de taco alto, pero sin pretensiones. Ese calzado era casi humilde. (El concepto de humildad corre paralelo con el síndrome de la miseria y no puedo dejar de rebelarme contra esto).

Bufaba interiormente, al dictar mi clase. Muy professional, diría yo, pero sólo de los dientes para afuera. (Por dentro me decía: "¿Y cuándo nos encatramos con esta mujer, en forma rápida y eficiente?")

Estaba leyendo el mensaje de tu mirada, esa llamada hecha por la hembra. (Está calculada para obligar al macho a pensar con la cabeza del pene: forma honesta de enfrentar la realidad. Allí no hay razón oscureciendo el entendimiento).

Primero sentí la violencia sexual. Así tuve un hemisferio del cerebro ocupado con fantasías sobre tu cuerpo extendido en mi lecho de lobo solitario; en el otro, tenía un claro concepto de la estructura sinfónica y sus problemas formales. De este modo seguí adelante, hasta el final, cuando me dirigiste una sonrisa y tus ojos dijeron ven, haz cuanto desees conmigo, pero ven (esa mirada dulce la hacía aparecer conquistada), para luego dar media vuelta con altivez. Te alejaste meneando las caderas. (En ese momento comprendí el universo: el movimiento de sus nalgas, ese apretar del vestido sobre la grupa, eran dignos de ser cantados por poetas. Lo han hecho desde que se inventó la poesía, pero por primera vez tuve conciencia de esa verdad eterna en el meneo y la canción).

Llevabas medias oscuras y adiviné las líneas de tu ropa interior, imaginado su color, completamente erotizado. Apenas saliste, acorralé al Chico Ariztía para preguntarle detalles, siempre con la seriedad propia del maestro bien intencionado, demostrando interés (meramente profesional) en una alumna inteligente (y de aspecto seductor).

Pero el Chico no era tonto. Se dio cuenta y dijo, con una sonrisa idiota:

"Está enamorada, señor ... "

El otro se llamba Humberto, pensaba casarse contigo, era profesional y tenía el futuro asegurado. ¡Un baño de agua fría! Yo, con cierto orgullo en mi cultura literaria, lo apodé Humbert Humbert (bautizo con hielo del Polo Sur).

Ese fue el primer dolor.

Como pertenecías a otro, no ibas a ser mía jamás. (Acepté la situación con mentalidad de ciudadano chapado a la antigua). Desde entonces, te hablé en términos pedagógicos. Debía prepararte para el examen de ingreso al Conservatorio Nacional y, al mismo tiempo, seguir desarrollando tus capacidades musicales. (Fui, pues, un lobito feroz, el cual se hundía en esos ojos, lamía en pensamiento la juntura de sus senos, soñaba con el sexo y sufría en medio de la soledad proporcionada por un matrimonio fracasado).

Me entregué a ese dolor. Tuvo, como todo sufrimiento, múltiples variaciones, matices, aromas y formas: una verdadera sinfonía de aflicción.

Pasó el tiempo, tal como sucede en estos casos, a paso de hormiga, pero una con patas de aplanadora municipal, destrozándome el corazón o cualquiera sea el lugar donde guardamos los amores subterráneos. (Seguí con mis clases: la teoría por aquí, el solfeo por allá; la armonía en este lugar, el contrapunto en ése otro; y el chequecito mensual como una burla ideológica). Soñaba con tus senos, todo a compás de vals lento con un acordeón en bambalinas.

En esas tardes, la clase era únicamente para tí. (Lo cual, a pesar de ser inmoral, resultaba emocionante).

Te decía, por ejemplo:

"Fumar es dañino, señorita. La estadística del cáncer no necesita una incidencia positiva."

Así, en seco, es insípido, pero ante los demás resultaba muy divertido. Tocaba tres corcheas en el piano, volcándolas sobre una blanca, (soles y mi bemol), lo cual aportaba los golpes del destino beethoveniano allí mismo. Eso era gracioso. Te reías, junto con los otros alumnos. (Teníamos al catedrático luciéndose frente a sus senos, ¡y cómo cruzaba las piernas!) Distribuía verdaderos tesoros de sabiduría, cacumen y perspicacia. De este modo, las clases resultaban interesantes, de gran originalidad y con excellente asistencia, lo cual me ponía en buenas relaciones con el señor Rector.

(Lo anterior es únicamente el reconocimiento de la realidad en el caleidoscopio del recuerdo).

Llegó la fiesta de fines de año. No hubo allí maestros y alumnos, sino simples compañeros, gente que deseaba divertirse. (La admiré desde lejos, mientras ella bailaba cumbias con meneos voluptuosos). Como de costumbre, yo estaba retraído. Miraba, copa en mano, con ojos de calamar y ansias de Casanova.

En eso se acercó el Chico Ariztía para decirme:

"Lo están esperando, don Santiago."

Me hice el tonto:

"¿Y quién puede ser, Ariztía?"

"No sé yo pues, don Santiago. Lo esperan, no más."

Seguí en la misma forma:

"Pero, ¿quién? ¿Dónde? ¿Cómo?"

El Chico se puso frenético:

"Por Dios, don Santiago, no sea leso. Ella lo espera. ¡Si se las están dando, señor!"

Y yo:

"¿Pero cómo se le ocurre, Ariztía? Soy un profesor serio. No puedo andar detrás de las alumnas. ¿Qué diría el señor Rector?"

El Chico siguió machucando.

Entonces le dije:

"Ella está de novia, Ariztía. Se va a casar ... "

Casi gritó:

"¡Cómo se va a casar, señor, si ese desgraciado la trata mal, vive con engaños y la hace sufrir!"

Por fin me dejó solo, abandonándome como si yo fuese una de esas causas que, por perdidas, inspiran desprecio. Puse la copa sobre la mesa y me fui. (El corazón me saltaba en el pecho, dándome patadas).

Estuve así en la vereda, apoyado contra un árbol. Respiré el aire nocturno a bocanadas, mientras escuchaba los ruidos de la fiesta mezclados con el tráfico de Alameda y te imaginaba como una seductora salida del infierno. (Mis fantasías habían tomado un rumbo tropical). Me alejé con lentitud.

Apenas pude dormir, presa de eso que los hombres sentimos, antes de lanzarnos sobre la mujer deseada. (Es previo a la primer alusión o al contacto definitivo, si puede decirse así. Tal como la hembra anuncia su disponibilidad, el macho también debe asegurarle su presencia: existe para ella, deseoso de satisfacer, conquistar y ser satisfecho). Estaba ansioso de ser tu rey y hacerte reina. (Lo cual era algo muy bueno, pero molesto para los testículos, sobre todo después de tres meses de celibato forzado).

El lunes siguiente, cuando repartí los trabajos escritos anunciando las notas finales, te embromé sobre la fiesta, hice mención a los conocimientos rítmicos del curso y terminé pidiéndote (con cierta seriedad) que no te retiraras después de clase: deseaba discutir contigo cierto punto formal importantísimo. No habías logrado comprenderlo, tal como podía apreciarse al estudiar tus respuestas concernientes al desarrollo de la sonata clásica.

Conversamos, sólo a modo de preludio para mi pregunta cumbre:

"¿Qué va a hacer ahora? Yo podría acompañarla al centro, si va en esa dirección."

Por casualidad, ibas hacia Ahumada.

Era de mañana, pero ya el calor derretía el asfalto y a uno se le pegaban los zapatos en la calle, al cruzar las esquinas. El aire apestaba con la concentración de hidrocarbones respirada por los santiaguinos. (A pesar de todo, era primavera en mi corazón: todo parecía un jardín lleno de pajaritos alegres).

Pasamos frente al York y te dije:

"¿Le gustaría ver esa película?"

(Cualquier cosa con tal de estar junto a ella a oscuras). Me miraste, algo incrédula: eran monos animados.

Agregué, rápido:

"Dicen que es muy divertida."

(Sus ojos decían sí quiero sí, a lo Molly Bloom).

Entramos y te agarré del brazo como un pulpo, guiándote en la penumbra (flor de la montaña).

Vimos algo de la función y reímos en los lugares apropiados. (La sentí esperar). De improviso cogí tu mano, sin control, en forma que te hizo saltar de susto.

Me incliné para susurrar:

"¿Se enoja?"

No quitaste la vista del telón, pero me apretaste contra el muslo.

Te besé con toda simpleza, no muy largo. Nos separamos como asustados de rozar las lenguas, contendores estudiándose después de haber tocado guantes. Entonces, enceguecidos por la pasión, nuestros corazones se unieron, precipitándonos en ese abismo de bocas púrpuras. La mano con que te estrujé el seno entró luego en el escote y por fin te sobó el pezón. (Estaba duro y era mío). Me apoderé de tus pechos (agarré sus piernas bien arriba y le acaricié el vientre) y tú, loca de deseo, te ofrecías ahí mismo. (Semejante a fruta brasileña, fluía en jugos vegetales, fundiéndose como si estuviese en el mercado del amor, esclava ante la impetuosidad del nuevo dueño). Salimos al fin, mareados de emoción.

(No logro recordar el título de esa película, sólo su presencia en la oscuridad).

En la calle, sin contemplaciones, te dije:

"Vamos a un hotel, mi linda, vamos . . ."

Y tú querías, me lo asegurabas con todo el cuerpo, lo cantabas en la mirada; pregonabas esa verdad con tu boca.

Dijiste:

"Hoy, no puedo; mañana, sí."

Te habría acusado de mentirosa, pero, después de esos besos, era imposible ser violento contigo. Tal vez leíste el dolor de mi soledad. (Podía ser mitigado únicamente por su carne más secreta y ahogado así en los jugos del sexo).

"Mañana, entonces. ¿A qué hora?"

Pensaste un momento:

"A las tres."

Era una promesa.

"Muy bien", murmuré, "¿dónde?"

(Sin poder esperar, se entregó entera):

"Donde tú quieras." Luego, cohibida: "Es tan raro tratarte de tú: voy a tener que acostumbrarme . . ."

(En ese instante, la veía junto a mí en el futuro). Miré tus ojos: el mundo desapareció, como si alguien cortara el sonido de la tele, dejando únicamente la imagen.

Te dije:

"A las tres, frente a la Biblioteca Nacional."

Sabía de un hotel cercano, en calle Guayaquil. Podíamos caminar hasta allí con toda calma.

Deseabas agregar algo más, pero sólo aceptaste:

"Muy bien . . ."

Tal vez querías usar alguna palabra cariñosa. Como ya se acercaba el bus, ardió en mi boca un beso rápido. Partiste sonriendo, la mirada muy verde en el calor. Y la primavera desapareció. Regresó el presente y con él mi soledad. (Me dejó con el recuerdo y el sabor de su boca madura, en Alameda con Ahumada.

Mientras te ibas en el sol (llevándose mi corazón), tuve esa pesadumbre cubriéndome con el velo tolerado sólo por gente de otro planeta.

Habíamos comenzado bien. Hubiera podido terminar en desastre si no hubiese sido por tu extrañeza al poder tutearme: aceptabas ser mía, tal como lo deseaba yo desde hacía tanto tiempo.

(Demasiado tarde, recordé que había olvidado preguntar su dirección y número de teléfono).

Al día siguiente estuve allí, frente a la Biblioteca, marcando el paso. Medí con cuidado los escalones, no fuera a encontrar algunos más altos que otros. Observé el ancho y espesor de las puertas. (En un momento, incluso caminé hasta el cerro Santa Lucía, para leer la inscripción cincelada en granito, con el fragmento de la carta escrita por don Pedro de Valdivia al rey de España). Al mismo tiempo, acariciaba dentro del bolsillo la misiva dirigida a tí la tarde anterior:

"Cuando pienso en tu nombre, una angustia tremenda me hace martillear la sangre. Siento la garganta apretada y el corazón me golpea el pecho ..." (Esa clase de comentario le gustó). "No creí poder sentir así nunca más, porque mi vida había llegado a un punto muerto. Estaba yerto en mi interior ..." (es curioso cómo asociamos la falta de amor con la muerte. Al mismo tiempo, el renacer de la emoción es comparable a la primavera, cuando los primeros brotes se elevan buscando la caricia del sol). "Has despertado cuanto estaba dormido, y así brotan en mí sentimientos y anhelos que ya no creía poder sentir otra vez en la vida ..."

(Era de un romanticismo juvenil, pero no le importó).

Tú, reina mía, llegaste tarde. (Iniciaba así una larga serie de atrasos injustificados precipitando dudas demenciales en mí. Tal vez anda con otro. No me quiere. Un accidente. ¿Qué pasa ahora? ¿Otra vez?)

Mentalmente, pronunciaba acusaciones en contra tuya: se trataba de cinco minutos hoy, diez mañana, quince, veinte minutos, y, si los sumábamos, eran horas, días enteros robados al amor. (Perdidos a la espera de una sonrisa, sus andares hembrunos y el sol de aquel sexo).

Torturado, aguardé hasta convencerme que no ibas a llegar: te habías convertido en espejismo. (Sin saber su dirección ni poseer el contacto etéreo del teléfono, resultaba una desconocida, promesa de algo que pudo ser y nunca fue).

Me sorprendí al verte, porque había perdido toda esperanza.

Te besé rápido, murmurando:

"Quiero amarte ..."

La alegría de tu sonrisa dijo: sí quiero sí.

Me retiré un poco para ver tus ojos. (Su boca entregada). Te necesitaba allí mismo, en la calle. Al mismo tiempo, noté esa humildad hiriente. (¡Cómo odio aquello! En realidad, me tortura aún hoy día). Deseaba una hembra altiva en mitad de la Alameda. No lo eras, avergonzada de tu belleza, cuando entramos por fin al hotel de calle Guayaquil. Pagué con temblor de manos. La encargada se admiró, lanzando una mirada curiosa. (Tal vez imaginaba que era la mujer de otro. Esto resultaba exacto, figurativamente).

Por fin solos, fingí ignorarte, aparentando confianza. Me saqué la chaqueta, mientras esperabas. Te abracé para hundirme luego en tu boca, pero muy rápido. (En un segundo beso pude sentir cómo se abría, punzándome con la divina víbora de su lengua). Te apreté los senos, el vientre. (Bajo el vestido, sentí hervir la juntura de sus muslos).

Pensé: voy a bañarte con mi lengua para secarte con la piel.

Atorados de pasión, caímos sobre la cama.

Sin la práctica de ser amantes, cohibidos ante nosotros mismos, entramos al lecho semidesnudos, lo cual era idiota, pero no podíamos reaccionar sino como el producto atávico de una educación insolvente.

Ataqué tu cuerpo con ansias de escolar. En ese momento sucedió algo considerado normal, según dicen, pero está escrito por quienes nunca parecen haber sufrido tal percance: mi virilidad desapareció. Tal vez te extrañaste, pero sin mostrar ningún rencor. (En realidad fue muy comprensiva, entregándome un cariño producto del amor). Me sentía morir, torturado por el fantasma de la impotencia. Lloré mis lágrimas de hombre. (Son muy dolorosas: nos han enseñado a no dejarlas correr, y así hieren por dentro, ardiendo en el fondo del alma).

Dijiste:

"No importa, mi amor. Otro día será ... "

Murmuré:

"No entiendo esto, mijita ... "

(La disculpa abyecta).

¿Cómo podía aceptarlo? Estaba a punto de fallecer.

Tratamos toda clase de estímulos cuya virtud había sido comprobada por expertos mundiales. (Todos mienten en este mundo, hasta el Kama Sutra de Vasyayana). Me consideraba herido y maldecía mi suerte. (El pene carece de conciencia, pero sin duda tiene una imaginación bastante perversa).

Por fin, ambos decidimos aceptar lo inevitable.

"Otro día será ... "

Derrotado, te besé por última vez. En ese momento, el animal pareció despertar por fin, irguiendo su cabeza insolente para reclamar un derecho de tirano.

Como un bárbaro, trepé sobre tí sin ningún escrúpulo. (Reaccionó con violencia ante la imposición de la carne). Yo era el monarca de tus deseos, vencedor de anhelos, conquistador del sexo y rapsodista del corazón. Al mismo tiempo, rogaba a los dioses para que me permitieran satisfacerte, rezando por un poco más de tiempo, a punto de vencer ya, casi triunfante al fin, cuando me di cuenta cómo habías levantado las piernas hasta mis hombros (para tener más de mí y entregarse vencida). Enloquecido, la conmoción me agotó de súbito en un orgasmo de lava multicolor. Rígida, experimentaste aquello tan íntimo, resistente a toda descripción. (Con la respiración detenida, el mundo mismo aguardaba, admirado). No gritaste. (Eso vendría después, en nuevas tardes de pasión, cuando el placer le desgarraría la garganta). Tampoco me rasguñaste como una gata salvaje. (Dejaba aquellos desmanes para otras veces, y así la entrega iba a ser más completa). Tuviste un goce de crema. (Humilde, no tengo otra palabra para describirlo). Tu abandono fue dulce y nunca lo olvidaré, porque estuvimos todavía más unidos en ese instante, con la certeza de haber comenzado algo definitivo. (Había mayor substancia que la encontrada en un amorío pasajero, propio de burócratas vespertinos). Era, en consecuencia, un sentimiento profundo.

Luego de explorarnos por segunda vez, cuando estábamos descansando, escuchamos un alarido cercano, sofocado a duras penas por el beso del amante desflorando a su querida. Ese grito nos unió todavía más.

Dijiste en un murmullo:

"Era la primera vez para ella también, ¿no crees tú?"

(Tampoco he olvidado esas palabras, tal como nunca olvidamos los detalles importantes que estructuran esta larga soledad llamada vida).

Siguieron meses de voluptuosidad.

A través de los sentidos, abandonamos cadenas, prejuicios, complejos y vergüenzas. En conceptos políticos, hicimos arder nuestra burguesía en la hoguera del placer. (Esa práctica del amor me hizo descubrir un lujo inconcebible: la alegría proporcionada por una mujer multiorgásmica. Era un regalo de los dioses, concedido al mortal indigno).

A veces, al salir casi arrastrándonos de algún hotel clandestino, todavía lograba tener conciencia de los tipos volviendo la cabeza para mirarte por detrás, cuando caminabas a mi lado y yo te rodeaba la cintura en señal de posesión.

Ocultaba también mis celos. Sabía que Humbert Humbert te rondaba. (Según me contaba, a veces iba de visita; otras, lo divisaba en la calle). Más de una noche, al llevarte a casa en taxi, él estaba allí, en las sombras, acunando seguramente su dolor. Si yo lo conociera, imaginabas, tal vez podría pensar en forma diferente y no sentir desprecio.

"No es un mal hombre y todavía me quiere ... "

Había algo que podías intuír: yo de ningún modo deseaba una vida entera a tu lado. No podía atarme con la seguridad engañosa del matrimonio. Si recién salía de uno, ¿cómo iba a meterme en otro?

De este modo, arrastramos algunos secretos desde el comienzo, durante un año entero. (Como toda mujer con sentido práctico, buscaba una posición estable: mi anarquismo no le convenía. Esto para explicar los acontecimientos siguientes).

La felicidad tiene matices como el atardecer. (También es e-fímera: se asemeja al pétalo de una rosa). Puede poseer la deli-cadeza conocida por las mariposas, o, similar al vacío dejado por un relámpago, su ausencia es inmediata y la oscuridad permanece.

Cuando estuviste en mis brazos aquella tarde, te sentí extraña. (Tal vez la expresión apropiada sea la de lejanía espiritual). Aunque tus reacciones fueron las mismas, faltaba algo. Estabas en otro lugar. Eramos cuerpo y alma, debías sentir conmigo.

"¿Qué le pasa? ¿Me va a contar alguna cosa?"

Inocente, dijiste:

"Nada ... "

Pero estabas faltando a la verdad (ambos lo sabíamos) y me dio frío.

Es curioso recordarlo de ese modo, pero fue mi reación ante la primera mentira.

"Dígame, pues, mi amor ... "

"Si no hay ninguna cosa ... "

(La miré con ojos de inquisidor).

Tenías vergüenza.

Entonces, decidiéndote de súbito, dijiste:

"Ayer, salí con él ... "

(Sin mencionar su nombre, tal vez para no tenerlo en la cama. Pero allí estaba, de todos modos).

"¿Ah, sí? ¿Te llevó a un hotel?"

Quería herirte. (Escurrió la vista). Tuviste valor para asentir con la cabeza. (Sin embargo, ella no tenía miedo, pese a mis ce-los, inmensos como pesadillas). Tal vez sentías haber hecho algo indigno de nuestra unión.

Presioné:

"¿Te encatraste con él?"

Resultaba curiosa aquella vulgaridad repentina. (El esqueleto salía de su tumba y la abrazaba con pasión mortuoria, por eso yo estaba helado).

"Anduvo detrás de mí todo el año ... "

Era una disculpa inaceptable.

(Claro, suena melodramático ahora, pero en ese momento, al saber cómo había consumado la traición, se me congeló el alma. Tal vez eran sus ofertas de matrimonio, recalcando la seguridad económica, mientras yo me debatía inútilmente ante la situación en que había quedado, cuando el Ministerio de Educación me dejara cesante).

Necesitaba saber algo, con la insistencia propia del macho:

"¿Te hizo gozar?"

Entonces dijiste:

"Al final ... cuando acabé ... fue tan fuerte ... "

Eso me hirió en forma definitiva. Era un clavo en el centro del alma.

"¿Te volviste loca gritando?"

Moviste la cabeza en muda afirmación.

Murmuré:

"Quererte tanto y haces una cosa así ... "

Te hería con mi dolor, a propósito. (También deseaba dejar en claro esa bifurcación de nuestras vidas: ella iría hacia otro lado con su soledad, dejándome correr en pos de la mía).

Murmuraste, como una explicación:

"Los quiero a los dos ... "

Yo dije:

"Tenemos que terminar esto ... "

(No deseaba aceptarlo, pero me pareció el modo correcto de actuar).

Hubieses deseado seguir desnuda en mis brazos, pero no podía permitirlo. (Su sexo me esclavizaba).

Te llevé hacia la Alameda para decirte adiós con la voz reservada para esas ocasiones y el sentimiento proveniente no del corazón, como desean hacernos creer, sino de un lugar metafísico en el cual se encuentra anidada esa locura sublime llamada amor.

Vi tus ojos tan melancólicos, cubiertos por nubes de lágrimas. Comenzaron a correr y, por ser humildes, me hirieron todavía más. Imposible describir esa tristeza invernal en mitad del verano, cuando llegó el bus. Di media vuelta. Si esperaba tu llamada, estaba equivocado. Tal vez lo hiciste en voz baja, (el orgullo me obliga a creer eso), pero no te escuché.

Así fue como nos separamos.

Me alejé, diluviando por dentro al recordar tu dulzura, esa presencia fecunda en pasiones, llena de jugos y dueña de una boca más voraz que otras bocas.

No podíamos terminar tan simplemente, en realidad. (Estaba allí, era mía, lista para responder a mis requerimientos).

Nos vimos tres veces (todas con desesperanza, cada una más lejos que la anterior), siempre con miedo, porque habías dejado de tomar las píldoras: Humbert Humbert no se preocupaba por tales cosas. (Al principio, feliz de verla traicionar a mi enemigo, pensaba en una posible reconciliación. Tenía un asomo de esperanza). Pero el último encuentro es el que vale.

Ocurrió en el lugar de nuestra primera cita, frente a la Biblioteca Nacional. Llegaste con diez minutos de atraso. Te besé cariñoso, esperando una respuesta pasional. Estabas reservada.

"¿Vamos al hotel?", te dije, picado.

Te negaste: deseabas conversar.

Yo lo sabía. De algún modo podía leerte como un libro abierto.

Pedí perdón, agregando:

"Tú sabes ... tenía que pedirlo ... "

Asentiste con la cabeza.

Era una mañana de abril y la neblina ocultaba el sol. De la mano, te llevé hasta el cerro Santa Lucía. Nos sentamos en un escaño.

Me preguntaste:

"Y tú, ¿cómo has estado?"

(Recordé la extrañeza del primer tuteo, esa intimidad casi prohibida). Deseaba saber de Humbert Humbert, el profesional con futuro asegurado. Quería casarse pronto, dijiste. El matrimonio se acercaba como un acontecimiento histórico.

En el fondo, pensabas contarme un secreto, pero no te atrevías. Me divertí durante un rato, estirando la conversación.

Por fin, murmuraste:

"Tengo algo que decirte ... "

Puse cara de inocencia:

"¿Sí?"

"La última vez ... me dejaste embarazada ... "

Curiosamente, ese anuncio me hizo feliz.

"¿Estás segura?"

Como si pudieras estar equivocada.

"¡Yo tengo que saber ... !"

(Recuerdo ahora esa tarde, breve, sin importancia, un amorcito clandestino, hacía dos meses atrás. Pero estábamos apurados, ansiosos por cortar la cuerda umbilical de nuestra pasión. Fue demasiado corto para una despedida digna de ser recordada con cariño. Tal vez comenzábamos a sentir vergüenza, veneno indispensable para asesinar cualquier amor).

Agregaste rápido, como si desearas perdonar:

"Le eché la culpa a él ... "

Sin nombrarlo, para no tener aquella sombra entre nosotros.

(Dijo que la había llevado donde un médico, el cual arregló el asunto sin mayor problema).

Murmuré algo calculado para alejarte de mí, pero no pude evitarlo:

"¿Por qué no dejaste al guachito?"

Eso te molestó:

"¿Estás loco? Me sentía pésimo ... "

Todavía deseaba herirte:

"Me hubiera gustado tener un hijo contigo ... "

Cosas dichas mientras no exista el deber de criarlos, por supuesto. (Excepto esa vez, cuando expresaba el sentimiento en una forma idealizada).

Nos miramos, cada vez más lejos. En ese instante se acercó una pareja de turistas japoneses. Deseaban tomar una fotografía de nosotros. Te abracé. Sonreímos con aparente felicidad ante la cámara. (Ahora estamos juntos, el único recuerdo posible, al otro lado del mundo, dentro de un álbum ignorado). Nos agradecieron con una pequeña reverencia. (Gente muy bien educada).

Permanecimos en silencio durrante un rato, como si las palabras se hubiesen terminado. (Dijo algo acerca del tiempo, confusa y sin ánimos). Nos miramos entonces, para estar seguros. (Supimos que sí: era el fin).

Caminamos hasta el paradero, todavía unidos por las manos y la mirada. Llegó el bus. Hubo un beso de labios fríos. (Los viejos amantes han compartido cuerpo y alma, terminando por agotar la copa de la pasión).

Prometí:

"Nunca te voy a olvidar ... "

Sonreíste con tristeza, imaginando tal vez que era una mentira dicha para caer bien. Subiste rápido, pero vi tus ojos cuando volviste la cabeza para consevar mi imagen. ¡Conocía bien tu mirada humilde! Alcé la mano en señal de adiós, fingiendo esa alegría tonta usada en los momentos más graves, como si todo fuese pasajero.

Pensé en nuestra despedida: había durado tres meses y ahora resultaba irreversible. (Se trataba sin duda del último dolor, el más fuerte). Permanecí clavado, en tanto el bus se llevaba tu recuerdo, y la mañana a fines de abril fue insoportable.

El tráfico de pronto cobró vida y fluyó por todas partes.

(Junto a él, descendió mi soledad).

Pasaron quince años de amores, otros tiempos, viajes, un Golpe de Estado como puñalada en el pecho de Chile. Nuevamente el matrimonio, hijos, estudios, trabajo. Nunca te olvidé, reina mía. (Esa juventud compartida durante un año de amor).

Desde el extranjero, me preocupaba la situación del país. Tuve algunos contactos con exiliados. (Yo pertenecía al Grupo de Acción Urgente de Amnistía Internacional y conocí verdades como bayonetazos). Mi labor era modesta: algunas obras que nadie publicaba, sirviendo sólo para hacerme sentir la agonía del escritor ignorado, lo cual es una muerte constante. Recibía boletines con listas de prisioneros, interrogados, torturados o desaparecidos. Trágico destino de gente con dolores anónimos al otro lado del mundo. Compartía ese compás de espera con un millón de exiliados. (Como una muestra de protesta, cambié de ciudadanía, sin dejar de ser chileno en el corazón). Tristezas propias de estos tiempos.

Esa tarde recibí un boletín, igual a tantos otros.

Tu nombre encabezaba la lista.

(Había sido detenida a raíz de una manifestación organizada para lograr que el gobierno militar se hiciese reponsable por los prisioneros desaparecidos). Furtivamente, como lo prescribe el reglamento, te hicieron desvanecer. Se temía por tu vida; tal vez estabas siendo torturada. Pedían solidarizar con tu causa por medio de cartas dirigidas a las autoridades chilenas.

(Según aprendí en ese momento, el crimen de rebeldía es la bienaventuranza de los patriotas).

Tengo los dedos adormecidos de tanto escribir a los burócratas del gobierno militar que resultan impenetrables. (Nunca ha estado detenida, dicen). No existes, me indican.

Tengo los ojos secos. El río del dolor corre dentro de mi alma, en ese lugar mítico donde guardamos las penas causadas por nuestra desgracia nacional. ¡Qué torpes resultan quienes ven en la violencia la única solución para los problemas sociales, como si los cadáveres pudieran forjar el destino de las naciones!

Y ése es el tercer dolor, más brutal por ser ciego.

He dejado de escribir cartas, excepto ésta, la última y la única que no despacharé jamás, porque tu dirección se encuentra en mi corazón. (No sé dónde está: si la han enterrado en un cementerio o en un lugar desconocido, tal vez bajo un sauce o por pedazos, los brazos aquí, el torso por allá, la cabeza en el fondo del océano). Han cumplido su objetivo: como no existes, solamente eres una fantasía creada por mi imaginación.

(Nunca la olvidé y he cumplido la promesa hecha tanto tiempo atrás, en una fría mañana de abril).

(¿Por qué me llueven cuchillos dentro del pecho?)

Freddy Rodríguez

Freddy Rodríguez maintains a fine-tuned critical balance between aesthetics and politics, the art of painting and it social content. Using lush colors to depict blossoming flowers and serpentine leaves, the artist evokes the tropical splendor of the Caribbean. At the same time, he mourns the rape of this paradise by colonialism and its long lineage of dictatorships. Issues of freedom of expression and the processes of forging artistic and cultural identity converge in Rodríguez' work.

These political messages are subsumed by the artist's desire to create beautiful paintings fusing Renaissance and modern traditions. Integrating illusionistic space with flattened surfaces, and contrasting loose and tight brushstrokes, the artist enters a dialogue with centuries of art concerned with these same pictorial issues. Rodríguez' complex style and approach can be appreciated on both formal and thematic levels.

Layered with imagery, the paintings challenge the viewer to decipher their configuration and meaning. Beneath a thick and transparent pigmented surface, collaged text and newspaper photographs emerge as ghost images. These elements, heightening the symbolism of light and dark, are intrinsic to the paintings' message and subtly balance the tonal value of the composition. Rodríguez then paints over this background the dense colors mixed with sawdust for texture. He sometimes uses writing as a final unifying device in a process that culminates in a rich dimensional surface.

Although the themes in Rodríguez' paintings reflect violent upheavals in society, they are sublimated into an atmosphere of compositional harmony. Rarely strident, the artist conceives of his works as warnings for the future. His critical political consciousness and empathy for his cultural roots are communicated through a seductive visual language. By defining an alliance between art and politics that does not displace either concern, Rodríguez makes an important contribution to contemporary art.

Freddy Rodríguez

1989: mixed media on canvas, 60" × 42"

Courtesy Scott Alan Gallery, New york (212 226-5145)

Things of Paradise

Adelaida López Mejía

Bucólico ajedrez

¡Bucólico ajedrez!
Entre penachos sube
una espiral de humo en los pantanos.

Empieza la guerra
en los tembladerales.

País de maravillas.
Entre íncubos
de hongos venenosos,
patas acolchonadas como felpa,
piel como lombriz,
brillan luciérnagas en la lejanía.

En otro mundo fue
la guerra espléndida
de batallas puntuales.

Sólo la reina cumple,
general de corazones,
plenipotencia
paticoja detrás de escaramuzas.

El caballo noble,
destructor de imperios,
todavía es un fantasma en el pantano.
Su inmensa cabeza inspira terror
entre la infantería.

En noches sin luna
aparece un cuerpo blanquísimo,
entero o sin miembros,
sobre el vaho del agua.

Y nuestro enemigo

¿quién es?

¿No somos nosotros
en el mismo pantano
o en otro
lugar idéntico
de idénticas lianas?

La familia

Más adentro de mí,
al cruzar el semáforo,
se me aparece la familia.

Se me acercan,
limosneros y mendigos.
Me gritan
—si con huesos de pescado
has hecho sopa,
¡sírvenos la cena
que robaste!

En el cruce de la calle
los choferes se enloquecen
y golpean la bocina.
Ni este rendir de cuentas
es el suyo,
ni esta ceremonia.

Mis escasos huesos tiemblan.
La catedral bajo la calle
me recuerda
ocasiones
más dolorosas.

El viento me despeina.
Mi familia innumerable
sube conmigo a pie
por una calle.

En una sola alcoba vamos a vivir.
En una sola cama en el futuro.

VI

Cuando la calma vuelva
si es que vuelve,
cuando las cosas
por antiguos nombres
comiencen a llamarme
a repartirme
en solidario sur
sobre el aroma
y lo que he sido
vuelva a ser de nuevo
al íntimo engranaje
de las norias:
sobre el eterno rostro
de las aguas,
en caracol, entonces
desataré
un lenguaje de mareas
que habitará
todas la playas,
todos, los hermosos ahogados,
que las siembran
y en lentas manos
donde el vacío
lo reune todo
y Dios es
un andrógeno sonido
según la posición
que inventa el ojo,
tejeré una distancia
a cada esquina,
un letal movimiento
hacia el asombro.

XXII

De una Isla
jamás
nadie se escapa
es como una mujer
de la cual nunca
podemos deshacernos
por completo;
su verde
nos retiene abiertamente
fuera de todo amor
logra existirnos
ser algo de la calle
y de las gentes:
se levanta contigo
te sorprende
frente al espejo
peinas
su silueta
pretendes olvidarla
pero escuchas
en tus zapatos
el eco de su huella
que imperturbable
a todo sobresalto
te sigue, sin ayuda,
a dondequiera;
es parte
de la cama o el armario
la más antigua risa
que has tenido
el más nuevo dolor
que a ti se acerca
mientras
te roba el modo
de soñarla
y te busca, te mira,
se te enfrenta
o te reintegra
en latitud de barca
a un erótico

impacto de mareas
como única manera
de encontrarla
en el filo absoluto
de la espera.

Residencia plural

Como te contaré
de ésta mi casa,
esta ciudad
que nadie quiere
en fija residencia,
mi rechazada casa
donde amigos y gentes
que aún no encuentro
viven planeando
como irse de ella.
Mi violenta ciudad,
como esos fuegos
que nadie quiere ver
quemando bosques.
Mi desmembrada casa
donde todos se sirven
en bandeja
asesinatos, besos, amarguras
y una ternura
que a mitad de cuerpo
nos sorprende
el viaje en equilibrio
de los ojos.
Mi casa definiendo
el horizonte
de rostros por venir
y de otros rostros
que jamás rodarán
por el amplio cuchillo
de estas calles.
Aquí tuve un olor,
una presencia
y diez y ocho años
sobre el pecho,
aquí aprendí a perder
todas las cosas:
los perfiles más simples,
las ausencias,
las ventanas,
los mástiles,

ciertos tonos de azul
que tiene el agua
y la manera
de tocar la vida
tan sólo
con el ruido
de la vena.

Miami Mimesis

Miniature porcelain clowns
crowd the heart shaped bowl,
hands and legs confused.
Their white faces painted
with russet cheeks and violet lips
and the teal eyes,
defined by penciled-in brows,
stare.
Golden ruffles crown their necks
and red, green, black lace
forms their tiny bodies.
But the radiance of these colors,
the carefully drawn smiles
do not fool me.
This small multitude overflows
with eyes that shout.

A Visit to West New York

The Virgin of Charity, in blue,
and her three fishermen rest
on the wooden dresser.
I can hear salsa on
the neighbor's radio.
I try to decipher the faces
covering the night table.
The single bed hardly fits
in this room, cluttered,
clothes hanging, off the closet doors,
on the red felt arm chair. I turn
to face the flowered wall
and sleep.

The ring of the phone, her voice,
loud and energetic, waken me.
I quickly dress, follow the scent
of expresso and buttered toast.
It's Jose's mother I meet in the kitchen,
her eyes glistening with mischief.
We have just met, but she talks of life
back home, her arms waving as she
urges me to eat more toast.
Jose seems embarrassed.

Then, it is time to leave.
He opens the door.
I confront the landscape:
a lean street with urined curbs,
a jagged fence and skies of
worn and pitted bricks.

Alma Mater

Half past three at school,
in an oversized blue t-shirt,
navy polyester shorts,
she sees a crowd of mothers.

I see me,
six again with tears,
searching, my mother with a
flowery wide skirt and flats,
waiting in a 67 Ford,
under the same black olive trees.

I return to her
now
running, smiling, waving.
For hers are not hollow hallways.

They hold the echoes.

Finding Home

I have travelled north again,
to these gray skies
and empty doorways.
Fall, and I recognize
the rusted leaves descending
near the silence of your home.
You, a part of this strange
American landscape with its
cold dry winds,
the honks of geese and
the hardwood floors. It's more
familiar now than
the fluorescent rainbow on the overpass,
or the clatter of politicos in the corners,
or the palm fronds falling by the highway.
I must travel again, soon.

The Old Order

A man enters through the kitchen
and closes the door behind him,
afraid of letting the outside in.

Onions and peppers simmer,
fries and plantains sizzle,
pork grease drips off the window panes.

He places the yellow cap on the formica
and waits his turn.
Finally, he hollers above the clatter;
a young plump waitress serves him a mountain of rice.

After his meal, he wipes the grease off his lips,
gulps down his expresso and
shouts his goodbyes.
Outside, now he tilts his cap and walks away with ease.

Edgar O'Hara

Tornado Watch en Saragosa, TX

Venir a Texas a morir de viento
En estas casas que son de mentira.

La de ladrillos tampoco es segura
Si el lobo y el chanchito vanse al cuerno.

Valió la pena, como Pedro Rojas,
Escribir nuestro epitafio en el aire.

Blanco y negro tiritando juntos
en un paradero de East Austin

Lo que nunca hermana la piel
Que lo consiga la pobreza.

Endechas texanas para un despechado al pie de una Wurlitzer en la frontera

El Coyote
Persigue al Correcaminos
Por vergeles de osamentas
Del amor.

Así terminan los bravos
Como tú:
Resignados
A rancheras y boleros.

La patria

Cuando le preguntaron
por el mar,
le contestó
que aún
no, que
todavía
no se lo habían llevado
y ofreció
entregar
sus ojos.

Retornos

Y después de las amenazas,
los tiempos hundidos por un
lenguaje muerto,
ellos regresaban
en el resplandor.
Eran como un comienzo en la fragancia misma del
agua,
eran tan hermosos mientras jugaban en las
espumas de agua viva.

Ella le sacudió
las heridas, secó
los olores de la muerte.

II

El le abrió el cabello
como si estuviera
despedazando dos ramas de ágatas,
jugaron a ser los
ríos
a ser actinias
en la rosada textura
de las
mejillas del
agua.
y entonces
el aroma, las olas, haciendo un color de sol y maderas
entonces
ya nada me era extrañezas,
porque también la memoria y yo misma
habíamos emigrado
a estos paisajes de agua
a las cercanías de las caletas
y a esos precisos impenetrables, viajes de travesías
prestadas junto a la orilla de las costas
en busca de plumas salvajes
y la fresca compañía
de las desprevenidas gaviotas
y entonces supe que la lluvia

iba en mi alma
como un silencio o una brisa
entonces supe que había llegado
al mar
y el agua de la tierra muy al alcance
al alcance de mi mano,
alejada del albergue de los pies
y desperté en todas las patrias
en todos los sargazos.

La extranjera
pide un trago
de agua
un trozo de tierra
flotando en la intemperie
de sus destierros
y el agua la acerca
a la vida de sus regiones inventadas
y la invención es una isla pequeñísima
haciendo un mapa,
geografías,
tatuajes de sus
dolores.

Prefería ver el mar de las extranjerías,
imaginarlos en las
tierras de otros.
y en los atardeceres del azar,
se perdía en los puertos llagados,
llevaba en sus hombros los grandes lienzos de nieblas,
y en las huerfanías,
pensaba en los mares de la patria.
y su boca
era una
herida
sin banderas.

José Quiroga

Escrito en llamas

a joseph

Apuntar la flecha en el arco a la cuna donde nacen las
   estrellas,
De una línea en la arena, de una sombra, de un cinto
   en la arena,
lleno de luces, de esa sombra invertida que destila su
   arena,
en la página que he escrito, en honor a tu silueta.
Regresar a tu delgada figura, risa de arena en la alcoba,
mientras se disuelve, tu cuerpo en su cuna.
Besar la inquieta superficie, en el fuego de una calle,
   entre paredes
que regresan a un velo, y detrás de un sueño a una mirada.
¿Qué lanza ha dado contra el sueño que el tiempo ha
   desgarrado?
En el espacio de mi pecho entre dos balas, en una calle
   hirviendo, te busco.

*   *   *

Los hombres golpean el pavimento, un mar de ceniza
   cubre
los techos y los árboles, las aves, bajan de norte a sur.
Es el ruido de una noche en el día, antes que la noche
   se lleve el silencio.
Se ha encendido la forma de un túnel, y al fondo, sobre
   el lomo de un tigre, duerme la bala asesina.
Y este sitio en que nos hemos amado, quién lo salvará
de las cercas de papel y de los sellos, quién lo protege.
Cómo es posible rescatar su abrigo en esta cárcel de alas
   que acechan:
dos líneas y en el centro de una rama la garganta.
El suelo que ya no pisamos, una lluvia de cristal en el
   suelo.

*   *   *

Navegar en tu camino de estrellas, escribir una carta
que nunca saldrá de mis manos.
Al abrigar esa orilla, el arco de tu espalda henchido
a un viento sin palabras.
El cuerpo al mástil, sus flechas abriendo los párpados,
llenando
la carne de sal y arena,
debajo de las sábanas, mientras al dorso, el fuego cruza
la noche.
Es el fuego de antes del recuerdo que vuelve, que disuelve
la mentira de esta nube.

*   *   *

Mi respuesta a la noche en esta noche: ni una sola bala
podrá evitarse en esta línea.
Ni alimento, ni abrigo, ni consuelo mientras desembarcan
en la página desierta, llena de sombras ahora.
Ni desanclar el nudo, rescatar la voz del túnel, ni una
piedra
puede hacerse estrujando el papel de esta carta,
que rompa el cristal de esta ventana donde pájaros y
ceniza
resbalan por los techos.
Talismán sí. El brillo de su coraza invisible. Repetida
franja de noche,
el cinto de estrellas, la ola que impulsa el barco,
la arena invisible de tu pecho, una lluvia de luces que
sólo vemos tú y yo, oculta al enemigo.
Mi rosa entre palabras. Mi sábana a tu cuerpo tendido
sobre el fuego de las calles.

*   *   *

"El horizonte ciego y débil", señala una voz que me
acaricia.

Palpo la dureza de su costado, mientras desembarcan,
buscando una sombra,
una línea móvil, la trinchera.
Advierto la suma de fronteras que componen su espacio: la hora del baño,

su risa, el horizonte en su pupila,
La manera en la que su cuerpo se pierde en el lecho que
    no lo sostiene,
la voluntad formal del sueño, como el aceite, mientras
    cubre sus brazos de harina para hacer una casa,
la fragante alborada en su talle, la parra en su cuello.

Nacimos dentro de un arco imborrable pero también
    ausente:
su hosca resonancia llegaba al refugio nuestro, como
    una hoja se permite quebrar una ventana.
Desde entonces la memoria y el tiempo se separan.
La permanencia de lo frágil: el tintero, la mesa, la nube
    hirviendo
del café, la sombra de una mano que se alarga
en el instante cifrado, el terreno que se mueve, la co-
    lumna de humo
en la que somos siempre ese horizonte.

*   *   *

Soñé que el reino del sueño me había sido vedado, que
    buscaba entre
la opacidad misma un cristal opaco.
En la antesala del sueño había visto un trono y un cetro,
    y una alfombra roja y unas alas extendidas.
Pero el brillo cedió a una fuente negra, a una cortina
    hecha de la ausencia de luz,
hasta que el material mismo se evaporaba.
Sin que fuese todavía la nada, no dormía.

Pero siento el martilleo de la construcción, me dije, son
    los obreros
del edificio vecino, los empleados de la compañía de
    teléfonos
en la calle, con los ojos cerrados, estoy en el sofá de mi
    cuarto, en la ciudad
en la que habito, no quiero despertar.

Quise dormir, digo más bien, quiero soñar,
pero ni una sombra
vino a mi rescate, sin terreno, sin franja, sin espacio
Y ni siquiera, contenido en el deseo del sueño, pura
    lumbre de la nada

Flotando entre palabras, la torre de sus consonantes, la
 sábana
henchida en su tilde, el gorjeo de una flecha en el acento.

Basta desear sobre la nada para andar en este reino pero
 no basta.
Así en la lejanía de esta celda, la sombra de una enre-
 dadera,
un brazo que enciende una playa.
Porque amar sin el sueño, noche a noche, es robarle la
 arena
al agua, abrir una puerta, darle cuerda a un reloj.

*   *   *

Aún faltando su silueta en la corriente, la forma eterna
 del jardín.

Van cayendo, uno a uno, los objetos en la noche: una
 paz incierta
los sostiene, de nunca haber cedido al tiempo,
entre una orilla y la otra, el grano opaco en el centro de
 la mesa,
el lago que una sábana dibuja, la estrella que soñaba en
 una isla,
este desafío al azar que supone encontrarla,
Su calma incierta inamovible en el fragor de tantas
mentiras.

*   *   *

Dónde evocar la noche y el árbol, enterrados en un
 mapa de hielo, sus corrientes internas.
Qué libertad ha marcado a su anhelo: la orquesta siembra el deseo, en un salón muy blanco,
el terreno de un mapa que se extiende a un mundo más
 allá de una costa.
Ofrece rosas blancas al diamante en sombras que co-
 nozco:
mangas de camisa, pulseras heridas por la luna que re-
 flejan.
Y afuera la noche se cifraba en una lámpara en el mar,
 sobre una calle de plata, y era Beirut o La Habana,
pero no importa su nombre, la sucesión teatral lo ha
 devorado todo,

se ha convertido en poesía, espectáculo,
negación poética o afirmación política, abrasada a un
 terreno sin fondo,
cosida al mismo lienzo, sí, con sus variantes,
pero inscritas en la misma tela del regreso, como su
 imagen
imposible,
el fuego y su retorno luminoso y vedado.

agosto, 1990

Alfredo Gómez Gil

Se me acaba España

Se me acaba España
cuando piernas carecen de agilidad
para saltar Pirineos.
Cuando espaldas
desprovistas de alas
no pueden despegar
para conocer de cerca
poetas de América.

Se me acaba España
en el graznido de una gaita gallega,
en el sobresalto de un martinete,
en el crujido de los Xiquets de Valls
rompiéndose la cabeza en el suelo
o en el pájaro de una folía
que no se atreve
a penetrar por el cráter del Teide;
si el declinar vigoroso
de una jota compartida
termina de hablar de humanos
y siempre que aiztcolaris
no talen
la pericia de sus hachas.
Los panochos de la huerta de Murcia
son golondrinas desorientadas
y sus "alborás" la insignia de su solapa.
En la larga Mancha de D. Quijote
se me acaba España ... se me acaba
No puedo dormir
ni en Escalas de Oscar Esplá,
provocada susceptibilidad ulcerosa
irresistible a fabada, paella, gazpacho
y tanta gastronomía concreta
que aburre el estómago,
embrutece los gustos;

sabiéndome el vino
de Sandeman, Osborne, Terry, Domecq
a Commonwealth convencional.
Los gitanos de sobremesa
prontos a la exportación
acicalados con cremas de broncear,
hacen de mi indigestión
rabia de risas
y el rubio de sus mujeres morenas
inaguanta la procacidad
de sus pensamientos más diminutos.
  Se me acaba España
en sus cortes envalados
de colores cromáticos y acromáticos.
Se me acaba en San Isidoro
Vitoria, Suárez, Balmes por supuesto
y hasta en Unamuno, Ortega y Zubiri.
Las torturas graníticas de Gaudí
cierran más mi corazón
que el suyo.

  Se me acaba España
en el impotente imán fabricado
para atraer valores huidizos
de Ochoa, los Pablos, Sert ...
y del pataleo por su postura.
  Se me acaba España
cuando la lente de un Buñuel
para crear
tiene que arrojar el rollo por el tragaluz
porque el hombre que parió
un sistema jurídico sin esquemas
tiembla por un ruidillo de miniclaustro
o por un taco
de minero asturiano.
¿Que tendrá que ver? ... —Por eso
por eso, se me acaba España;
  Se me acaba España
en el sol que está en todas partes
de Benidorm,
en el agua fría de Biarritz
en la Concha,
que no pasan de ser un vano

fatuo e impreciso,
utensilio decadente
de las dos aristocracias,
guitarra y limonada,
de modelos de Balenciaga
e hijos que además del título
serán mañana ingenieros
o de incansables sátiros tostados.
    Se me acaba España
en su estudio preñado e impuesto
pensamiento monárquico de sangres podridas.
    Se me acaba
en su incesante manifestación de virilidad
cuando Europa nos manda sus mujeres,
siendo las nuestras,
más calientes y parturientas,
las que pueblan
el mundo de la trata de blancas.
    Se me acaba España en el
oligárquico intento de graduar los pasos
a la cristalina formación universitaria
rigiéndola por lacayos incompetentes
que amasen y confundan
siervos de un fin distinto a su citado
a una juventud
para que no sepa
lo que quiere,
despistándola
para que en su fondo
tampoco desee saberlo.

    Moralidades bien delimitadas
para agotar un universo de Titanes
encadenadamente indefinidos.
Por eso al amor
le cuesta horrores
hacerse un sitio,
porque el espacio
lo ocupan entero
unas enormes tablas de cartón
fabricadas por una Comisaría de Policía
y decoradas
por un grupo

de señoras del Opus Dei
ocultación lucrativa
de rezos color oro.

   Se me acaba España
en la proliferación de sus ismos,
ismos malogrados, ismos contumaces,
ismos
inventores de sotanas.

Pero el privilegio de la Fe,
no es España.
La cabeza de un hombre,
no es España.
El sol y el olivo,
no son España.
El Amor
no habita en España.

Por todo
se me acaba España
   me acaba España
    acaba España
     España
      . . .
      . . .
     España . . .

José Paredes

Huída hacia adelante

Me iré de ti una tarde de junio cálido
y no dejaré de oir el último vuelo de tu pálpito
cuando el silencio roto por mis pasos calmos
me orillen al insondable abismo de tus cantos.

No. No dejaré de sentir el vuelo de tu hálito
adherida a mí estarás; más, solo breves horas,
porque para perderte mejor buscaré otras olas
que contengan sabias el misterio de mi cántico.

Cuando otro silencio hiera mi bravo paso
estaré libre de ti, de tu compleja sombra.
la herida que en mí tuve ya no te nombra
y la muerte huyendo va de mi diestro lazo.

Iba mi fuga orillando abismal tiniebla
aquel extraño atardecer de junio claro.
Hoy me pregunto: ¿Sólo rocío fue tu abrazo?
Y ahuyento mi paso de tus olas ciegas.

Luis Cruz Azaceta

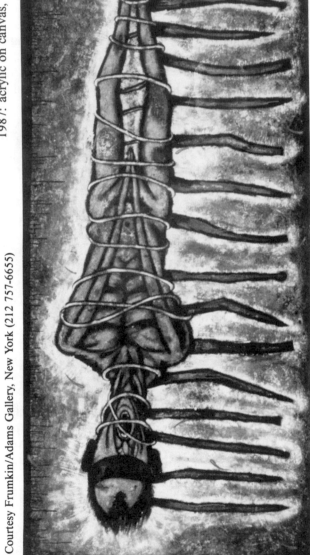

Courtesy Frumkin/Adams Gallery, New York (212 757-6655)

1987: acrylic on canvas, 76" × 168"

Latin American Victims of Dictators, Oppression, Torture and Murder

Luis Cruz Azaceta

Like many other Cubans, Luis Cruz Azaceta was at first sympathetic to the new government. But economic turmoil, rumors of Castro's pro-Soviet orientation and the promise of elections that failed to materialize soon made him skeptical. Not wanting to join the militias, he decided that, if he could not commit himself to revolutionary aims, he ought to leave the country. In 1960, he spent three days and nights in a line at the American Embassy and received a visa to settle permanently in the United States.

Azaceta worked for three years in a trophies factory in Hoboken, New Jersey, for $1/hour, then was fired for his effort to unionize the factory employees. Unemployed for two weeks and desperate to do something, he wandered into an art supply store. "I became an artist out of boredom,» he admits. Working nights as a clerk in a library, he graduated in 1969 from the School of Visual Arts, New York. "I had all kinds of teachers,» he states, ranging from the expressionist painter Leon Golub to the minimalist Robert Mangold. "I got out totally confused.» He was then painting geometric abstractions, but returned from Europe in 1969, which included an exposure to Goya and Bosch, feeling that he had to do something different: "I started wondering why I was painting stripes. It wasn't myself. So I started painting more from the guts, from feelings. I wanted some kind of iconography that would be mine.»

The artist's early works were cartoon-like images rendered in bright, flat pigment with black outlines. More recent arcylics exhibit thick, multicolored layers of paint, the images almost carved in relief. The figures portrayed are almost always tormented in some way: pierced by nails, eviscerated, flagellated or decapitated. Many are self-portraits, though the artist is not so much portraying himself as using his own image to represent everyone: "By showing brutality, I really want to call for compassion. I want to present the victim—that is always my theme.»

From John Beardsley & Jane Livingston, *Hispanic Art in the United States: Thirty Contemporary Painters & Sculptors* (New York: Abbeville Press, 1987).

Luis Cruz Azaceta

Oppression

Juana Rosa Pita
o Penélope reescribe *La Odisea*

Jesús J. Barquet

El mito de Ulises y Penélope ha estado presente en la literatura cubana desde el siglo diecinueve hasta nuestros días, y ha servido muchas veces para representar de manera metafórica la experiencia histórica de la Isla, marcada desde entonces por exilios, retornos y esperas como las padecidas por los protagonistas del mito homérico.

Si bien la revolución de 1959 cerró un período de exilio entre los cubanos, otro comenzó a abrirse ese mismo año provocado por dicho hecho histórico, en lo que parece constituir una fatalidad cíclica de la Isla. Este exilio aún vigente ha encontrado también su representación literaria a través del mito antes mencionado en el poemario *Viajes de Penélope* de Juana Rosa Pita.[1] Pero en nuestro estudio de la función del mito de Ulises y Penélope en VP no nos limitaremos exclusivamente a esta referencialidad históricoespacial y sus ulteriores implicaciones teóricas, sino que describiremos también cómo gracias al mito la autora se inserta en cierto espacio literario cubano descrito por José Lezama Lima y establece allí sus propios derroteros en temas tales como las relaciones —presentes ya desde el *Diario de a bordo* de Cristóbal Colón— entre historia, mito y poesía, y entre paisaje y escritura; el sentido ético de la resistencia desde la cultura; y la posibilidad de definir una sensibilidad insular cuya existencia constatable sirva, como señala Lezama Lima, "para integrar el mito que nos falta."[2] Asimismo señalaremos algunas de las mutaciones que Pita provoca en el mito de Ulises y Penélope al incorporarlo, no como una imagen pasajera en su libro, sino como el código fundamental al que cada poema y paratexto se afilia ya explícita, ya implícitamente.

Frente al aspecto parcial y/o erróneamente generalizador de muchas definiciones del mito, hemos preferido adoptar una postura ecléctica, que nos parece la más apropiada al objeto de este estudio.[3] Por otra parte, la incorporación del mito de Ulises y Penélope que realiza Pita no es afín al principio romántico de originalidad a ultranza, sino a otro más apropiado de tradición literaria que, comenzando con el propio Homero cuando retoma y fija literariamente los mitos que le precedieron, llega hasta nuestros días con autores como Joyce, Rilke, Borges y Roa Bastos.[4] También es afín a la propia naturaleza repetitiva del mito, la cual le permite su infinita renovación o adaptación a los diferentes contextos culturales que con nueva voz, intención y función, lo convocan. Pero esta sucesiva renovación del mito atenta, paradójicamente, contra otra faceta de su naturaleza: si bien el hecho de que un autor retome ciertos mitos constituye una manera de revitalizarlos, el fijarlos de forma escrita "les resta vida," lo cual ha venido ocurriendo ya desde Homero y los trágicos griegos.[5] Trataremos aquí de determinar esa "vida", que llamaremos función, que el mito de Ulises y Penélope tiene en el contexto cultural de su autora, es decir, dentro del exilio cubano posrevolucionario.

Primeramente debemos señalar las transformaciones producidas por la nueva voz autorial que en VP convoca al mito, y por el género elegido, la poesía lírica, con un "yo" presente desde el primer verso: "Me ha dado por creerme Penélope" (15). No estamos frente a la narración omnisciente y externa propia de la épica, sino frente a una identificación sicoemocional del "yo" autorial con uno de sus personajes míticos, Penélope. Una consiguiente encarnación del mismo ocurrirá más adelante cuando el "yo" de varios poemas pueda relacionarse con la voz autorial y con Penélope indistintamente.

Este proceso de confluencia de "yos" requiere analizarse según los tres tipos de "yos" que John B. Vickery detecta como consecuencia directa de "the subject-object relation obtaining between poem as utterance and myth as story or report": el "yo" histórico o personal, el "yo" mítico o metapersonal y el "yo" creativo o metamórfico, los cuales no se presentan uniformemente en todos los autores sino que se caracterizan por sus manifestaciones proteicas, multiformes.[6] Si bien el "yo" histórico o personal descrito por Vickery no se refiere necesariamente al autor de un poema, sí constituye en VP la voz de su autora, en ambivalente movimiento de lo íntimo a lo colectivo.[7]

Las maneras de autoenunciarse esa voz autorial son diversas y enmascaradoras. Se autoenuncia, por ejemplo, en su oposición inicial al "yo" mítico o metapersonal constituido por la figura de Penélope.[8] Pero esta oposición tiene sólo la intención de dejar constancia de la existencia de dos "yos" diferentes en su inmediata referencialidad externa, ya que más adelante ambos convergerán en lo esencial íntimo o mítico. De ahí que en los primeros poemas del libro, la autora asuma su "yo" frente a un nítido "tú" dialogante, que es Penélope: "Penélope que tienes / a Ulises siempre lejos o allegándose / destéjeme este sueño" (17), "tú —tejedora máxima" (22). Y ratifica su no-ser Penélope cuando, tras decir que le ha dado por creerse Penélope, emplea la siguiente prótasis condicional contingente: "Si yo fuera Penélope / suelo que yo pisara sería Itaca" (15). Una vez establecidas las dos personas (histórica y mítica), se apresta Pita a dar un salto metamórfico en el poema 6 (25): en éste, el "yo" parlante comienza a imprecisar su referencialidad y la nítida oposición antes mencionada comienza a hacerse equívoca y a mostrar su función primordial: convocar el mito, hacer que la figura mítica se encamine "a la estancia del poema" (70). Es por esto tal vez que la sección inicial del poemario se titula "Profesión de mito". Ese salto metamórfico constituye el momento en que los dos "yos" analizados tienden a fusionarse en el tercero, el "yo" creativo.[9]

Otra forma de autoenunciación del "yo" histórico se realiza mediante una circunlocución parcialmente enmascaradora que aparece de manera esporádica en el poemario: sabemos que dicho "yo" se refiere a una poeta porque afirma ser "tejedora" (15), y tejer remeda en algunos versos el acto de escribir: "voy tejiendo sílabas sin rumbo" (29), "enlazar cada hilo del poema" (84). Pero este autoenunciarse como tejedora la conduce inequívocamente también al arquetipo o figura mítica que mejor la expresa e incluye: Penélope. De ahí que la llame "tejedora máxima" (22). Insertarse en el mito constituirá en lo adelante un acto de economía factual y verbal. Gracias al mito,[10] el "yo" histórico puede definirse a partir de lo que considera esencial a su ser íntimo-colectivo: "tejedora sí soy para que alienten / los que habrán de morir / y es la mía la almohada / más llorada del siglo" (15). Su proceso de automitificación es asimismo un paliativo intelectual para su incomprensión del sentido de la existencia.[11] De ahí que la voz autorial busque explicar(se) la naturaleza problemática de su ser empleando diferentes mitos: "Yo Eurídice ... / soy Isis ... / vivo Penélope" (5). Esta constituye también la forma más vacía o teatral en que el "yo" histórico se autoenuncia. Nos hace ver claramente que las figuras míticas que utiliza son sólo máscaras, disfraces, papeles previamente escritos que reparte según la ocasión entre las diferentes facetas de su personalidad escindida. Eurídice e Isis establecen el nexo entre VP y sus dos poemarios anteriores,[12] pero a la vez inician el conflicto entre esa previa denominación adoptada, la verdadera identidad existencial de la autora y su experiencia vital, percibida por ella como un acto equívoco entre lo volitivo y lo impuesto (mar: exilio): "porque aún hay tanto mar / vivo Penélope" (5). Sea como fuere, su autopostulación final como Penélope dinamiza en su ser una capacidad fundadora que desemboca en la firme convicción de poder crear un espacio propio en medio de tanto mar, un espacio que sustituya a su Isla perdida y garantice el regreso de su amado Ulises. Tal capacidad fundadora constituye una mutación en el patrón mítico incorporado. Por eso afirma: "Si yo fuera Penélope / suelo que yo pisara sería Itaca / al regresar Ulises / se quedara" (15). Que ese espacio sea el poema mismo, la metafórica tela que teje Penélope mientras sueña o se lanza a sus "viajes revelantes" (74), parece ser la intención de la autora, quien cierra su libro con la presencia vibrante y solitaria del paso de dicha tela sobre el mar dejando una "estela adamantina" (85). Tal vez esta estela sea la señal de tierra (Itaca) que guiará a Ulises, como antaño el famoso ramo de fuego en el mar supo guiar a otro marino, Colón, hacia las costas de Cuba.[13] Tanto en VP como en el diario de Colón,[14] el espacio o la tierra (¿prometida?) existe hecha metáfora en el mar. Para describir este espacio se necesita entonces una escritura que participe indistintamente de las instancias míticopoética e histórica.

Pita sabe además que el espacio creado, para sentirse completo o para ser o existir en la Historia, requiere su Colón. De ahí que el "yo" histórico exija, en lo mítico, la presencia de Ulises como contrapartida de su alter ego Penélope (la pareja masculino-femenino es elemento común al mito); y en lo personal inmediato, la presencia de nosotros, los Lectores, tan extendidos y repetidos en el tiempo y el espacio como cualquier otro personaje mítico:

> Pues en verdad si Ulises
> no planta su voz frente a la aurora
> y llena estas estancias
> quiere decir que Itaca no ha sido
> ni siquiera un deseo:
> Penélope no existe y todo lo tejido
> es gracia de la muerte ... (16)

> Del uno al infinito
> me bastaría Ulises ...
> para enlazar cada hilo del poema:
> cualquiera de los que han de morir
> me bastaría para no desatarlo
> o tú mismo
> que en un rincón del tiempo estás leyéndome. (84)

Pero cuando postulamos esta creación volitiva del espacio (y, por extensión, de las entidades míticas que lo pueblan) realizada por el "yo" histórico, no presuponemos en aquél una actitud pasiva sino todo lo contrario. Ya Lezama Lima comentó la múltiple función activa que tuvo el espacio (o paisaje) americano en la conformación de la literatura hispanoamericana.[15] Observó además que, una vez metamorfoseadas las entidades naturales de un espacio en entidades culturales imaginarias —como hace Pita al contrapuntear la experiencia cubana del exilio y el mito de Penélope—, "ese espacio tiene fuerza animista en relación con esas entidades"[16] que lo pueblan, llega a hacerlas partícipes conscientes —agregaríamos nosotros— de un contexto histórico superior que quizás antes no percibían ni comprendían pero que el paisaje les revela como suyo. De esta manera, el espacio es capaz de trazarles o mostrarles un destino a las entidades que lo pueblan. Este animismo y saber histórico del paisaje están presentes en la casa o espacio que compartían Penélope y Ulises en la Itaca de Pita. Refiriéndose a la casa, Penélope (o el "yo" histórico) le dice a Ulises que "nos mira la ventana," "la puerta que nos piense / se promete a jazmines" y la casa "nos sueña" (41) y "mueve las persianas si te acercas" (40). Penélope intuye que la casa "atesora un todavía / de canciones preciosas" y tiene "una invencible savia / por las sabias paredes" (38). Y concluye diciéndole a Ulises que "la casa está de vuelta / de todos los destinos / y sabe que hay justicia poética / y se sabe / la fecha que ignoramos" (38).

Todas las respuestas están en la mítica "casa", y, por consiguiente, todas las esperanzas o ilusiones ("only an illusion") de regreso definitivo ("la fecha que ignoramos") que el exilio cubano posterior a 1959 no ha podido verificar en lo real inmediato todavía.

Pero en el terreno cultural, la inserción desde fuera en el espacio literario cubano constituye, sin embargo, una posibilidad real no determinada por los límites geográficos del país ni por su actual coyuntura sociopolítica. Es decir, constituye una forma efectiva y libre de regreso, o más aún, de negar lo fenoménico del exilio al contraponerle el esencial cordón umbilical que une al artista con su tierra natal y que no logra cortar ninguna separación física ni decreto oficial.[17] Pita busca (y logra, como aquí nos proponemos demostrar) insertarse en esa tradición de escritores cubanos (Heredia, Martí, Carpentier, Sarduy) que, escribiendo desde fuera de la Isla, le han ayudado a conformar su espacio literario. Así como el vector del movimiento de Ulises lo dirigía hacia Itaca, Pita necesita a Cuba más para otorgarle un vector direccional a su creación, que para proponer como respuesta o solución el regreso físico o la permanencia en la Isla. Debemos recordar que en VP, Penélope, como Ulises, también abandona Itaca (ver poema 30). Y en su poemario posterior, *Crónicas del Caribe*,[18] la autora relata cómo en su "navegante cautiverio" (CC, 71) ha sabido preservar intactos su origen e identidad.[19]

Volviendo a las formas de autoenunciación del "yo" histórico, analizaremos ahora la función de tres textos del poemario que parecen ser las únicas referencias directas al entorno tempoespacial y cultural de la autora y que por estar colocados al principio y final del libro, nos permiten (y hasta obligan a) insertarlo en la problemática representacional del reciente exilio cubano. Esta específica referencialidad, obvia en el contexto total de la poesía de Pita, no implica una limitación en sus alcances estéticos y conceptuales, sino que por el contrario nos habla de la capacidad que tiene la autora de transformar estéticamente su circunstancia histórica personal —inclúyase aquí la de toda su comunidad— y expresarla, gracias al mito, a través de un código universal fácilmente identificable. En la propia naturaleza del mito existe una fuerte interrelación entre lo particular y lo general.[20]

Los dos primeros textos son en realidad paratextos: una cita introductoria de Lezama Lima: "Nuestra isla [sic] comienza su historia dentro de la poesía" (6); y el prólogo del libro, "Los viajes revelantes de Juana Rosa Pita" (9–11), escrito por Reinaldo Arenas en el exilio. Sorprende la curiosa (o tal vez errónea) inserción del prólogo dentro del corpus poemático del libro, como si formara parte del mismo. Los dos autores (Lezama y Arenas equivaldrían a Penélope y a Ulises, respectivamente) remiten a un espacio literario e histórico inicial, el cubano, en el que el material mítico procede a insertarse. Arenas, ya desde el título de su prólogo, transfiere explícitamente "los viajes revelantes" de Penélope a la autora y afirma que ésta "ve a través de Penélope a ella misma" (9–10). Señala además que "el gran acontecimiento" de esta epopeya es la resistencia, "el viaje inmóvil de Penélope" (10), haciendo así resaltar el trasfondo ético del poemario y su pertenencia a una tradición. Lezama Lima ha señalado ya "la carga de eticidad que entraña" dicha resistencia desde la cultura en la historia de Cuba.[21]

Por su parte, el paratexto lezamiano presenta no sólo un posesivo ("nuestra") que colectiviza y da nacionalidad al "yo" personal o histórico, sino también una transformación equívoca en la palabra "isla" al registrarla con minúscula. Lo que exclusivamente era Cuba (la Isla) en el ensayo original de Lezama, será en VP no sólo Cuba sino también Itaca u otra "isla" cualquiera entre las muchas presentes en los mitos o en la realidad; por eso un verso dice: "tejiendo la marea entre las islas" (85). De igual forma que pasamos de Isla (con I mayúscula) a islas, en las entidades míticas pasamos de Troya a "troyas" (26), de Penélope a "penélopes" (31), de Helena a "helenas" (71), como señalándonos el espejeo o repetición de la historia, y dentro de ella el exilio cubano como una instancia más en la serie infinita de exilios y regresos que el mito de Ulises, en tanto que arquetipo, representa.[22]

El paratexto de Lezama Lima también introduce un tema esencial de la cultura cubana que forma parte de la poética de Pita: la confluencia de historia y poesía, o expresado de otra forma, la escritura de nuestra historia a través de la poesía, tema al que volveremos más adelante.

El tercer texto que nos remite a las circunstancias tempoespaciales del "yo" histórico, está colocado al final, fuera del corpus central del poemario como un exergo explicativo, y pertenece a la propia autora: "Este que fuera cuento es vida en mí / y de una cierta isla hará la historia" (87). De manera altamente sintética, Pita hace idénticos el mito (en tanto que fábula, relato o "cuento") de Penélope y Ulises, su "yo" personal e histórico ("vida"), y la comunidad representada por éste ("historia"). La función del mito de Penélope es, pues, no sólo conformar una historia personal y colectiva, sino también explicarla y universalizarla mediante el patrón genérico referencial e interpretativo que el mito ofrece.

Es de notar también que este afán historizante y arquetípico de VP provoca en el plano teórico un movimiento contrario que nos devuelve a la naturaleza misma del mito, al restituirle a este su aspecto original de experiencia vivida.[23] Historia y mito se confunden, como les ocurrió a los primeros historiadores (léase cronistas) cuando experimentaron y trataron de expresar la peculiar realidad americana a la luz de los mitos entonces en boga en Europa.[24] Para Pita, el mito y su expresión hecha poesía constituyen además una fuente histórica mejor o más sustancial que el mero dato positivo. Insatisfecha con la historia oficial que no logra desentrañar el sentido del caos en que se vive, quiere reescribir la historia de su pueblo a través del mito y la poesía,[25] e imitando a los cronistas intitula "crónicas" a su próximo libro, CC.

Concluyendo podemos afirmar que los tres textos anteriormente estudiados (cita de Lezama, prólogo de Arenas y exergo de la autora), en la medida en que contribuyen a crear ese equívoco o identificación entre historia y mito (es decir, entre determinadas circunstancias tempoespaciales y la fábula arquetípica), constituyen una forma más de manifestarse el "yo" creativo o metamórfico definido por Vickery.

Por otra parte, el lado subconsciente y subjetivo de la experiencia histórica que revelan el mito y la poesía se opone a la actividad racional y supuestamente objetiva de los tratados de Historia.

Constituye su reverso, el cual es para Pita más fidedigno que el anverso. Con este procedimiento de inversión la autora busca revelarnos la verdad de su drama colectivo y afirmar que la necesaria y buscada comprensión o respuesta no radica en lo histórico propiamente dicho sino en lo íntimo humano:

> Las troyas recurrentes
> los asuntos del hombre no pretendas
> que pueda comprenderlos:
> Penélope no siente la deshonra de Ilión
> siente a Telémaco
> manoteando en el centro de su sueño ... (83)

La clave de la historia está en su reverso: "Ocultos son los rumbos de la épica: / el revés de la historia urde la danza / de los cantos futuros" (55). Ni Ulises ni sus viajes exteriores cantados por Homero poseen la respuesta, sino Penélope inmersa en su intimidad. De ahí que Penélope-Poeta emerja líricamente como centro (sujeto y objeto, voz y tema) del poemario, y afirme que su onírico viaje, asociado indistintamente al mítico tejido y a la escritura de la autora ("navegas tejiéndole" [52], "volar la pluma" [62]), es "chalupa más sutil / cóncava y ágil / que las viriles naves de Ulises" (62). Según ella, el supuesto gran viaje de Ulises es sólo un torpe producto del "desatino humano" (34), de los "asuntos vanos" del hombre (27); mientras que los viajes de ella se atreven "por el más ceñudo océano" (51) y constituyen "los viajes revelantes" a los que Ulises debe acogerse: "Agota los prodigios del gran viaje / y quédate a los viajes revelantes" (74). Ella es también, para mayor ironía, "la que urde los viajes / tejiéndole la historia a contrasueño" (72). A diferencia del "cándido Ulises" (47), Penélope no actúa con ingenuidad sino con una clara conciencia de destino:

> No te llamen ingenua
> Penélope
> sólo porque le das tu pleno día
> a tejer y olvidar la absurda tela:
> bien sabes el destino de esos hilos
> que rehusas perder. (69)

Al desplazar el punto de vista de la narración del mito —del antiguo Homero a la poeta encarnada en Penélope—, puede Pita proceder a desmitificar la versión del vate griego y refutar su supuesta autoridad sobre la interpretacion de los hechos. Así ocurre cuando se refiere a la sexualidad insatisfecha de la solitaria Penélope, la cual había sido eludida eufemísticamente por Homero:

> Ya le comprendo el signo
> a tu quehacer nocturno
> Penélope:
> si te invita la sembrada blancura
> tus senos se despiertan hacia el cuarto
> horadando la sombra . . .
> Sólo que un tal Homero
> porque es ciego y es noble
> dirá que es Atenea —¡oh epopeya!—
> quien te da el dulce sueño. (37)

Estamos así frente a un personaje que busca independizarse de su creador y escapar del diseño que se le había previamente asignado. Cuenta para ello con la fuente divina que anida en su amor por Ulises y en su capacidad de reescribir la Odisea: "No es Homero el cantor: / es Dios que crió voz en nuestro abrazo / y se vistió de ciego para el canto" (73). No sólo logra Penélope con sus viajes escapar de la fijación verbal de su ser mítico realizada por Homero y en la cual ella no era más que el necesario complemento pasivo del héroe masculino, sino que también logra invertir esta relación de complementariedad al erigirse ella como centro rector y a Ulises como su frágil correlato masculino:[26] ella lo crea, le conforma su memoria de la isla (22), lo guía aun a distancia (42). Los viajes de Ulises tienen entonces un solo fin, Penélope, y en función de ella hallan su razón de ser:

> Cuánto país tendrás que descubrir
> cuánto ardid y prodigio reeditar
> para no errar la ruta de mis senos:
> cuántos años por tardas geografías
> de circes y calipsos . . .
> sólo por redimir
> cándido Ulises
> un minuto en mi lecho. (47)

La inversión[27] que coloca a Penélope en el centro del mito responde a la capacidad que este personaje tiene de representar, frente a la dispersión vivencial del desislado Ulises, la presencia resistente de la isla natal, del hogar previamente fundado.

Como Penélope, la isla también preserva intacta en su memoria la identidad original del desterrado:

> Podrá extraviarse Ulises
> todo lo lejos lejos
> de la que urde los viajes . . .
> pero Itaca le guarda
> acento viejo y piel
> sobre las playas jóvenes

que lo vieron crecer hacia el destierro. (72)

Y la isla es depositaria de esa memoria porque todo desterrado, en el ciclo infinito de los exilios, siembra su epopeya antes de partir (ver poema 48).

Otra mutación que la autora realiza en el mito se produce cuando desplaza física, aunque no síquica ni emocionalmente, a Penélope de Itaca. Para sorpresa del conocedor del mito, Penélope —como la autora— no vive en la isla, sino que ha tenido que ausentarse de ella para sobrevivir. Su presencia es la imagen resistente de una ausencia: "Queda en la isla mi imagen / y aléjome de tanto pormorir: / salvo mi hermoso cuerpo de la ruina" (53).

Al representar e interpretar mediante el mito de Penélope y Ulises la experiencia histórica de su comunidad, la autora descubre un destino ineludible de exilios sucesivos: ve a su pueblo como a Ulises, "dado a la pasión de los espejos" (48). Es la trampa que le han tendido la representación mítica y el empleo de una denominación previamente fijada. Por eso, dudosa ante su intención mitificadora inicial, le pide más adelante a Ulises que se desmitifique: "Ah si te desbautizaras ... llegarías" (48).

Frente a la historia como repetición de los mismos arquetipos (helenas, troyas, penélopes) y contra la fatal capacidad fijadora del signo lingüístico, crea Juana Rosa Pita en VP un cosmos poético donde lo particular y lo general, así como los significantes y los significados, se entrecruzan, indefinen sus contornos y reacciones, se metamorfosean en su opuesto. Aunque utiliza los nombres propios míticos de referencia única (Penélope, Ulises, Itaca), prefiere crear un magma impreciso de sustantivos comunes multirreferenciales (penélopes, troyas, islas, casa, odisea) y de pronombres personales con sus respectivas variantes pronominales. La multirreferencialidad de los sustantivos comunes (entre los que incluimos los nombres propios transformados en comunes por la eliminación de la mayúscula y la pluralidad) y la significación vacía de los pronombres eliminan cualquier posible fijación e identificación definitivas. Los pronombres (yo, tú, él, ella, nosotros) entran en el discurso de manera equívoca, por lo que nuestra recepción no logra muchas veces identificar ni a los interlocutores ni a la persona de quien se habla. El aspecto actualizador del pronombre crea así un texto que no pretende fijarse más allá del brevísimo instante de su emisión. La posible referencialidad de un poema es prontamente subvertida o (re)emplazada por el poema siguiente. Mediante ambos recursos lingüísticos, Pita logra escapar del fatalismo que el mito parecía determinarle, y expresar al mismo tiempo la dinámica interna de los tres "yos" que intervienen en su texto.

Pero en el exilio fatal del cubano, la autora detecta otro elemento común con el mito de Ulises: el origen insular de ambos. Aun cuando comprende que la presencia de un máximo censor en el suelo natal constituye una causa importante del exilio de sus compatriotas (ver poema 11), Pita prefiere priorizar como razón última del exilio un supuesto mito insular que opera de manera determinante sobre sus habitantes. Ve como innata a la isla, una oscura sinrazón telúrica o fuerza centrífuga que arrastra a sus pobladores al exilio:

> Madre isla que estás venida a remos
> convertida en solar de pretendientes
> infundiendo los viajes
> ¿quién guardará tus playas de naufragio? (62)

Pita continúa así las reflexiones tempranas de Lezama Lima sobre la necesidad (y posibilidad) de definir un particular comportamiento y sensibilidad insular en el cubano.[28]

Con la poesía de Juana Rosa Pita estamos frente a una de las más consistentes poéticas contemporáneas que ha decidido instalarse en el ámbito del mito, es decir, adoptar como suya una perspectiva mitológica que contrarreste y subvierta esta época preferentemente científica y tecnológica. Las afirmaciones de Mircea Elíade sobre el comportamiento mitológico del hombre contemporáneo[29] se corroboran de manera explícita en VP. Mediante el mito de Penélope y Ulises, Pita revela en las estructuras sicoemocionales del cubano exiliado el reflejo de un comportamiento arquetípico universal que lo lleva a repetir, partiendo de sus específicas circunstancias históricas y geográficas, motivos míticos clásicos como el viaje, el paraíso perdido y el eterno retorno. El viaje, aventura o destierro en busca de una vida mejor (y que lanza incluso a la Penélope de VP); el paraíso perdido (no necesariamente relacionado con un período histórico abolido o por venir, sino con la pérdida del hogar, del solar materno); y el eterno retorno (que hace repetir a Ulises: "Y yo llegaré a Itaca" [45]) son motivos presentes no sólo en el poemario de Pita sino también en gran parte del discurso cubano del exilio.

En lo metafísico, este comportamiento mitológico entraña, como también señala Elíade,[30] la eterna lucha humana contra el tiempo y la muerte. Por eso Penélope dice que "hay magia que cortar / y si nos falta el tiempo / le alegamos ahoritas a la muerte" (74). Pietro Civitareale analiza también la poesía de Pita en función del carácter metafísico que encierra el motivo odiseico de la peregrinación y del viaje, entendiéndolo "no tanto como expresión de una inevitable condición existencial, como objetivación ineludible de su estado de exilio, cuanto como reclamo de un absoluto: búsqueda baudelariana de otra parte, capaz de transformarse en el plano sicológico en una posible verdad."[31]

La rebelión y la búsqueda de otro espacio son constantes de la obra de Pita que ella observa también en todo poeta exiliado cuando afirma que éste

> nutre su realidad reinventando el pasado, domina el arte de proyectar su ensueño sin perder el equilibrio, mantiene a su alrededor un espacio libre de la mugre del siglo: espacio sólo abierto al ser humano, mantiene a raya a las máquinas, los dragones, los ogros.[32]

Se trata, pues, de la búsqueda y consecución de un espacio personal y libre de toda sujeción o atadura, salvo la de la página en blanco; o sea, de un espacio que parece compartir las virtudes últimas de la poesía. Para Pita, la palabra poética también "enmienda la realidad, tanto para quien la dice como para quien la escucha, si en vez de darse a la muerte se da a ella," es "vida intensificada y enmendada desde una perspectiva de infinito": la poesía es "¡dos veces vida!"[33]

El poema es además "aquel sitio perdido" donde se resuelven (o podrían resolverse) amorosamente y fuera del "río del tiempo" y sus contingencias, todos los desencuentros y desacuerdos humanos: "Ese cuarto infinito / de sábanas benditas por milenios / de amor es el poema."[34]

---

[1] Juana Rosa Pita, *Viajes de Penélope* (Miami: Solar, 1980). Prólogo de Reinaldo Arenas. Todas las referencias de página serán de esta edición y aparecerán dentro del texto; abreviatura empleada: VP.

[2] José Lezama Lima, *Obras completas*, II (México: Aguilar, 1976): 51.

[3] En su *El mito: su significado y funciones en las distintas culturas* (trad. Antonio Pigráu Rodríguez, Barcelona: Barral, 1973), G. S. Kirk señala que "los mitos difieren enormemente en su morfología y su función social" y "no hay ninguna definición del mito, ninguna forma platónica del mito que se ajuste a todos los casos reales" (21). En este sentido, en su *Mito, literatura y realidad* (Madrid: Gredos, 1965), Marcelino C. Peñuelas habla no sólo del carácter exclusivista de las numerosas definiciones del mito que existen, sino también de nuestra imposibilidad de reducir su ser "camaleónico" a elementos fijos y constantes, "porque al parecer su esencia es racionalmente inaprehensible, inefable" (10). Por tales razones consideramos improcedente también el criterio de algunos mitólogos que, siguiendo sus cerradas definiciones, excluyen del Parnaso mítico a la figura de Penélope por carecer de un origen divino. Preferimos repetir con Kirk que "muchos episodios humanos de (o implicados por) estos poemas [homéricos] han adquirido categoría mítica arquetípica sobre todo a causa de la especial textura conferida a la leyenda por la presencia

de los dioses: episodios como el rapto de Helena, la elección de Aquiles, su amistad con Patroclo, la muerte y mutilación de Héctor, la ruina que se cierne sobre Troya, el regreso y venganza de Odiseo, la perseverancia de Penélope." Todos estos episodios, sigue diciendo Kirk, conservados de una forma u otra en la tradición oral y escrita, "se han convertido en paradigmas míticos en el pensamiento y literatura subsiguientes" gracias a un proceso secundario de desarrollo que les ha otorgado "los altos tonos de fantasía que muchos otros mitos poseen desde el principio, en virtud de sus propios temas o de su esencial contenido de poderes sobrenaturales" (op. cit., 49–50).

[4] Así lo ha percibido también el crítico italiano Pietro Civitareale en su artículo "La escritura mágica de Juana Rosa Pita" aparecido en *El Gato Tuerto*, núm. 10 (1988): 9: "el discurso poético de Juana Rosa Pita se ha venido paso a paso enriqueciendo con un motivo centralísimo de la tradición literaria mediterránea e hispanoamericana: el odiseico de la peregrinación y del viaje."

[5] Al respecto, véase Peñuelas, op. cit., 108.

[6] La clasificación que seguimos pertenece a John B. Vickery, *Myths and Texts. Strategies of Incorporation and Displacement* (Baton Rouge, La.: Louisiana State University, 1983): 187. Según Vickery, el "yo" histórico o personal "postulates a temporal and singular identity for its voice which may be either actual or hypothetical. This locution may refer to the poet as an existent person, that is, the voice in the poem as that of an unspecified person who yet at some level is the poet, if only by the very fact that the poem is his poem" (187–188).

[7] "Sucede en mi poesía: aunque yo no lo busque, mi voz personal cede a veces a mi voz comunal," escribe Juana Rosa Pita en carta del 12 de mayo de 1987 dirigida a mi persona.

[8] Para Vickery, "the mythic or metapersonal self is the I of the mythic figura represented in the poem, and may exist in either an affirmative or a negative relation to the personal self" (op. cit., 188).

[9] Para Vickery, el "yo" creativo o metamórfico es "the reflexively aware intersection point of the actual and the potencial, the determined and the anticipated, and the known and the unknown, which taken together make up the three dimensions of the thinking world of consciousness. Because of its protean nature, generalization about the creative self is difficult. One thing we can say perhaps is that it is that quality of linguistic intentionality envisaging both symmetrical and asymmetrical relations between the personal and mythic terms of the self" (op. cit., 188).

[10] En su *Mythologies* (trad. Annette Lavers, New York: Hill and Wang, 1979), Roland Barthes señala que el mito "abolishes the complexity of human acts, and gives them the simplicity of essences" (143).

[11] En su *Myth and Meaning* (New York: Schocken Books, 1978), Claude Levi-Strauss afirma que el mito "gives man, very importantly, the illusion that he can understand the universe and that he does understand the universe. It is, of course, only an illusion" (17).

[12] Juana Rosa Pita, *Eurídice en la fuente* (Washington: Solar, 1979) y *Manual de magia* (Barcelona: Ambito Literario, 1979).

[13] En su *La cantidad hechizada* (La Habana: UNEAC, 1970), José Lezama Lima da su interpretación de ese hecho histórico en un ensayo

brevemente citado (y no casualmente) en VP: "Nuestra Isla comienza su historia dentro de la poesía. La imagen, la fábula y los prodigios establecen su reino desde nuestra fundamentación y el descubrimiento. Así el almirante Cristobal Colón consigna en su *Diario*, libro que debe estar en el umbral de nuestra poesía, que vio al acercarse a nuestras costas un gran ramo de fuego en el mar" (215).

[14] Véase Cristóbal Colón, *Diario de a bordo*, ed. Vicente Muñoz Puelles (Madrid: Generales Anaya, 1985): 47.

[15] Hablando de las primeras crónicas, Lezama Lima dice que "en los cronistas el asombro está dictado por la misma naturaleza, por un paisaje que, ansioso de su expresión, se vuelca sobre el perplejo misionero" (*Obras completas*, II, 298).

[16] Lezama Lima, *Obras completas*, II, 283.

[17] Por eso Severo Sarduy puede afirmar que nunca ha salido de Cuba, en su artículo "Severo Sarduy: lluvia fresca, bajo el flamboyant", *Escandalar*, núm. 3 (1978): 65.

[18] Juana Rosa Pita, *Crónicas del Caribe* (Miami: Solar, 1983). Las referencias de página serán de esta edición y estarán insertas en el texto; abreviatura empleada: CC.

[19] "En bandolera de papel / llevo todo lo que amo (amé amaré) / y el universo en su callada música / Sólo un milagro de espesura leve / es capaz de preservar el arca / de materia impregnante en el diluvio / No tiene potestad la historia / en la capilla transparente donde vuela / la mariposa que secuestró al mar" (Juana Rosa Pita, CC, 74).

[20] En su *Mythology. The Voyage of the Hero* (New York: Harper & Row, 1981), David Adams Leeming afirma que "myths spring from the particular problems and concerns of a given race or tribe, but on a deeper level their source is the universal soul of the human race itself" (4).

[21] Asimismo señala Lezama Lima que esa resistencia "había de ser característica de todos los intentos nobles del cubano" (*La cantidad hechizada*, 215). Un texto clave sobre el desarrollo de la eticidad cubana es Cintio Vitier, *Ese sol del mundo moral. Para una historia de la eticidad cubana* (México: Siglo XXI, 1975).

[22] En su próximo poemario, se produce un movimiento inverso: Pita restituye la mayúscula a la palabra Isla y la ubica geográficamente: "Trasvolando el Caribe / pasé sobre mi Isla que dormía / y repoblé su sueño" (CC, 18). También sabe ser muy específica con dicha palabra: con motivo del premio literario "Ultimo Novecento" que le fue conferido en Italia en 1985, escribe lo siguiente: "Italia descubre de nuevo mi Isla: trozo cautivo de nuestra América" ("El código vibracional de mi poesía", *La prensa literaria*, Managua, mayo 25 de 1985, 2).

[23] En su *Introduction to a Science of Mythology: The Myth of the Divine Child and the Mysteries of Eleusis* (Londres: Routledge & Kegan Paul, 1951), Carl Gustav Jung y C. Kerenyi afirman que "the primitive mentality does not invent myths, it experiences them." Es decir, los mitos constituyen parte de la historia de una comunidad en la medida en que son "original revelations of the pre-conscious psyche, involuntary statements about unconscious psychic happenings" (101).

[24] Lezama Lima observa en los primeros cronistas una "tendencia a tener una perspectiva mitológica, aun en la realidad de lo que [les] rodea,

paisaje, flora, fauna" (*La cantidad hechizada*, 216).

[25] Pita afirma que "la poesía es la otra historia: creación sin fin, revela el Sentido bajo el caos aparente" ("El código vibracional", 2).

[26] Ya Pita había ensayado en su *Mar entre rejas* (Washington: Solar, 1977), la incorporación de un complemento masculino (el poeta entonces preso Angel Cuadra) a su voz lírica. Esta segunda presencia, como la de Ulises en VP, es imprescindible para lograr el valioso contrapunto ético y emocional y la unidad ficcional que presentan ambos poemarios.

[27] Un poema posterior de Pita ("De cómo dar con el mito moderno") está basado precisamente en la inversión: en vez de ser la princesa rescatada por el príncipe, éste resulta ser rescatado por ella. Incluido en Carlota Caulfield, *El tiempo es una mujer que espera* (Madrid: Torremozas, 1986), 9.

[28] Lezama Lima, *Obras completas*, II, 51.

[29] En su *Aspects du mythe* (París: Gallimard, 1963), Mircea Elíade señala en ese afán mitologizante del hombre contemporáneo una forma de rebelión que atañe tanto a lo físico como a lo metafísico: "On devine dans la littérature une révolte contre le temps historique, le désir d'accéder à d'autres rythmes temporels que celui dans lequel on est obligé de vivre et de travailler. On se demande si ce désir de transcender son propre temps, personnel et historique, et de plonger dans un temps étranger, qu'il soit extatique ou imaginaire, sera jamais extirpé. Tant que subsiste ce désir, on peut dire que l'homme moderne garde encore au moins certains résidus d'un comportement mythologique. Les traces d'un tel comportement mythologique se décèlent aussi dans le désir de retrouver l'intensité avec laquelle on a vécu, ou connu, une chose pour la première fois, de récupérer le passé lontain, l'époque béatifique des commencements" (232).

[30] Elíade, op. cit., 232.

[31] Civitareale, op. cit., 9. Continúa diciendo que "en la invitation au voyage el ser humano ha visto siempre, reflejados, los extremos emotivos y cognoscitivos de la propia existencia, en cuanto que su propia vida, más allá de toda evidente determinación espacial y temporal, no es otra cosa que un aventuroso tránsito por el enorme e insondable dominio del alma, mirado y reencontrado en la realidad especular del mundo" (9).

[32] Pita, "Paraíso de exiliados", en ·*El Miami Herald*, Miami, junio 16 de 1986, 4.

[33] Pita, "El código vibracional", 2.

[34] Pita, *Mar entre rejas*, 24.

The Structure of Antonio Skármeta's
Soñé que la nieve ardía

Donald L. Shaw

In 1976, Antonio Skármeta complained that "quand toute l'A-mérique se débat dans une lutte difficile contre ses oppresseurs dans laquelle le prolétariat est protagoniste, héros et fréquente victime, les nouveaux écrivains n'ont pas su l'interpréter."[1] He himself was not guilty of the charge. Of his first novel, *Soñé que la nieve ardía*,[2] written in exile after the fall of the Allende government, he was to write: "En [*Soñé* ...] se expresan estratos d⊂ la juventud proletaria que contrastan con la figura de Arturo, un futbolista provinciano, que viene al Santiago convulsionado y transido por la solidaridad dispuesto a triunfar confiado en sus valores individuales."[3] Refer-ences to a "contrapuntal" technique in the novel are readily found (for example in *Del cuerpo a las palabras*,[4] or in the review of *Soñé* ... [5]); but they tend to refer to the contrast between the young people in the *pensión* where Arturo lives and a couple of variety artists who have also found refuge there. A closer examination of the novel's structure, however, reveals that the most important contrapuntal effect is gained by contrasting Arturo with one in par-ticular of the politically active young people, el Gordo Ossorio. This modest and attractive young man, "un buen revolucionario y un buen trabajador" (39) functions as the standard against which Arturo is measured. This is the basic structural principle of the novel.

Its narrative organization reveals a certain symmetry. Of the twenty-two chapters, chapter eleven, the middle one if we count the pages, together with chapters twelve and thirteen, constitute the pivotal section of the narrative. Chapter eleven centers on Ossorio both because here he assumes the narrative voice and be-cause here he assumes his function as the figure in terms of whom we are to judge Arturo. He has the task of calling to order one of his fellow-workers guilty of selling cloth on the Black Market. He succeeds brilliantly, leaving the culprit convinced and contrite. The whole chapter is an illustration of how the threshold of po-litical consciousness in the masses can be raised. The fact that Ossorio is the agent of the process indicates him unmistakably as the role-model for the central character. In this central chapter Ossorio appears in his social guise, that is, as a worker in the context of the embattled collectivity, in direct contrast to Arturo as a non-productive, individualistic, modern gladiator. Not for nothing is the latter placed in the context of commercialized, professional soccer, where collective team-spirit has been eroded by the star-system and the commodity-value of single outstanding players. The roots of Arturo's character are egocentricity, materialism and lack of concern for others. In terms of his (non-existent) love life, this means that only a physical relationship with a girl has any attraction for him. In chapter twelve his obsession with simple sexual gratification is made explicit to don Manuel, the owner of the *pensión*. During their conversation Arturo on the one hand mentions the possibility of selling his sporting talents to the highest bidder (the USA). On the other, when don Manuel offers him some poems by Neruda with the suggestion that they could give him ideas for chatting up the other sex, Arturo replies laconically "No creo que me interese, don Manuel. Yo no quiero hablarles, usted ya sabe lo que quiero" (125). Thus, as chapter eleven is the crucial chapter for Ossorio, chapter twelve is the crucial one for Arturo. Together they constitute the "strong center" of the novel, around which the plot as a whole and Arturo's character development revolve.

In chapter thirteen Susana, whom Arturo is attempting to seduce, is seen dancing with the narrator (transparently Skármeta himself) who writes her a poem on a napkin, explaining that "pop" poetry can play a role in bringing about personal and presumably social "liberation." Arturo, on the other hand, makes a clumsy attempt to instrumentalize a stanza from Neruda in order to bludgeon Susana into accepting his advances (that is, into submission). He fails ignominiously. In the last incident of the chapter he turns to Ossorio to find out how he succeeded in establishing a relationship with his girl-friend, María. Ossorio, in his character as role-model, reads him a blunt lecture on socio-political solidarity (he had met María while both were working for *Unidad popular*, so that their affair concides symbolically with the Allende regime). But more especially he insists on the need for simple honesty and affectionate sincerity in sexual relationships. It leaves Arturo unmoved.

Chapter thirteen, then, is functionally connected to chapters eleven and twelve via the contrast between Ossorio's emotional and sexual fulfillment with Arturo's frustration. Together the three chapters form a narrative unit, the importance of which is underlined by its central position. Structurally speaking we can see it as a nodal point which divides *Soñé* ... into two halves. What is extremely interesting is that each of these halves contains a strategically situated sequence of three chapters, also functionally connected with each other and also having to do with the contrast between Arturo and Ossorio.

The first of these two sequences comprises chapters six, seven and eight. Its opening is signalled by the first shift of narrative voice. Chapters one through five are related retrospectively in the third person from the conventional standpoint of omniscience. In complete contrast, chapter six is told in the present tense, from inside the mind of Ossorio, in a kind of reported thought and speech, as he sits on a bus along with other young people from the *pensión* (excluding Arturo, who has of course refused to participate). They are on their way to help break an anti-Allende transport strike. As the chapter unfolds we gradually come to recognize that it centers on the recent shooting of a comrade and the shocked grief which it causes his friends. The theme of the chapter, in other words, (associated with Ossorio, who tries to comfort the others in spite of his own distress) is unselfish sacrifice on the part of the working class. The young people mourn their comrade's sacrifice of his life as they prepare to sacrifice their rest day in the cause of distributing vegetables to the needy.

Chapter seven initially functions as a brutally ironic contrast. While the other youngsters go about their humble and unselfish collective task, Arturo is seen advancing towards his dream of individual fame, wealth, and sexual success as a soccer star. The narration at the opening of chapter seven takes the form of a radio commentary on Arturo's first important game. Skármeta's intention is plainly that of juxtaposing two kinds of activity. One is collective, unselfish and self-sacrificing; the other individualistic, self-centered and self-seeking. One serves the ends of the mass of the people; the other, served up by the media to a passive audience, is part of the social control-mechanism which distracts the masses by means of commercialized spectator-sport and keeps their discontent off the boil. The language applied to Arturo by the commentators: "grandeza," "valentía," "coraje," "un elemento potencialmente valioso" (76) is designed to ring hollow in the context of his lack of socio-political commitment. Similarly the first radio commercial, inviting listeners to patronize an expensive restaurant, is an unavoidable contrast to the need for the young people of the *pensión* to spend their Sunday distributing vegetables to the poor.

In this chapter Skármeta first begins systematically underlining the difference between Arturo and Ossorio. On the bus, the latter had exhibited a deep emotional solidarity with the others. Arturo, on the other hand, symbolically refuses a pass to the team captain, Jáuregui, because he wants the glory of the goal for himself and in consequence loses it for his own side. In the locker room Jáuregui modestly asks him to share his skills with the rest of the team. But Arturo's reply reveals not only his selfish individualism, but also that he had learned it at high school, while Jáuregui admits that he has only had primary education. Arturo goes on to mock both the older man's job in a factory and his left-wing political ideas. This last produces the retort: "Me da la impresión de que no te importara el país" (80), which Arturo does not in effect deny. But Jáuregui's last shaft hits home when he humiliates Arturo by drawing attention to his virginity.

Chapter eight completes the earlier of the two narrative units under review by linking the question of Arturo's lack of sexual experience even more specifically to his class and ideological situation and thus heightening the implicit contrast with Ossorio. Arturo's over-confidence in himself as a star football player goes together with a lack of self-confidence at the sexual level. This is expressed by his tendency to want others to solve his sexual problem for him. On the train to Santiago at the beginning of the novel, he shared his provisions with a fellow traveller on the understanding that the latter would put him into contact with women after they arrive. Similarly in chapter eight, after a meal with a middle-class friend, he begs him: "salgamos a buscar mujeres" (94) and finally gets him to go where they can pick up a prostitute. The result is still more failure.

Structurally, the importance of these three chapters is easy to overlook until we notice that they are balanced by another such functional sequence in the second half of the novel. Comprising chapters seventeen, eighteen, and nineteen, it is closely connected in several ways with the sequence we have just discussed. In the first set of chapters Arturo is on his way up in the world. In the second he is headed for failure. The contrast is emphasized using radio commentary by the same speakers in both cases. In the first sequence Arturo refuses to cooperate with the other young people, preferring to concentrate exclusively on his own career prospects. In the second he agrees, albeit reluctantly, to train the Amateur League soccer team belonging to the factory where Ossorio works. In the first sequence he is sharply rebuffed·by Susana. In the second he is accepted by her and consoled. As the first sequence ends, he is seen leaving to try and lose his virginity with a prostitute. As the second ends, he loses it with Susana. There can be no question about the intentionality of the patterning here. The underlying movement in *Soñé* ... is that of a see-saw, with a fulcrum in the middle and a shift of movement around it.

Chapter seventeen begins logically with Arturo and Ossorio together. Once more we notice Skármeta's deliberate emphasis on Ossorio as a natural leader of his fellow workers, diligent, tactful, undogmatic and non-authoritarian. That is to say, before signalling Arturo's small and half-reluctant shift away from individualistic self-interest towards collective solidarity, Ossorio is once more presented as the figure by comparison with whom we are intended to gauge the former's progress. That it is still slow is underlined by his reluctance to use the term "compañeros" instead of "señores," but this is brushed aside by Ossorio, who reveals his satisfaction with Arturo's decision to act as trainer for the team (the expression of his dawning recognition that his talent must be used for the benefit of the proletariat) before leaving to help coordinate a large political rally. Arturo accompanies him, conscious for the first time of participating in the warmth of the collectivity. But the sensation is short-lived. It is followed dramatically by the crucial episode in his development: as Ossorio is beaten up by a gang of right-wing thugs, he stands paralyzed with fear and then cravenly runs away. In chapter seventeen, that is, the contrast between Ossorio and Arturo (between socially-committed virility and a-political lack of it) reachess its peak. Ossorio is symbolically martyred for the cause, though he is not actually murdered. Arturo commits his most ignoble action, symbolically betraying both his comrade and the cause towards which he has just begun to gravitate.

We have already suggested that, despite its appeal to the masses, professional soccer (as seen through the eyes of the radio commentators) is identified with the individualistic, manipulative world of the bourgeoisie. The next stage of Arturo's evolution is manifested by his expulsion from this world. There are a number of ironies implicit in the incident described by the commentators in chapter eighteen. The grotesquely inflated style of the commentary itself produces an ironic contrast with the simplicity and directness of the workers' discussion in the previous chapter. The very factor of self-interest which we saw governing Arturo's attitude to the game in chapter seven now proves his undoing. Finally the aggressivity which was so absent when Ossorio needed it explodes when the referee awards a penalty against Arturo.

In chapter eight, after his first triumph on the football field, Arturo had turned to his bourgeois friends for a celebrative meal, his pleasure sharpened by the hope that his prospective stardom would be complemented by his sexual initiation. In chapter nineteen, after his expulsion from the field, he turns to his proletarian friends, specifically to Susana, Arturo finds not only the final integration of his personality (no longer in a selfish context, but through outgrowing his individualism and reaching out towards another), but also absolution for his cowardice in chapter seventeen. Susana's embrace symbolizes the warm embrace of proletarian solidarity. Arturo's achievement of it carries the promise, ultimately brought into effect at Neruda's funeral, of political commitment on behalf of that solidarity, despite the fall in the meantime of *Unidad Popular* and the establishment of the Pinochet regime.

To conclude: *Soñé* ... is really a development-of-consciousness novel. Arturo's initial individualism and lack of solidarity with the others of his age group is gradually replaced by a less self-centered, more socially-committed stance. The arrangement of the chain of episodes through which this change takes place, the main unifying strand of the plot as a whole, is characterized by the use of three crucial narrative sequences. In each of them Ossorio functions as a role-model for Arturo. By structuring the plot in this way, Skármeta is able to highlight the essential stages of the protagonist's evolution. At the same time he provides a symmetrically balanced pattern for the narrative, into which the other aspect of the plot can be integrated. The result is a first novel by a leading post-Boom writer which is not only memorable for its theme but is also interesting as a literary artifact.

[1]"La toute nouvelle génération," *Europe* 570 (1976): 197.

[2]*Soñé que la nieve ardía* (Madrid: LAR, 1981); all page references in the text are to this edition.

[3]"Narrativa chilena después del golpe" in *Primer coloquio sobre literatura chilena (de la resistencia y el exilio)* (Mexico: UNAM, 1980): 73.

[4]Raúl Silva Cáceres, ed., *Del cuerpo a las palabras: la narrativa de Antonio Skármeta* (Madrid: LAR, 1983): 16, 53.

[5]Lon Pearson, "Chilean Literature in Exile," *Chasqui* 15.1 (1985): 47–54.

Roots Uprooted: Autobiographical Reflections on the Psychological Experience of Migration

Oliva M. Espín

> ... each of us confronts our respec-
> tive inability to comprehend the expe-
> riences of others even as we recognize
> the absolute necessity of continuing to
> do so.
>
> —Linda Brodkey

Ethnic minority and women researchers frequently find themselves dissatisfied with the traditional methods of research that are
considered valid by other social scientists while struggling to establish their legitimacy in the academic world. The result, more often
than not, is that we find ourselves involved in research projects that
do not feel methodologically "right" to us in order to achieve this
legitimacy. Or, alternatively, devote ourselves to what "feels right"
at the risk of losing tenure battles or other academic "blessings"
from our colleagues.

Shulamit Reinharz, discussing a research method that she de-
nominates "experiential analysis" (1979, 1983), states that "the
first step in articulating a new method (of research) is to understand
that one's personally experienced dissatisfaction with conventional
methods is not an intrapsychic, private problem but derives from
structural inconsistencies and skewed assumptions underpinning
the methods themselves" (1983, 166). In her formulation, the personal experience of the researcher is not only valid but essential
in the development of studies that would be contextual and relevant. For Reinharz, a relevant research project should provide "an
opportunity for catharsis or self-discovery" (1983, 176) for both
researcher and subjects and a "research product likely to provide
resources or answers to pressing problems in living" (176). "The
record of the researcher's feelings and ideas is also data" (175) because "all knowledge is contingent on the situation under which it
is formed" (177) and, for all researchers, "one's own race, class,
religion and gender predispose us to consider some settings more
interesting and important than others" (179).

Denzin's (1986, 1989) and Runyan's (1982) work, using life narratives for sociological and psychological research, respectively, have demonstrated the value of studying life histories and biography for the social sciences in general and psychology in particular. Through their psychobiographical and interpretive interactionist studies they have demonstrated that the data provided by life narratives produces a richness that could not be obtained through the use of other methods.

I am sure that, by now, we are all disabused of the notion that "value free" research exists at all. But we are probably very well trained to doubt the validity of our personal experiences and life as sources of data. Interestingly enough, if we were not the researchers, probably some outsider to our cultures could get some grant money to study our lives and get a few good publications out of the analysis of data based on interviews about our experiences. Why not then, take the role of that "outsider" while remaining ourselves, combine the perspectives of experiential analysis, interpretive interactionism and psychobiography, and do some experiential studies of data provided by our lives and the lives of individuals with similar experiences?

As a social scientist, and on the basis of my own personal experiences, I believe that there is much to be learned from the individual narrative. For the last few years I have been engaged in the experiential analysis of my own migration story as a research project. I believe there is a void in the literature that could be filled through the use of life narratives to understand the psychological impact of the experience of uprootedness from a scientific (as opposed to just human interest) point of view. That is why I would like to share with the readers the results of my own experiential analysis of this process and the life narrative on which it is based. My intention is to demonstrate both the importance of studying this topic and the usefulness of this methodology for its study.

In 1984 I returned to Cuba for a two-week visit for the first time after an absence of 23 years. I left Cuba when I was 22 years old, so at the time of this visit I had lived, roughly, half of my life in Cuba and half of my life away from Cuba. This coincidence made the time and timing of the visit particularly significant. The visit provoked in me innumerable reflections on the experience of uprootedness in my life and on the significance of having lived half of my life away from my country of birth.

The purpose of this essay is to share some of those reflections and some of the experiences that led to them. The experiences I want to share refer to the uprootedness of the second half of my life as well as to the intense experiences involved in that two-week trip to Cuba. I believe that these reflections can shed light on the experiences of exile and uprootedness in the lives of others.

I do not intend to discuss Cuban politics, to take positions pro or against the Cuban revolution or even argue the soundness of my decision to leave Cuba in 1961. Obviously, my life experiences, like anybody else's, are deeply connected to a specific time, place, and historical event. However, any discussion of the specifics of this historical event (i.e., the Cuban revolution), would distract from the subject of this essay, namely, some psychological consequences of uprootedness and historical dislocation and the description of a methodology to study them.

Even though my experience of uprootedness is in one sense absolutely mine, individual and unique, it is, in another sense, generalizable to any person who has ever undergone the effects of historical dislocation. Because I am a psychologist, and I see the meaning of my experiences mostly in psychological terms, I will describe the psychological impact on me of historical dislocation in the hope of generalizing my experiences to those of other people, particularly women, who have experienced similar events. Reinharz (1979; 1983) and Runyan (1982) have amply demonstrated that the experiential analysis and psychobiographical approaches used in this paper are valid forms of inquiry for the social sciences.

After this preamble, let me describe briefly the experiences of historical dislocation and uprootedness as I have felt them in my life and as they became intensely obvious to me as a consequence of my visit to Cuba in 1984.

I was barely 20 years old when Fidel Castro came to power in January 1959. By then, I had already experienced a number of events that had created in me the sense of instability that usually precedes actual uprootedness. For example, Batista's first take over and his dismissal of my father from the Armed Forces, and that of all others who were not his sympathizers just two years after my birth; Batista's defeat in the presidential elections of 1944; his second take over in 1952, after the suicide of one of Cuba's most honest political leaders; the terror and tensions of the Batista years and, finally, the entrance in Havana of Castro's Rebel Army in January 1959, a joyful event also characterized by suddenness and intense emotions. The Bay of Pigs invasion in 1961 culminated for me a series of unexpected changes and surprising turning points. Through all those years, historical events had transformed the course of my life. Although I had previously been aware of the dangerousness of other historical events, such as the Second World

War, Roosevelt's death, the atomic bombs in Hiroshima and Nagasaki, these events were happening far away and their impact on my life was not the same as that of the political events happening in Cuba.

I—like other Cubans of my generation, like thousands of young people in Europe before and during World War II, like thousands of young people yesterday and today in Central America, the Middle East, Southeast Asia, throughout the world—had learned to live immersed in a situation of constant danger, without being consciously aware of that fact. I first recognized that I had been living in daily subliminal terror while watching a film in a theater in Madrid, Spain, when I left Cuba for a brief period in 1958. I was suddenly overcome by the realization that I could enjoy the movie without needing to keep a part of me on the alert, worrying about the possibility that a bomb might go off, that the police might raid the theater or that something similarly dangerous might occur. Mind you, in my years in Cuba I was never hurt by a bomb, nor was I ever arrested. yet bombs had killed and maimed many young people, some of my adolescent friends had been executed or imprisoned and I *knew* it could happen to me too. The most amazing aspect of this experience was the realization that I had learned to always be alert *without even knowing* that I had learned it.

Elie Wiesel has written that once you have been in a situation of constant danger, you never feel fully safe again (Wiesel, 1984–5). His description, although referring to the incomparable horror or the Holocaust, fits my experience. Rahe and Holmes (1967; 1972), who have done research on the effects of stressful events on illness and health, tell us that events such as getting a new job, moving to a new place or losing a partner, create stress that can lead to the development of physical illness. Needless to say, the stress created by living under the fear of bombs, government persecution or other similar life-endangering situations is probably greater and capable of producing even more dramatic effects. Studies of learned helplessness demonstrate that when individuals find themselves trapped in situations they cannot control, they tend to become seriously depressed (Seligman, 1975). Since I have never been seriously ill or particularly depressed about these issues, and neither have been most of the people I know who grew up under similar conditions, it seems that there are inner resources that sustain people in these extreme situations of which we psychologists do not know much about. Studies involving children and adults who have been exposed to situations incredibly more dangerous than anything I have ever experienced shed some light on how psychological survival, development and growth are achieved in spite of the negative effects produced by violent events created by disruptive political situations and historical dislocation (See, for example: Coles, 1986; Dimsdale, 1980; Loomis, 1962; Reinharz, 1971; Williams & Westermeyer, 1986).

The most immediate feeling experienced after leaving such a situation of constant danger is relief, together with sadness and grief for those left behind. Confusion and frustration about all the new places and people and customs encountered soon add further burdens. But then, slowly, the unfamiliar starts becoming familiar, daily events start blurring the intense feelings of the first few weeks and years, and life settles into a new routine. Years go by and life goes on.

I lived in several countries after leaving Cuba, earned several higher education degrees, got married and divorced, developed important relationships and friendships along with a sense of better self-understanding, worked hard and enjoyed life. Cuba was not constantly in my mind. For the most part, I remembered the events of my 22 years in Cuba as intrapsychic events of *my* individual life. Here and there I was confronted with my uprootedness, but it was not a constant or acute pain.

Perhaps I was lucky; if I lived away from Cuba, at least I was living in other Latin American countries. The sense of being "different" was not as vivid there as it later became in the United States. But in spite of similarities in language, customs and values, I always had a sense of not fully belonging. There was the sound of popular folk music that was familiar to everyone but me. And there was my memory of another popular folk music that only I knew. There was the unfamiliar taste of food that was a daily staple for the others. And there were tastes that I longed for which were unknown or inaccessible in that particular country. Even though we were all conversing in Spanish, there were words and expressions that seemed unusual and even offensive to me. And there were expressions I used which did not have any meaning for my closest friends.

So I learned to speak my Spanish with a Costa Rican accent while my Cuban one receded and I learned to enjoy Costa Rican food and to love Costa Rican music. My friends, co-workers, and classmates forgot to include me in their list of foreigners. And yet, once in a while, the subject of my nationality would come up when someone was angry with me or when I could not remember events in Costa Rican history. To this day, those years in Costa Rica are very close to my heart, my Costa Rican friends continue to be central in my life. But they know, as I know, that I am not really Costa Rican.

There were things I shared with them, however, that I cannot share now with my close friends in the United States. No matter how fluent I am in English, my innermost feelings *are* in Spanish, and my poetry is in Spanish. This deepest part of myself remains hidden from people who are extremely important to me, no matter how hard we all try. I can translate, but translated feelings like translated poetry are just not the same. If there was a difference between me and my friends in Costa Rica, there is an even greater difference between me and my friends in the United States. It is amazing how much hamburgers and Coke versus black beans and coffee remind an uprooted person of that difference!

Indeed, the loss experienced by an uprooted person encompasses not only the big and obvious losses of country, a way of life, and family. The pain of uprootedness is also activated in subtle forms by the everyday absence of familar smells, familiar foods, familiar routines for doing the small tasks of daily life. It is the lack of what has been termed "the average expectable environment" (Hartmann, 1964) which can become a constant reminder of what is not there anymore. It is the loss of this "average expectable environment" that can be most disorienting and most disruptive of the person's previously established identity. In some cases, this disruption of the "average expectable environment" and its impact on the individual's identity (Garza-Guerrero, 1974) can be at the core of profound psychological disturbance. Although the lack of my "average expectable environment" was not destructive for me in this way, I have experienced its loss, more or less keenly, throughout the second part of my life. My return to Cuba in 1984 brought into focus what this loss had entailed for me.

After twenty-three years away from there, I realized that I needed to go to Cuba. As if I did not trust my own decision to go, I planned for my trip hastily. But, the more I had to wait for my permit from the Cuban government, the more I knew I needed to go. I was not sure how it would feel to be there, but I knew that I had to do it and I knew that I had to do it alone. Without friends. Without people who had never been to Cuba before. Without people who had also been born in Cuba and thus had their own feelings about being there. This was my own emotional journey.

My journey back to Cuba did not start with the actual trip. For weeks before it I had sudden flashbacks of familiar scenes, places, events that I had forgotten or at least not remembered for the last 23 years. During the year after the trip I also had flashbacks of the events and places of my trip and of my previous life in Cuba. These flashbacks were so vivid and powerful that they absorbed me and distracted me from the activity of the moment. They made me think of the flashbacks, of almost hallucinatory quality, that are sometimes experienced by people suffering from Post-Traumatic Stress Disorder or involved in mourning and bereavement (Parkes, 1972). In fact, it seems that I have been involved in a grieving process, no matter how unaware of it I may have been, and it is possible that I will continue to be involved in it for the rest of my life whenever these feelings are reactivated.

After a 45-minute flight from Miami, I arrived in Havana around 5:00 a.m. The transition was quick and dramatically abrupt. You have to understand that for me there had been not 90 miles between Cuba and the United States, but almost a quarter of a century and a dense wall of memory. The lights of Havana brought tears to my eyes. They had been so close and so out of my touch for so many years ...! By 7:00 a.m. I had checked in at the hotel, taken a shower, had breakfast and cried, because for the first time in 23 years I had had Cuban sugar in my morning coffee. The moment I stepped out of the hotel I knew exactly where I was, what corners to turn, what buildings would be waiting for me on the next block, and which one of the buses going by would take me to which place in the city. In a few hours I had walked through my old neighborhoods, I had gone by my school, I had walked familiar streets and had come back to the hotel without ever having the slightest confusion about where I was or getting lost.

Cuba had been like a forbidden paradise for half of my life. Suddenly, this forbidden paradise was all around me. For years Cuba had been a dark and painful memory. Suddenly, it was present, and clear, and the sky was blue, and everything was as it always was and as it was always supposed to be. And everyone spoke with a Cuban accent! This deep sense of familiarity, of everything being right, of all things being as they are supposed to be was something I had never experienced since 1961.

The experience of total familiarity was, of course, facilitated by the fact that there has been minimal construction in most Cuban cities during the last 30 years. But, aside from the familiarity of the physical environment, there was something more to my experience than just the same buildings and the same bus routes, probably best illustrated by my intense reaction to Cuban sugar and the Cuban accent. Strangers almost always assumed that I was not a visitor, only on a few occasions did some of my clothes give me away. I was even told at one of the dollar stores in Santiago that they could not sell me the t-shirt I wanted to buy; didn't I know that these stores were only for foreign visitors?

But the joy in this sense of belonging was made painful by the realization that it will never again be part of my life on a continuous basis. I believe that, in the deepest sense, this is what uprootedness is all about; that you do not fully fit or feel comfortable in your new environment and that most of the time you do not even know that you don't. It takes an experience like my going back to Cuba to realize that what you have mistaken for comfort does not compare with what the feeling of belonging really means.

On my first morning in Havana I went to the school I attended from first grade to senior year in high school. The main door to the school was closed, but the door of what had been the chapel was open. The statues of the Virgin Mary, the Sacred Heart of Jesus, Saint Joseph and the Crucifix were not there. Neither were the pews or the confessional boxes. The floor was covered wtih mattresses, the room was full of gymnastics equipment and a small group of girls about 5 to 8 years old were graciously exercising to the rhythm set by music and a teacher's voice. I had visions of myself and other little girls receiving our First Communion in that same space, and I could not stop thinking about what my life would have looked like if I had done gymnastics rather than Communion in that place. And I wondered what the lives of these little girls would look like in the future.

As part of my emotional pilgrimage, I also wanted to visit the homes where I had lived. In spite of all the previous experiences, nothing had prepared me for what I would encounter in the apartment where we lived before leaving Cuba. I went there for the first time on the evening of my second day in Havana. As I walked to the door, a shadow on the side attracted my attention. It was too dark to see, but I knew what it was. I touched it and my fingers confirmed what I had realized in a fraction of a second: my father's nameplate was still affixed to the column at the entrance. Nobody was home that evening, so I returned the next day. And there, in the daylight, was my father's name on a bronze plate. It had not been removed after 23 years! This time a young man opened the door, and I told him the purpose of my visit and asked for his permission to come in. If the sight of my father's name on that bronze plate had sent chills through my spine, the insides of that apartment provided me with an even stranger experience. All of the furniture was the furniture that we had left, the same furniture that had been part of the first 22 years of my life. In fact, the man who opened the door had been taking a nap on my parents' bed, the bed on which I was conceived!

I am sure some of you own pieces of old family furniture. I am sure some of you have gone back to old family houses. But I do not know if you have ever experienced the impact of a physical space where nothing has been moved an inch, in a quarter of a century, since you were last there, yet where other people and their lives are now occupants.

A daughter of the poet Carl Sandburg had shared a cab with me from the Havana airport to the hotel. When I had told her that this was my first visit to Cuba in 23 years, she had told me that the house of her childhood, now a museum of her father's life, was both a familiar and strange place for her. At that moment, I had not fully understood her. Two days later, standing in the middle of the apartment that had been my home for several years, I knew what she had meant.

In addition to what I have described, my trip to Cuba made me realize that my memories had a geography. That what I remembered had actually happened in a definite physical space that continues to exist in reality and not only in my memory. That Cuba, in fact, exists beyond what I think or feel or remember about her. This realization, which may seem all too obvious, was the more powerful because before my return I never knew that I felt as if Cuba did not have a real existence beyond my memory.

My trip evoked other strong feelings, as well. It may not come as a surprise to know that in spite of the intense and powerful sense of belonging that I experienced in Cuba, I was always alert and vigilant. Among everything that Cuba triggers in me, the need for being vigilant and alert is always included.

Beyond this powerfully intense experience of familiarity and strangeness, my trip put me in touch with childhood friends and made me reflect about the differences in our lives, about the choices to stay or leave that have dramatically influenced our life projects. None of us has any way of knowing what our lives would have looked like without the historical dislocations that have marked them. The only known fact is that powerful historical events have transformed the life course of those of us who left and those of us who stayed in Cuba. Those who stayed, if not uprooted, have also been under the effects of dramatic historical transformations. It is impossible to know if our decisions have resulted in a better life project for any of us, although we each hope and believe to have made the best decision. Bandura's (1982) discussion on the importance of chance encounters for the course of human development addresses the impact that chance may have as a determinant of life paths. For some people, chance encounters and other life events are additionally influenced by historical and political events far beyond their control. It is true that all human beings experience life transitions, but for people who have been subjected to historical dislocations life crossroads feel, intrapsychically, as more drastic and dramatic.

It seems rather obvious that the impact of sociocultural and historical change on psychological development should be incorporated in any discussion of human development (Elder, 1981). As Bandura (1982) asserts "a comprehensive developmental theory must specify factors that set and alter particular life courses if it is to provide an adequate explanation of human behavior" (747). This is particularly important if we want to understand the experiences of individuals whose lives have been dramatically influenced by traumatic historical and political events because "the danger of any period of large-scale uprooting and transmigration is that exterior crises will, in too many individuals and generations, upset the hierarchy of developmental crises and their built-in correctives; and [make us] lose those roots that must be planted firmly in meaningful life cycles" (Erikson, 1964, p. 96). It seems that the use of a methodology that includes life history narratives and an experiential analysis of those experiences could provide social scientists with a tool to understand what the experience of historical dislocation and uprootedness entails for psychological development. Considering that these experiences are part of so many lives in the world in which we live, the importance of such endeavor for the social sciences seems quite obvious.

In my case, what I learned once again from this trip is that who I am is inextricably intertwined with the experience of uprootedness. And what this uprootedness entails, particularly after this return trip, is an awareness that there is another place where I feel at home in profound ways that I did not even know or remember. That place, however, is not fully home anymore. And this reality is, precisely, the most powerful reminder of my uprootedness. My daily routine is not the daily routine of people in Cuba; their way of life is not my way of life; their perceptions of reality sometimes clash dramatically with mine; I have learned new things about myself—and what is important for me—that do not fit in Cuban life anymore. Even if I wanted to adapt in order to be there, I do not know if they have any use for someone like me. I would love to have the possibility of being back in Cuba for a longer period of time, but I know that Cuba could never be my permanent home again. Believe it or not, I missed my daily life here while I was in Cuba.

Let me also say that I do not believe I have "a corner on up-rootedness." In fact, I do not believe that my experience has been particularly difficult. During the past 30 years I have been lucky enough to secure reasonably good jobs, I have developed meaningful friendships that I deeply treasure, I have learned new things about myself and the world that I might not have learned had I stayed in Cuba, and I have evolved valuable adaptive skills as a result of coping with so many changes. It is precisely because my adaptation has been relatively successful and yet so painful at times that I am convinced of the profound psychological impact that uprootedness can have. If I, who have been able to survive and make sense of my experiences in a productive way, have felt and experienced what I have just described for you, it is reasonable to assume that the pain and confusion experienced by other women less fortunate than I will be more extreme and difficult to survive.

The obvious next step for me as a researcher is to collect life narratives from other people who have undergone similar experiences, particularly from individuals who may have returned to their countries of birth after many years of absence, and compare those experiences. I believe there is invaluable data to be gathered through this process and powerful generalizations to be made that would further our understanding of human development in general and of the impact of the experience of uprootedness in psychological development in particular.

I have found that sharing my own experiences produces a cathartic and self-exploratory effect in the audience as well as helps clinicians empathize with patients who have undergone similar experiences. I have also had several conversations with women who have returned to their countries of origin after long periods of time. Their experiences parallel mine to a remarkable degree. It seems evident to me that the details of my own narrative, as well as other life narratives may provide invaluable information to understand the experiences of other immigrants and possibly be useful in structuring programs of psychological assistance and mutual support.

I hope I have succeeded in demonstrating that there is value in the data provided by our own lives and that these data can be a point of departure for valuable analyses of other lives. By incorporating our own experiential perspectives to the research enterprise, ethnic minority researchers can thus innovate not only the focus of social science research but also the methodological approaches with which to study its content. This approach, both in content and process, constitutes a creative endeavor necessary to include new points of view in our disciplines rather than just adapting an established paradigm that, both in content and process, does not fully include the lives of our communities.

Allport, G. (1942). *The use of personal documents in psychological science.* N.Y.: Social Science Research Council.

Brodkey, Linda, "Writing critical ethnographic narratives." *Anthropology and Education Quarterly* 18 (1987): 67–76.

Bandura, A. (1982). "The psychology of chance encounters and life paths." *American Psychologist,* 37(7) 747–755.

Coles, R. (1986). *The political life of children.* N.Y.: Atlantic Monthly.

Denzin, N.K. (1986). "Interpretive interactionism and the use of life histories." *Revista Internacional de Sociologia,* 44: 321–337.

Denzin, N.K. (1989). *Interpretive interactionism.* Newbury Park, CA: Sage.

Dimsdale, J. (1980). *Survivors, victims and perpetrators.* Washington, D.C.: Hemisphere.

Elder, G.H. (1981). History and the life course. In D. Bertaux, *Biography and society: The life history approach in the social sciences.* Beverly Hills, CA: Sage.

Erikson, E.H. (1964). *Insight and responsibility.* N.Y.: Norton.

Espín, O.M. (1987). "Psychological impact of migration on Latinas: Implications for psychotherapeutic practice." *Psychology of Women Quarterly,* 11: 489–503.

Garza-Guerrero, C.A. (1974). "Culture shock: Its mourning and the vicissitudes of identity." *Journal of the American Psychoanalytic Association,* 22: 408–429.

Hartmann, H. (1964). *Esays on ego psychology.* N.Y.: International Universities Press.

Holmes, T.H. and Rahe, R.H. (1967). "The Social Readjustment Rating Scale." *Journal of Psichosomatic Research,* 11: 213–218.

Levy-Warren, M.H. (1987). "Moving to a new culture: Cultural identity, loss, and mourning." In J. Bloom-Fesbach & S. BloomFesbach, Eds. *The psychology of separation and loss.* San Francisco: Jossey-Bass.

Loomis, C. (1962). "Toward systematic analysis of disaster, disruption, stress and recovery—Suggested areas of investigation." In G. Baker and L. Cottrell, Jr., Eds. *Behavioral science and child defense.* Publication #997. National Academy of Science-National Research Council.

Ortiz, K.R. (1985). "Mental health consequences of the life history method: Implications from a refugee case." *Ethos,* 13: 99–120.

Parkes, C.M. (1972). *Bereavement: Studies of grief in adult life.* N.Y.: International University Press.

Plummer, K. (1983). *Documents of life: An introduction to the problems and literature of a humanistic method.* London, England: Allen & Unwin.

Rahe, R.H. (1972). "Subjects recent changes and their near-future illness susceptibility." *Advances in Psychosomatic Medicine,* 8: 2–19.

Reinharz, S. (1971). *Coping with Disaster,* Unpublished manuscript. Department of Psychology, University of Michigan.

Reinharz, S. (1979). *On becoming a social scientist.* San Francisco: Jossey-Bass.

Reinharz, S. (1983). "Experiential analysis: A contribution to feminist research." In G. Bowles and R.D. Klein, Eds. *Theories of women's studies.* Routledge & Kegan Paul.

Seligman, M.E.P. (1975). *Helplessness: On depression, development and death.* San Francisco: W.H. Freeman.

Ticho, G. (1971). "Cultural aspects of transference and countertransference." *Bulletin of the Menninger Foundation*, 35: 313–334.

Wiesel, E. (1984–5). "The refugee." *Cross-Currents*, 34.4: 385–90.

Williams, C. and Westermeyer, J. (1986). *Refugee mental health in resettlement countries.* Washington, D.C.: Hemisphere.

(Re)Writing Sugarcane Memories: Cuban Americans and Literature

Eliana S. Rivero

From Exiles to Ethnics

In 1988, an anthology with the title *Veinte años de literatura cubanoamericana* was published. The introductory essay to that volume described Cuban American writers as possessing certain characteristics: they were mostly first generation immigrants, they wrote mostly in Spanish, and were more interested in their country of origin than, say, Mexican American or Nuyorrican writers. Two statements in particular attracted the reader's attention in that essay:

> a pesar de que los rasgos de su literatura nos muestran que *el cubanoamericano no se ha asimilado ni lingüísticamente ni culturalmente a los Estados Unidos*, la asimilación estructural de muchos de ellos, es decir, su éxito económico y su participación en la actividad comercial y financiera de este país ha sido casi total ...

and

> A diferencia de la literatura mexicanoamericana y la nuyorriqueña, en la literatura cubanoamericana la etnicidad queda definida *no como diversidad y diferencia en continuo choque con la cultura dominante*, sino como apego a los antepasados y las tradiciones del país de origen.[1]

I fully understand that these words were written before the publication of *Raining Backwards* (Arte Público, 1988) by Roberto Fernández, *Crazy Love* (Arte Publico, 1989) by Elías Miguel Muñoz, and the anthology *Los Atrevidos: Cuban American Writers* by Carolina Hospital (Linden Lane-Ediciones Ellas, 1988). These recent works easily belie the assertions above. But since 1977, Dolores Prida had been writing and directing plays that not only incorporated bilingualism and Cuban American slang into the speech of the dramatic characters, such as *Coser y cantar*, but that also showed a very definite flair for feminist satire—American style— in her musical *Beautiful Señoritas*.[2]

In these pages, I not only depart from the above quoted assumptions on Cuban American writers in general, but I contradict them, to come up with what I consider a more updated and realistic perspective on their works. The reflections I offer also deal with the issue of whether such texts can be considered "exile literature" or not, and although I use illustrations taken mostly from the literature of Cuban American women, my objective is to arrive at conclusions engaging Hispanic ethnic writings in the U.S. as a whole.

In a 1989 article appearing in the volume *Breaking Boundaries*,[3] I argue precisely the opposite from the authors' viewpoint in *Veinte años*: I say that *Cuban American* [women] writers are those who indeed treat the experience of being ethnic minorities, and do so by availing themselves of a bilingual register of voices. That they sometimes write by mining nostalgic sources for thematic and stylistic purposes is not a sufficiently weighty reason to group them with *Cuban* women of a different generation, who not only use Spanish exclusively as their literary medium, but that also—and this is most important—identify themselves as members of an immigrant or exile literature with basic links to their native country.

Between 1959 and the early eighties, when several waves of immigration from Cuba included writers in various degrees of career development and/or practice, many works appeared in the United States or elsewhere (for example, in Spain) that confirmed the establishment of what could be termed "immigrant or exile literature": *literatura del exilio*. This was written in highly developed literary Spanish, and either recounted, for the most part, the painful process of uprooting from the mother culture, or described—with tinges of nostalgia— pre-revolutionary island life.[4] In some instances, such as in the case of Lydia Cabrera or Belkis Cuza Malé, the authors' trajectory continues the line of writing begun in the fifties or sixties, and their literature can be said to belong to the wider panorama of Latin American letters as it comprises Cuban literary production before the Revolution. In other words, these authors consider themselves emigrés, or transplanted writers, and they have a niche in their own national literature—whether this is written inside or outside the homeland. Their work is primarily defined by their native, *Cuban* experience.[5]

Such writers possess names that are well-known in the literary world arena, and their texts have been marked by the inevitable affective connection with Cuba, its society and its people. The vital experience of such Cuban authors in the country of adoption does not parallel that of the native Hispanic, such as the Mexican American/Chicano or the mainland Puerto Rican, but rather one could say that their literary discourse is aligned with nostalgia, and that their world vision either ignores or rejects the conditions of margination from the mainstream under which the other Hispanic native groups operate. Their discourse often recreates those spaces which gave birth to the poet, both in a physical and in a spiritual sense; as an illustration, the poem "Frente al mar" by Ana Rosa Núñez, is a configuration of living, yet absent, images, distant in time and in miles. It is a collage of motifs that paint a scene of the main Cuban city and its characteristic port outline—the Farola del Morro, a lighthouse which guides ships in their entrance to the bay. This famous lighthouse is an emblem on many tourist postcards, and in the poetic text, a symbol of light in the darkness of lost memories:

> En la Antigua Casa del Mar, tú,
> vara del Alcalde que vas diciendo Habana
> con la voz más clara (*Veinte años* 29)

In addition, many immigrant Cuban writers share a thematic thread of denouncing political realities in the island, or they contemplate— with deep sorrow—the uprooting of cultural values that have resulted from immigration to this country. One can also mention, in this respect, those women who had begun to publish before leaving Cuba, such as the novelist Hilda Perera or the above quoted poet Ana Rosa Núñez, in what I call the "over fifty-nine" generation.

Women authors who were born in Cuba between 1935 and 1945, but who share in these characteristics, include the poets Pura del Prado, Rita Geada and Juana Rosa Pita. Their texts either recreate inner and outer landscapes of their native land, whether social or personal, or live within a space populated with the inner demons of self-analysis. Their works often bespeak an existential alienation still struggling with nostalgia; as, for example, in the following text by Geada entitled "Contrastes," which is dated in New Haven, 1967, and describes a snowy day:

> El corazón,
> apretado por la música lejana,
> es nieve que se derrite lentamente.
> ¡Qué lejos los puentes de la infancia!
> Desde nuestra ventana
> los autos cruzan raudos
> quebrando con sus colores
> la sinigual blancura. (*Veinte años* 130)

One singular characteristic of this group of writers is that their own view of themselves is not akin to that shared by many native

Hispanic women in the U.S. Most of these Cuban authors write outside the concerns of either gender or ethnicity, not feeling the need to express their identity in either terms. In contrast to what other critics affirm, I classify them as Cuban immigrant writers, and *not* as Cuban Americans.[6]

Nevertheless, from the midseventies on, and similarly to what has occurred with the rich and varied literatures of other immigrant groups— for example, Chinese Americans—Cuban texts have been published that manifest the process of transition in which their writers are engaged. Some of the younger Cuban immigrants, by their assimilation or adaptation, and by their adoption of certain linguistic and cultural patterns prevalent in the United States among other Hispanics, exhibit a consciousness of change. This is sometimes linked, for women authors, to a feminist awareness that perhaps stands in conflict with middle class values or a more conservative ideology. At times a detail, as subtle as a North American geographical name or a song title, appears in the poem or short story: such is the case in the works of Maya Islas (*Sola ...desnuda ...sin nombre*, 1974; *Sombras papel*, 1978), Mireya Robles (*Tiempo artesano*, 1973; *En esta aurora*, 1978; *Hagiografía de Narcisa la Bella*, 1985), and Uva Clavijo (*Versos de exilio*, 1974; *Ni verdad ni mentira y otros cuentos*, 1977; *Entresemáforos*, 1981; *Tus ojos y yo*, 1985; *No puedo más y otros cuentos*, 1989). In different texts, for example, Islas speaks about "el threshold de mis miedos" ["the threshold of my fears"]; Robles reflects about "Feelings, una canción escrita para el subway" ["Feelings, a song written for the subway"]; and Clavijo writes a short story in Spanish entitled "1342 Park Road."[7] Islas' *Sombras...*, Robles' *En esta aurora*, and Clavijo's *Versos de exilio* and *Ni verdad ni mentira...* are among the first works published by Cuban women in the U.S. that document American society through the authors' literary *personae*, bearing witness to the cultural impact of a very different lifestyle.

In the above group the reader can detect—if sometimes vaguely—a certain consciousness of belonging to an immigrant generation that is slowly ceasing to be, because its younger members are, to a greater or lesser extent, becoming used to the feeling of permanence that a prolonged stay in the country of adoption has produced. We (I count myself among them) began to be conscious of our being different from the dominant groups in the seventies, and internalized this difference as a first step in becoming members of one of the largest ethnic minorities in America. In the seventies, some of these women also began to write as feminists; that is the case of Robles, Islas and myself. We are consciously biculturals, and bilinguals in varying degress, although for those of us who migrated in our late teens or early twenties Spanish continues to be the dominant, preferred language for writing. In the political spectrum, our generation is divided; some profess liberal ideas nurtured during college years in the sixties, and yet some others feel closer to the conservative ideology of their parents. Among some of us, in this group, there appears already the occasional text written in English, and a more or less effective utilization of a bilingual discourse that captures our sense of hybridism, or even alienation, with respect to the predominant Anglo culture. Thematic richness for these authors implies direct experiences of their ex-centric life; that is, an existence that is functional within the system but *not* at the center, and which the system—and the Anglo majority—can neither assimilate nor understand. It is at this juncture, I argue, that *Cubans* begin the process of becoming *Cuban Americans*.

And it is precisely at this juncture that linguistic functionality and standard performance in English becomes a key issue in being "ethnics"—that is, hyphenated Cuban-Americans. In the theater, as previously noted, Dolores Prida had been writing, acting and directing in a bilingual mode since 1977. By 1981, both bilingual and original English texts by Cuban-born women had appeared, in the form of poems and short stories. In quite a few of them, there was a thematic insistence on the conflict of immigrants who at first confront hostility or indifference from the dominant culture. As a concrete illustration, here is a fragment of a poem I wrote in English between 1979 and 1980, a text recreating realities from the early sixties—our Cuban immigration experiences in Florida:

> ... the jars of peanut butter and the boxes
> of rolled oats   U.S. DEPARTMENT OF AGRI-
>   CULTURE—
> SURPLUS COMMODITIES   I learned to read them
>   carefully
> every fifth of the month
> and I liked their cardboard flavor because
> it came from the Midwest and heartland of the country
> (it was free anyhow and it made for good cookies) [...]
> years make it seem so unreal but
> it existed: Miss Miller who at fifty-five
> swore never to rent her nice one-bedroom apartment
> to another Cuban: the tenant had strange ways of
> celebrating hurricanes with a party and
> her strong coffee made stains in the sink
>   the upstairs neighbor (very proper high school
>   administrator) had a visitor
>   every Thursday evening   and my living room rafters

would screech with the jolts of the bed
and middle-aged white Anglo-Saxon
passionate Protestants making love
over my head
    another uncle of mine was married
to a Puerto Rican lady who shopped at Jordan Marsh
and scolded me for studying too much (most of all *Spanish*,
    of all idiotic things) and she recited every time I was
     her captive audience   "marry a doctor,
nice, Latino parents but American ways"   and then
proceeded to engage in solid conversation for two years
reciting   all the wonderful values she had learned
as a bicultural   and I was still
chewing cookies made with oats from the USDA (...)
and all is oh so far beyond
my present and   north from the river
where I live   and suddenly exist in memories (...)
this is
another land of plenty   where I reap and am reaped
where I deal in my words   and forget
that I ever ate surplus commodities ... and still
the two circles surround   me the dual love-and-hate
relationship   my languages the mother that I rec-
    ognize
as real   legitimate and splendid   and the sur-
    rogate
the tongue that lets me be two times   the person
    that I am ...[8]

For those of us who have been involved in this transformation, it is a process that started with emotional and psychological pain, continued with resignation, and seemed to end with the acceptance of unchangeable realities. It continues unfolding today, however, with the realization of a divided self, one that must exist in two cultural and linguistic environments.[9]

The greatest difference between this group, whose numbers grow steadily as years go by, and those I refer to as "Cubans," is the latter's distancing from mainstream U.S. cultural—*not* socioeconomic — perspectives. A Cuban writer tends to be more a critical observer of, rather than a participant in, North American realities. And she or he will enter more into a writing dialogue with the Cuban insular past and/or present, feeling more affinity with Latin American or European modes of work and socializing than with the "American way of life." On the other hand, a Cuban American writer would be the younger, more easily adapted individual, who immigrating as a child or young adolescent, is only part time practitioner—if at all—of the Cuban nostalgia discourse. She or he possesses finely honed linguistic skills in English, due mainly to

American secondary schooling, and in their works one can notice that peculiarly fluid character of a biculturalism and bilingualism that still, after almost thirty years of original immigration, constitutes an impossibility for older emigrés. In a few cases, their position vis-à-vis the establishment, which links them to other Latino minorities in the U.S., distinguishes them from the majority of Cuban Americans, and certainly from the Cubans.

Most of all, I argue, Cuban-origin writers—both men and women—who go on to become Cuban *Americans* do so on the basis of an acute awareness: that of a double identity. This becoming conscious of their difference usually begins on the trail of nostalgic discourse, manifesting often as a sense of belonging nowhere—neither here nor in Cuba. Their place and time had been defined by a cultural space that is no more: the decade of the fifties. Perhaps this sense is best expressed in the prose and poetry of Lourdes Casal, who in the seventies began publishing works marking the transition from a consciousness of immigration to a certainty of permanent, unresolved dualism. This hybridism was felt by the writer on two levels: existential and sociocultural, and was illustrated first in her book *Los Fundadores: Alfonso y otros cuentos*, published in 1973, which contained significant recreations of childhood under the shadow of grandparents who were immigrants to Cuba themselves. This was a form of nostalgia that was continued in contemplations facing the Hudson River, in New York, while thinking of the clear Caribbean water at the Cuban beaches of youth. The male narrator muses in "Love Story Según Cyrano Prufrock":

> Aquí frente al Hudson verdinegro, hay olor a yerba buena y el sol un poco tímido me despierta recuerdos bajo la piel, te has ido y recuerdo mi rostro entre tus pechos   el sol y hace doce años que no nado, te recuerdo juegos bajo el agua y el Caribe transparentes Guanabo   el agua azul   la arena al fondo y las piedras multicolores   nácar y el agua bañándome los ojos[10]

The reader notices how American and Cuban images flow into one continuum, and U.S. geographical spaces are a conduit for the stream of memories that pervade the immigrant's consciousness.

Casal's experience of living alternately in two radically different cultures profoundly affected her view of reality. Her poem "Para Ana Veltfort," first published in 1976, best portrays the dichotomy lived by a Cuban outside her primary cultural milieu. Her poetic *persona* functions in two distinctly different environments, but fits completely in neither. The text, full of recollections and rememberances, tells about her sense of double identity:

(. . .) Nueva York es mi casa,
Soy ferozmente leal a esta adquirida patria chica.
Por Nueva York soy extranjera ya en cualquier parte (. . .)
Pero Nueva York no fue la ciudad de mi infancia,
no fue aquí que adquirí las primeras certidumbres,
no está aquí el rincón de mi primera caída
ni el silbido lacerante que marcaba las noches.

Por eso siempre permaneceré al margen,
una extraña entre estas piedras,
aun bajo el sol amable de este día de verano,
como ya para siempre permaneceré extranjera
aun cuando regrese a la ciudad de mi infancia.
Cargo esta marginalidad inmune a todos los retornos,
demasiado habanera para ser neoyorkina,
demasiado neoyorkina para ser,
—aun volver a ser—
cualquier otra cosa.[11]

Havana is the mother city of identity, but New York is an experience that will forever define the writer's sense of marginality. The poet feels somewhat alien, a stranger—a foreigner—in either place, whether the native or the adopted space of life, and yet both sites are familiar and very much part of her being.

Such a marked self-awareness of hybridism appears explicitly in the fabric of poetic texts as the one above, although it was also beginning to be interwoven by Casal in her fiction as early as 1973. In the above quoted "Love Story According to Cyrano Prufrock," a double discourse of recreation about Havana and New York is already present. In that narrative, a male narrator goes in search of love and identity, and is evidently much influenced in his speech and perceptions by Casal's own studies of Guillermo Cabrera Infante's *Tres tristes tigres*, that classic Cuban novel of nostalgia for the lost past. Casal's reader finds in "Love Story . . ." allusions to a complex web of readings, and notices an American cultural presence in which, nevertheless, Cuban/Hispanic elements are basic to an understanding of the totality of the text:

Ay poetisa, los tigres no eran tres sino miles . . . me senté a tu lado a declamarte discursos impresionantes sobre el destino de la década, lo que se nos habían vuelto los sesenta (fíjate, piba, terminamos con Nixon de presidente), los gallardos caballeros que se fizieron (te regalé un poster de Malcolm X), la sociedad de consumo lo deglute todo (te regalé un disco autografiado por Marcuse que se estaban liquidando en Marlboro), Peter, Paul and Mary se separaron y los Beatles ya no existen . . . (Capítulo I. "Beatriz encontrada with a little help from my friends, from Johnny Weismuller to Jean-Luc Goddard") (*Fundadores* 72-73)

Allusions to French film directors and Hollywood actors, American civil rights leaders, New York stores, and legendary musical figures can be found alongside memories of the native city, references to night life, popular song lyrics from the sixties, and speech imitation of medieval literary texts.

But English appears still as a point of contact; the second language functions as a cultural tool that has not yet become part of the author's "natural" literary voices and rhythms. Casal wrote mainly in Spanish, but her works—whether essays, film reviews, poems, short stories, or articles—are thoroughly permeated, during the last five years of her publications, with the double vision of a bicultural. To the end of her life, Casal's painful awareness of an unsurmountable dual reality—one that had to be lived out daily—was still best expressed in her reiteration of motifs belonging to Havana and New York. Her own tale of two cities reflects her ultimate fear: the erosion of time, that inexorable leveler that makes contours disappear under the dust, that erases all known things. She had explored this theme since writing the poem "La Habana 1968":

> Que se me amarillea y se me gasta
> perfil de mi ciudad, siempre agitándose
> en la memoria y sin embargo
> siempre perdiendo bordes y letreros (*Palabras* 49)

The same fear of not capturing reality, of losing all memories, was still assaulting the poet years later. She yearned to name the features of her adopted city, her second source of identity. And so we read in the text "Domingo":

> Recorro las calles de este New York vestido de verano,
> con sus guirnaldas de latas de cerveza, (...)
> obsedida por la pasión de nombrar,
> azotada por la furia de fijarlo
> y recrearlo todo en la palabra,
> esta batalla irremediablemente perdida
> contra la caducidad de todo,
> esta batalla incesante y dolorosa
> contra la erosión,
> el tiempo,
> y el olvido,
> que lo devoran todo. (*Palabras* 58)

In her expressed anguish, bent on capturing ephemeral images of life, Casal confronts the reader with her fearful experience of losing identity; an identity defined, for the Cuban in America, by spaces tinged with the essence of both cultures, both countries.

It is, then, with Lourdes Casal that Cuban writers in the United States can begin to claim their cultural dualism as immigrants. Even more importantly, her works give witness to the first full-fledged step in the direction of becoming Cuban Americans in the truest sense of the term. Ethnic dual names (formerly "hyphenated Americans") point to a recognition of existential and socio-cultural hybridism in varying degrees, and since the midseventies some Cuban writers in the U.S. have been involved in the process of recognizing themselves as "others"; not only because of ethnic and/or gender imperatives, but—more crucially for them at this stage—because of their irrevocable historical situation.

In the works of the other U.S. Hispanic writers, it is usually the emergence of bilingual texts that signals for them an established conscientization of minority status; in other words, the political consciousness of being "dual" or "other" is clearly expressed at the linguistic level. This phenomenon was first registered for Cuban women authors with the theatrical presentations by Dolores Prida, a journalist and poet who has distinguished herself mainly as a playwright, and who has brought to her work a feminist worldview that is also unmistakably ethnic. The first play she wrote, *Beautiful Señoritas*, was a one act musical produced in 1977, which poked fun at the long-standing Latin women stereotypes—"from Carmen Miranda to Cuchi Cuchi Charo to suffering black-shrouded women crying and praying over the tortillas to modern day young Latinos trying to redefine their images" ("The Show" 182). Of all the plays she has written since, only two are in Spanish, and they cover the gamut of different social and cultural themes. *Coser y cantar*, in spite of its title, is a bilingual production featuring two characters called "Ella" and "She," and it mostly "elaborates the construction of a Latina subjectivity in the United States"[12] . Prida herself characterizes it as dealing with "how to be a bilingual, bicultural woman in Manhattan and keep your sanity" ("The Show" 185).

Dolores Prida represents, in my view, the conflictive hybridism of Cuban Americans at full play. Her "bilingual fantasy for two women," *Coser y cantar*, presented in 1981, poses questions on being Cuban, or Latin, at the interfacings of gender, ethnicity and class. Most of all, the two dramatic *personae* represent the two faces of the bicultural, and they must fuse together to continue existing: according to Sandoval, they must come to terms with "intercultural understanding" ("Mapping" 214). Although "Ella" affirms that if return to Cuba were possible, "She" (the unreal, acquired part of her own self) would disappear, the Anglo side of the equation—in turn— rejects most of the nostalgic mode of discourse:

> (She): But, if weren't for me you would not be the one you are now. No serías la que eres. I gave yourself back to you. If I had not opened some doors and some windows for you, you would still be sitting in the dark, with your recuerdos, the idealized beaches of your childhood, and your rice and beans and the rest of your goddamn obsolete memories![13]

"Ella" and "She" are clearly two halves of the real being; since the speaking voice of the Cuban American does "configure and articulate herself in two languages,"[14] she must then write in a bilingual mode. And yet, language is only one feature of this text which crosses boundaries and breaks with the past. *Coser y cantar* is definitely an indictment of two cultures which constitute themselves as expressions of male paradigms; for this reason, a note of denunciation of inequality is voiced in the play. This turns out to be, at once, an argument against the suffocating, yet culturally-enshrined, boundaries of traditional ethnic values dealing with sexual propriety as defined by gender roles, and also—important to Cuban American men as well as to Cuban American women—a rebellion against rigid ideological molds passed down to younger Cuban immigrants by the older generations. As Luis Santeiro, another Cuban American writer, puts it:

> My family came to Miami from Habana when I was 13, that means there are at least two sides to my personality—one that is conservative and relates to traditional beliefs, another side that is rebellious and secular.[15]

The end result of this seemingly schizophrenic situation is a writer who, whether woman or man, is not only continually aware of her or his own hybrid self, but at the same time obliged to be constantly constructing this bicultural self—deconstructing the original Cuban one and reconstructing a new American one, only to reverse the process according to circumstances and to situations arising in the family or ethnic community, or in the public sphere of work and mainstream encounters. It boils down to a matter of re-emphasizing or de-emphasizing the Cuban self at the expense of the American one, and vice-versa: Cuban Americans are ever experiencing, as Sandoval reminds us, "the reality of two socio-cultural territories and two linguistic horizons" ("Mapping" 217).

Another Land, Another Time

This process of Cuban American ethnic awareness and affirmation, with its subtle temporary rejection of the old to embrace the new, is for me best described as "(re)writing sugarcane memories." Let me explain the term, which serves both as a nucleating motif and as the title for this piece. In the nostalgic discourse of Cuban writers residing in the United States, whether one considers prose or poetry, the presence of palm trees and sugar cane is a constant. One only has to read a variety of works written by Cuban authors in the U.S. , such as Pura del Prado, Emilio Bejel, Maya Islas, José Corrales, Ana Alomá Velilla, and quite a few others, to find these motifs of "Cubanness": the geographical, topographical and socioeconomic symbols taken from the Cuban flora, and utilized as poetic objects for remembrance and recreation. In addition, sugar is not only the main source of survival for the Cuban economy—the basis for its island culture—but is also a metaphor for life's enjoyment: the very word "azúcar" [pronounced "¡asúca'!"] is oftentimes used in popular music as an interjection to convey to the listener, or dancer, the sweet ecstasy of sensual joy experienced in the exhuberance of musical sound. It can be said that the words *sugar* and *sugar cane*, and the images created by them, are metaphors for the essence of what it means to be Cuban. As the old political saying in the island proclaimed, "sin azúcar no hay país"— without sugar there is no country.[16] In the works of Cuban authors, then, and in those by younger Cubans in transition, "writing sugarcane memories" is an image that figuratively represents the re/creation of mother country motifs in a subtle form of nostalgic discourse. Thus Cuban American literary discourse, one that remembers and observes objectively at the same time, one that confronts and synthesizes Cuban tradition and American innovation, and that lives in the duality of both cultures, as the characters in Dolores Prida's play, would be best represented by the metaphor "(re)writing sugar cane memories."[17] And it is precisely in the work of one of the youngest Cuban immigrant authors, Achy Obejas, that the reader finds a text exhibiting all those characteristics of Cuban American discourse. No small coincidence that one of her texts, a (quasi)bilingual poem with the distinctive features of English linguistic dominance, is entitled "Sugarcane": hence, I use the term as a single word.

In the mid-eighties, poems and short stores written by Achy Obejas started appearing in various Latino women's journals and magazines. She was described in the Contributors section as a Cuban American writer (or as a Cuban poet, journalist, and playwright) who lived in Chicago. As of this writing, she has published only a book of poetry which has apparently not circulated widely (*Come The Fox*, 1982), but her works can be read in *Woman of her Word: Hispanic Women Write* (1983, 1987), *Third Woman* (1984, 1986), and in *Nosotras: Latina Literature Today* (1986), an anthology of works by Hispanic women in the United States which features—according to the editors—literature that portrays the experience of Cuban American, Chicana and Puerto Rican women.[18] One of the poems she published in 1983 was "Sugarcane," and the readers could notice immediately that this was highly crafted evidence of a bicultural world vision similar to that of other well- known U.S.-born Hispanic women poets, such as the Chicana Lorna Dee Cervantes and the Nuyorrican Sandra María Esteves. "Sugarcane" constitutes a synthesis of the searching for roots and the consciousness of hybridism that we have characterized as typical of the "hyphenated" ethnic American. As it happens, it is an exemplary text to illustrate what I call the Cuban American "minority assimilation" experience; that is, a more defined individual awareness of U.S.-latino ethnicity, as experienced by a Cuban under the circumstances of marginal minority life in American society.

In the code-switching discourse that inserts words and phrases from Cuban popular speech into a standard street dialect of English, island and sugarcane motifs are mixed. They draw on an intertextual past of AfroCaribbean poetry, on song lyrics that portray the speaker's acquaintance with popular cultural icons and with the experience of midwestern and northeastern America.

> can't cut
> can't cut
> azuca' in chicago
> dig it down to the
> roots sprouting spray paint on the
> walls on the hard cold
> stone of the great gritty city
> slums in chicago
> with the mansions in the hold
> in the head of
> the old old rich left behind
> from other times lopsided
> gangster walls overgrown taken
> over by the dark
> and poor overgrown with no
> sugarcane but you
> can't can't cut
> cut the water
> bro'
> from the flow and
> you can't can't cut
> cut the blood

lines form this island
train one by one throwing off
the chains siguaraya
no no
no se pue'e cortar
pan con ajo quisqueya
cuba y borinquen no
no se pue'en parar (*Women Of Her Word* 48)

The words of a fifties' AfroCuban song by Celia Cruz—noted
Cuban singer, who reemerged as a famous entertainer in the heights
of *salsa* fever—constitute a takeoff point for the refrain "no se
pue'e cortar," which is the Spanish version of the opening verses
of the poem: "can't cut/cut the cane." The lyrics of Celia's song,
"siguaraya," refer to a tree especially revered for its magic prop-
erties in the belief system of the Yoruba religion, prevalent among
Cuban blacks. But whereas the words of "Siguaraya" affirmed the
cutting of the tree with permission of a deity ("Siguaraya, yo va
tumbá, con permiso de Yemayá"), Obejas changes the positive affirmation of the slave chant—"I am going to fell the tree with permission from [the goddess] Yemayá"—into a negatively phrased
reaffirmation of Caribbean cultural pride: "you can't can't cut/cut
the blood/lines from this island/train one by one throwing off/the
chains ... " The island, or islands, being Cuba, Puerto Rico and
the Dominican Republic, are cited here in the text by their Taíno
Indian names. What the text alludes to are not the islands *per se*,
however, but rather their cultural extensions: the Latino population of Chicago, made up to a great extent by large numbers of
impoverished Caribbean immigrants from the three island countries.

Siguaraya and sugarcane, two native, life-giving plants of that
region, are intimately tied to the economic, social, cultural, and
religious life of the Great Antilles. The three island peoples recognized in the poem are equated for what they share in the "magic"
life rhythms—represented by music and speech, and as such are
reproduced in the poetic text by the staccato pattern of the song
and the verses. At a less idyllic level, however, those island inhabitants are just part of the urban ghettos of the American Midwest;
a Cuban American ethnic consciousness, identified politically and
racially with other historically marginalized groups, is explicited
when the poem incorporates Hispanic dialectal forms originating
in Black English, such as "bro," and also with the reference to old
mansions of a once "prosperous" gangster city now taken over by
"the dark and poor." The cultural-political current that has united

the three Great Antilles in their history since colonial days is identified in Obejas's text as "this island/train..." from which "you can't can't cut/the blood/lines." In this manner, "sugarcane" refers the reader to an allegory of the slavery and oppression suffered in the Hispanic Caribbean by peoples of African origin; and at the same time, it subtly equates the Caribbean colonial system to American society, where large numbers of ethnic minorities with darker skin (Chicanos and Latinos as well as African Americans) are still in the lowest rungs of the socioeconomic ladder. This reality is especially evident in the largest urban centers of the country, such as Chicago, where extensive slum areas and tenements are populated by racial minority groups.

> I saw it
> saw black a-frica
> down in the city
> walking in chicago y
> la cuba cuba
> gritando en el solar
> I saw it
> saw quisqueya
> brown
> uptown in the city
> cryin' in chicago
> y borinquen
> bro'
> sin un
> chavo igual but
> you can't can't cut
> cut the water
> bro' (49)

The linguistic skills characteristics of the U.S.-born Hispanic are present in this poem, and specifically seen in the sound plays generated by means of idiom, slang, or phonetic chains; see for example, "the great gritty city," and the succession of "bro'," "flow," and "blood." Obejas, who immigrated from Cuba in her childhood, can interpret the expressive psychological dualism of the bilingual/biculturals, because she is one of them. She is looking for connections between her "Cubanness" and the conditions of other Hispanic minorities, especially those which come from the same geographical region of Latin America and are united by history and culture. Her consciousness of hybridism is poignantly illustrated by "Sugarcane" itself: a text where English language functionality and American cultural awareness are self-evident, but which internalizes some of the most typical elements of Cuban culture at the level of rhythm—"no no/ no se pue'e cortar"—to incorporate them in the written literary discourse. The poem ends on a reiterated note of cultural affirmation and rejoicing, taken from Cuban Spanish and from Cuban popular culture: "no/se pue'en parar/ ¡azuca'!," in the manner of the musical refrain at the end of a song.

On the other hand, Obejas has also published in standard Spanish, and has even dealt with the motif of the Cuban refugee who flees the island by "unofficial" means; see, for example, her poem "El bote" and her short story "The Escape."[19] Her work represents the other extreme from the writers I qualify as "Cubans," and is situated in a transitional zone between U.S. -born Hispanics and immigrant Hispanics.[20] Obejas' Cuban American discourse shares many of the distinctive features of the English-dominant Hispanic ethnic discourse, which in the eighties—with Lorna Dee Cervantes, Gary Soto, Sandra Cisneros, Miguel Algarín, Sandra María Esteves and Tato Laviera, to name just a few of the most recognized authors among Chicanos and Nuyorricans—defines what seems to be the future paradigm for Hispanic literature in this country.

Basic distinctions between a *Cuban* writer in the United States and a *Cuban American* writer are, thus, the full consciousness and practice of dualism, the sense of belonging to an ethnic minority, and the native use of English. As has been seen, Cuban-born women writers who belong to earlier generations still identify, for the most part, with a "writer-in-exile" definition. That situates them squarely within the realm of a Latin American status quo vision, whereas women minority writers in the U.S. usually speak from an experience of marginality and discrimination due to race, class, and/or gender. More to the point: Cuban immigrant writers—men as well as women—tend to identify with the establishment, reject the Third World stance of many native Hispanic writers, and do not feel part of an underprivileged ethnic minority.

In general, Cubans who were writers before they migrated preserve the literary notions and standards they learned in the intellectual and artistic formation period, and often consider themselves as part of the body of Latin American literature that is written in many countries of the world by authors who reside outside of Latin America. Still, some of the writing done by Cuban women in the United States presents a modified vision of cultural reality due to the prevalence of a feminist ideology in their texts, and to the naked, critical portrayal of sociocultural myths, such as the submissive petit-bourgeois wife and her pathetic DonJuanesque husband: an excellent illustration is *Hagiografía de Narcisa la Bella*, by Mireya Robles. This 1985 novel is a well-crafted, avant-garde work with ties to some of the best productions of Latin American prose fiction in the last decades (Puig, Donoso, Lynch, Vargas Llosa). Its locale is a provincial Cuban town in the fifties, and its plot ends with the terrible ritual death of the ugly, sensitive clairvoyant Narcisa, victimized in the hands of her family.

Robles represents, in the charactertization of Cuban authors offered in these pages, the immigrant writer who associates her craft with Latin American or Hispanic/universal canonical forms, while Achy Obejas symbolizes the other end of the spectrum: the Cuban American in her dually grounded vision of culture and society. To put it in more general terms: the most distinguishable feature that separates older immigrant generations of Cuban writers from their younger compatriots in the United States, beyond their choice of language, is the problem of their cultural/political identity and affiliations. These vital connections with their own inner and outer selves constitute an artistic motherlode of inquiry, rejection, and affirmation.

For Cuban American writers—both women and men—the process of establishing themselves in the multicultural U.S. literary scene has just begun to happen in the last ten years or so. They are already partakers of what Lourdes Casal defined in 1976 as a "marginality immune to all returns"; theirs are the bittersweet memories of otherness in which their very beings are rooted. They are struggling to deconstruct a former, prescribed way of being, to reconstruct—in their vital experience and in their writing—another discourse of memories. But for the present generation, the past identity is still too binding, and they must deal as best they can with their differentness in order to reach some semblance of integration. As a Cuban American rock star—Elías Miguel Muñoz' protagonist in *Crazy Love*, epitome of crossover dreams—puts it to himself:

> Don't resist the pull of history, Julian Toledo. Give up the treasured American realm of individuality. ... Julian Toledo would never be anything but a renegade Cuban ... always having to remember and return to the pain, having to face it over and over again (145-46)

The nostalgia ever present in the Cuban American's parents generation has given way to a split, hybrid cultural consciousness in the sons and daughers of exile. The literary symbols used by these "counter-exiles" are moving away from sugarcane; but other metaphors await them, even if only to confirm that they stand at the margins, at the crossroads of cultural dis/assimilation and on the path to full fleged minority ethnicity. In the meantime, Cuban American authors are eloquently (re)writing themselves into the present panorama of U.S. Hispanic literature—sometimes even into the mainstream discourse, with all its attendant discoveries (witness the "Mambo Kings" of Oscar Hijuelos, and his Pulitzer Prize).[21] Most importantly, however, Cuban American writers are delving into the mature awareness of their own collective and individual histories, saying their stories from bisected angles and in bilingual/bicultural modes of (re)telling.

[1]"Introducción," Silvia Burunat and Ofelia García, eds. *Veinte años de literatura cubanoamericana* (Tempe, Arizona: The Bilingual Press, 1988): 14; emphasis mine.

[2]See Dolores Prida, "The Show Does Go On," in Asunción Horno-Delgado et al., *Breaking Boundaries: Latina Writings and Critical Readings* (Amherst: University of Massachusetts Press, 1989): 181–88.

[3]Eliana Rivero, "From Immigrant to Ethnics: Cuban Women Writers in the U.S. ," in *Breaking Boundaries* 189–200.

[4]In "The Writer in Exile or the Literature of Exile and Counter-Exile," Claudio Guillén defines that first literature as the one in which "exile becomes its own subject matter," often expressing itself in an elegiac mode, *Books Abroad* 50 (Spring 1972): 272.

[5]For further elaboration of these categories, for Cuban American men as well as women authors, see my "Cubanos y cubanoamericanos: perfil y presencia en los Estados Unidos," *Discurso Literario* 7.1 (11 semestre 1989): 81–101.

[6]There is a younger generation of poets who could be considered in this group. Their Spanish *poemarios* are being published in Spain by Editorial Betania, and among them one finds Magali Alabau, Claudia Caulfield, and Alina Galiano.

[7]All three texts are reproduced by Margaret Randall in *Breaking the Silences: 20th Century Poetry by Cuban Women* (Vancouver: The Pulp Press Book Publishers, 1982): 25 (English); 31–32 (Spanish).

[8]Eliana Rivero, "North from the River, South Inside (Florida, 1961–Arizona, 1980)," in *Canto Al Pueblo: Antología* (Phoenix: Arizona Canto Al Pueblo, 1990): 108–09.

[9]This seems to be the conclusion that Mary Seale Vásquez reaches in a perceptive analysis of Elías Miguel Muñoz' *Crazy Love*, in her article "Family, Generation, and Gender in Two Novels of Cuban Exile: Into the Mainstream?" (forthcoming in *Bilingual Review/Revista Bilingüe*, 1990–1991).

[10]In Lourdes Casal, *Los fundadores: Alfonso y otros cuentos* (Miami: Ediciones Universal, 1981): 69.

[11]This poem appeared originally in *Areíto* 3.1 (Summer 1976): 52, and was later included in the posthumous volume *Palabras juntan revolución* (La Habana: Casa de Las Américas, 1981): 60–61.

[12]See Alberto Sandoval, "Dolores Prida's *Coser y cantar*: Mapping the Dialectics of Ethnic Identity and Assimilation," *Breaking Boundaries* 216.

[13]*Coser y cantar: a one act bilingual fantasy for two women* (New York: n.p., 1981): 30.

[14]Eliana Ortega and Nancy Saporta Sternbach, "At the Threshold of the unnamed: Latina Literary Discourse in the Eighties," *Breaking Boundaries* 14. My discussion in this article incorporates some ideas presented in this important essay.

[15]Testimony by Luis Santeiro in *Intar Now*, 3 (Spring/Summer 1987): 1.

[16]This often quoted phrase is attributed to the politician, philanthropist, and art collector Orestes Ferrara, an Italian man who migrated to Cuba in the 19th century, and amassed a considerable fortune in the island. I thank my friend and *maestro*, José Juan Arrom—professor emeritus of Latin American literature at Yale University—for providing this information, and as always, generously sharing with me his expertise in Cuban language and literature, folklore and culture.

[17]This is perhaps the closest Cuban Americans come to be (re)defined in terms of their migration/exile experience. Or, according to Claudio Guillén, these works would represent the literature of "counter-exile," the latter being that exile which "is the condition but not the visible cause of an imaginative response often characterized by a tendency towards integration, increasingly broad vistas or universalism" ("Writer in Exile" 272).

[18]"Kimberle" and "Sugarcane" [poetry], *Woman of Her Word: Hispanic Women Write* (Arte Público, 1983; 2nd. edition 1987); "El bote" and "China" [poetry], *Third Woman* 2.1, 1984; "Born in the Heat of the Night," "Biting" [poetry], and "Polaroids" [short story], *Third Woman*, 3.1–2, 1986); and "The Escape" [short story], *Nosotras: Latina Literature Today*, edited by María del Carmen Boza, Beverly Silva, and Carmen Valle (Binghamton, NY: Bilingual Press, 1986). A 1983 play that Obejas co-wrote, "Carnicería," was highly acclaimed and is considered the most successful play in the history of Spanish language theater in Chicago.

[19]Published respectively in *Third Woman*, 2.1 (1984): 33, and *Nosotras* 44–48.

[20]For explanation of these categories, see my article "Hispanic Literature in the United States: Self Image and Conflict," International Studies in Honor of Tomás Rivera, *Revista Chicano-Riqueña*, 13.3–4 (1985): 173–92. This model of analysis was later refined in "From Immigrants to Ethnics: Cuban Women Writers in the United States," *Breaking Boundaries* 191.

[21]It must be noted, however, that a writer like Hijuelos—born in New York in the early fifties—does not properly fit my description of Cuban Americans as acculturated immigrants: he belongs to a prerevolutionary immigration whose children are really "native born Hispanics" (see my 1985 article, cited above).

Exile as 'Permanent Pain': Alfredo Villanueva Collado's *En el Imperio de la Papa Frita*

Teresa Justicia

When Alfredo Villanueva Collado's second book of poetry, *En el Imperio de la Papa Frita* was published in 1989, William Rosa introduced it with the following comments:

> (Here) Villanueva Collado once again demonstrates his capacity to synthesize and summarize the anguish and desperation that the Puerto Rican exile suffers in the United States. However, this is not a book about exile, voluntary or involuntary, no; this book of poetry seems to aim at demystifying the paradisiac and unreal vision of a Puerto Rico struggling to maintain its national identity.[1]

I quote the above in order to begin my discussion of this superbly written book of poetry about Puerto Rico by a writer who has said, of his identity as a Puerto Rican poet living and writing in New York City:

> If one does, like I have, refuse to metamorphose, one must nevertheless choose some kind of official identity; mine carries with it an existential condition of permanent pain, pain that will only go away the day I return home. I define myself, then as a foreigner—un extranjero; and an exile—un exiliado ... But being an exiliado means I long night and day for a return to the land I have rejected.[2]

That yearning for a land and a culture that, in Villanueva's own words "is no longer" (40), has led him to write a book of poetry that not only translates his agony into words but also seeks to establish the double power of Puerto Rican poetry written in exile: its lyrical intimacy, born out of pain, and its attempt to explain a collective, problematic reality that in this case arises out of Villanueva's repugnance for "Puerto Rico's willing acceptance of its present vassal status" (40).

The first poem in Villanueva's *El Imperio*, "(el exiliado)," establishes the dominant tone of anguish and regret that serves as a leit-motif throughout this collection. It is narrated in the first person and is a lyrical description of powerful clashing emotions aroused in the poet by his exile:

El exiliado llora
como un niño pequeño.
Pequeño su mundo
grande su deseo.
El exiliado es niño
con memoria de viejo.
El exiliado es niño
que añora un terreno (11–12)

The poignant lyricism and nostalgia expressed in this poem culmi-
nate in the last two lines which delineate the intensity that lies at
the core of this narrator's pain: "Como llora el corazón / cada vez
que se desgarra" (12). With this poem, the poet has introduced
several themes and images which recur through the book; a strong
need to return to his native land paired with a longing for a new
land, a new landscape, and the pain that tears through his heart
as memory crushes him with the sights, voices, and smells of the
past.

In the second poem, "(la calle)," Villanueva ushers in a new
image, the city street, which becomes a symbol of the finite and
eternal boundaries of exile. It is both a confining and a liberating
image:

Toda la historia del mundo
comienza en una calle.
Hay evidencia rigurosa
de que la calle es eterna (...)
Uno podrá haber estado
en muchas grandes ciudades
con enormes avenidas
y altivos monumentos
pero uno siempre se encuentra
con su calle y con su gente (13)

Thus, the poem ends with the narrator stating that the street goes
with him wherever he goes. The street has become symbolic of a
certain permanence, a certain continuity, while it also generates a
feeling of being at home no matter where he is. This is a vision
of the street as coming to the rescue of the exile. It becomes a
simultaneous image of leaving and returning home.

In the poem "(bolero)" the poet begins his quest for identity
through a series of questions about his roots and the factors that
influenced him:

Cómo no voy
a ser como soy
si la vellonera

de cualquier esquina
me educó.
Una lingüística
mojada en cerveza
con sabor a llanto
me dio.
Cómo no voy
a ser como soy
si la radio AM
de cualquier por-puesto
me arrulló (15)

Here the poet condenses his experience of growing up Puerto Rican into images of the proverbial corner jukebox, the beer, and the AM radio station; and yet, all these images are glazed by the tears mentioned in the second stanza thus paving the way for the vivid finale where the raw fact of the poet's reality has already been transformed by his poetic vision and sublimely etched in the following image:

Una poética
mojada en la sangre
de un sol trasnochado
me dio. (15)

These lines suggest an image of the Puerto Rican sun as being engaged in a relentless bohemian vigil that leaves it fatigued, bleeding, thus immersing the reality around it in its blood. This image attempts to establish the permanence of being Puerto Rican, an identity created and sustained by blood, a mark that does not soon evaporate and leaves a trace forever.

And what about the night-watch that eternally wears this sun out? This is not the sun that is part of the traditional idyllic vision of an island surrounded by a beautiful blue sea, blue sky and a sun that shines bountifully on its people. This image is freighted with suffering, with pain; here the reader sees the sun as unconventional, almost as if some heavy burden were sitting on its breast. This marks the beginning of the poet's indictment of the "paradisiac vision" of the island which finds its mournful apotheosis in the poem "(recuerdos de mentiras)":

A mí me durmieron de niño
con historias de hadas.
me contaron el cuento
de una isla encantada.
Rodeada de un mar de turquesa
con montañas de un verde esmeralda.

> Con un cielo vestido de encaje,
> una brisa, mantón de fragancia.
> Cuando los cuentos traicionan
> queda el mar.
> Hay que mirar el mar.
> Hay que llorar el mar.   (30)

By the end of this poem both the exiled poet and the reader have been forced to accept a different kind of reality, one where all the usual national symbols have yielded to a poetic vision where all has been an illusion, the fairy tales, the enchanted island, the beautiful green mountains and brilliant blue sky. All is lost and yet not irretrievable; there is still the relentless, eternal power of the sea. Where myths have failed to sustain a vision, one can at least contemplate and mourn the sea.

Because the poems in this book do not seem to be ordered in any particular manner, it is not surprising to find the poet in the process of moving from the lyrical to the political, oscillating between Puerto Rico and New York without a fixed point. One is reminded here of Ana Sierra's commentary about Villanueva Collado's new volume of poetry *La voz de la mujer que llevo dentro*: "*La voz de la mujer que llevo dentro* originates in a subject in process; that is, a subject who is not fixed in the discourse but maintains mobility as his essence."[3] Sierra's observations could also be applied to Villanueva's stance in *El Imperio*, where he oscillates between opposite poles that form what William Rosa calls "paradoxical dynamics" created by the poet's exile. On the one hand, some poems, such as the ones described before, focus on lyrical feelings evoked by his plight; on the other, there are poems such as the ones that will be described below, that attempt to extrapolate what it means to live in New York/USA and how the poet goes about coping with and accepting his condition. In his own words:

> My role as an artist within an alien, hostile environment, is three-fold: I must describe the effect that environment has on me and those I love; I must bear witness to what has been lost forever; and I must voice as loudly and clearly as I can, alternatives to immigration (*Hispanic Writers* 42).

It is such an instinct to voice the influence of his present environment on himself and the ones he loves that originates poems such as "(octava avenida)," "(cuarenta y siete y octava)," and the bittersweet lyric "(los nombres)." "(octava)" and "(cuarenta y siete)" are poems which envision almost surreal images of New York. For example, from "(octava)":

> Calle irreal de Nueva York
> La noche quiere ser buena
> y no le llueve encima
> al pordiosero, que escarba
> en la basura buscando cena. (16)

and from "cuarenta y siete)":

> Allá van, apretujadas
> por el pasillo, las locas:
> el público las aplaude,
> ellas se ríen, comentan
> en otro idioma. (19)

Both these poems posit images of violence and human squalor. But it is in "(los nombres)" that Villanueva's pain becomes anger; this is a nostalgic and bitter poem about himself and his loved ones, all living in New York, burdened by the weight of the Puerto Rican myths that framed their initial encounters with reality. The language here is largely reminiscent of that "poetics immersed in blood" (my trans.) alluded to in the poem "(bolero)":

> Perdimos el jardín y perdimos la huerta,
> Joe fenecido, que me enseñaste
> una tarde mágica en tu pueblo,
> y nuestras flores son de plástico o cerámica (...)
> Nadie menciona
> la razón de la diáspora,
> de la ferocidad del animal isleño.
> Como nos gusta el desgarrarnos,
> hemos aprendido a comer nuestras carnes, (...)
> Hoy paso la muerte como paso una piedra.
> Hay que entregarse sin remordimientos.
> Nos ha tocado una herencia de violencia
> Ave Nueva York, los que van a vivir
> te saludan. (25–29)

Thus, exile has shamelessly transformed him and his friends. Nothing matters anymore, not even death, when Puerto Rico itself is slowly dying:

> Vamos a entregarnos a la debacle,
> hay que dejar que suceda el suceso.
> Que muera alguno no es tan importante
> cuando se muere un pueblo
> bailando la conga con Iris Chacón
> que va a la cabeza del bacilón. (27)

The anger and impotence the poet feels against this impending disaster brought about by Puerto Ricans' selfish betrayal of their own country, are the subject of most of the final poems in Villanueva's compelling book. He pursues this theme "(estado cincuentaino)," where he indicts Puerto Rico's chronic lack of action:

> Aquí no pasa nada.
> No hay sangre derramada.
> No hay grito que no tenga
> su tumba de cemento.
> No hay siquiera un lamento.
> Se han traicionado
> los unos a los otros. (31)

In "(meditación primera: el camaleón)" he likens Puerto Ricans to chameleons, much to the approval of the "northern crocodile":

> Entre el fuego y el agua
> el camaleón se torna salamandra.
> Entre el aire y la tierra
> el camaleón se torna equilibrista (...)
> El cocodrilo del norte
> ha dado su aprobación
> al opus camaleón. (33–34)

In "(meditación segunda: el pitirre)," Villanueva tears down another national symbol, "el pitirre," by once more alluding to all the lies he has been told about it:

> A quién engañan
> con la mentira
> de una historia
> a medias?
> En los libros
> de relatos exactos
> el pitirre
> es solo una palabra. (39–40)

This theme is also echoed in the poem "(y todo el resto es literatura)," where the poet begins by describing the simple, peaceful life of a country man living in the traditional rustic setting Puerto Rican writers have loved to extol; he's lying on a hammock in the porch of his wooden house built at the top of a mountain overlooking the sea, and he's offering a stranger the proverbial cup of coffee. Then Villanueva introduces an ironic, discordant note which jars the surface harmony of the moment he has created:

> Este hombre, cuyos hijos
> le rodean en la loma poblada
> de nuevas casas, (...)
> comenta:

> La verdad que la tierra es hermosa.
> No cambio por nada mi ciudadanía americana
> pero que no se hable mal de mi país (...)
> Ay patria, de pitirres traicionada. (42)

This theme of betrayal powerfully surfaces once again in the most violent poem in the book, "(algunas verdades duelen)":

> No me la llames puta, Silén,
> que no es mujer, sino isla,
> que no es isla, sino concepto,
> y no concepto sino dolor.
> Un sentimiento de vergüenza
> que no se menciona en público
> y que se llora en privado (...)
> Isla quieta, isla traicionada
> irredimida por ninguna sangre-
> sin cacique dormido en el hoyo,
> sin libertador muerto de hambre,
> pero con mercaderes de tu carne
> y un proletariado gordo
> gracias a la magia del mantengo. (35–36)

There lies his beloved country, betrayed by a selfish, tenacious clinging to the very myths that shaped it but that, as the poet perceives it, can serve it no more.

From this point on, Villanueva's voice becomes mournful and prophetic. In "(diógenes)" he sets out to look for a truly honest "jíbaro" or a brave "taíno." This poem's tone is so remorseful and bitterly ironic that he describes finding the first one in New York, on Fifteenth Street:

> Al primero lo encontré
> aquí mismo, en la quince,
> recostado contra una puerta,
> con la cerveza en la mano,
> la otra mano en la braguota,
> mirando pasar la gente. (43)

The man is a spectator, nothing more.. He has been reduced to watching life pass him by as he devotes himself totally to the fulfillment of his own desires. The fate of the "taíno" is even more ominous:

> Al segundo lo encontré
> con ambos pies en el aire
> pintado en una pared
> debajo de una calzada
> en una ciudad sin nombre,
> infestada de fantasmas. (43)

So much for the proud Indian. He's a ghost. he's dead.

This dirgeful tone extends to the next poem, "(réquiem para güiro y órgano)," where the exile laments the loss of his land and affirms his pain as he contemplates the sea:

> Pero el mar ladino
> con suave lengüetazo
> se escurrió por debajo.
> Me dejó tendido
> sobre una huella
> Me regresó al dolor
> de la tierra. (...)
> Tuve
> una isla con gente
> que era mía.
> Ahora tengo
> una gente sin isla.
> Qué me hago? (44–45)

Villanueva ends this collection of poems about Puerto Rico with the poem which gives it the title, "(en el imperio de la papa frita)." In this poem he asserts the power of words both to retrieve what we have lost and to possibly create a new kind of reality sustained by emerging myths:

> Parcha, guamá, ajonjolí.
> antes de que se pierdan
> hay que mencionar.
> Recao, corazón, caimito.
> en un diccionario
> hay que guardar.
> chayota, alcapurria, zurullito.
> Ingredientes nuevos
> de un nuevo mito.
> En el imperio de la papa frita
> quizás se estudie el bacalaíto. (46)

In short, *El Imperio* is poetry about pain; the emotional and cultural pain of exile; the pain caused by the conflict between illusion and reality, myth and realization, stasis and flow, life and death, past and present. And yet, in the final poem there is hope that a new myth will emerge, in a new space and time, symbolizing a different kind of reality. In this book the poet has oscillated between opposites that torture him; he has, as it were, deconstructed the limits of his reality in order to explore if it is possible to create new worlds, at least through language. At the end, in spite of all he remembers as lost, he seems to be closer to fulfilling his dream about a new land, a new landscape. Thus the book leaves the reader at the crest of this dream whose possibility the poet has subtly suggested throughout the poems but whose essence he refuses to reveal for us. At this point, he departs and leaves us to imagine that future, to dare to create a new myth ushered in by a new world. Until such a time, however, the only recourse left the exile is the state of permanent pain evoked by the double burden of remembering where he comes from and realizing where he is:

> A las cinco de la mañana,
> pintado el cielo de claro,
> un día raro de lluvia,
> el aire sobre la quince
> huele distinto, a salado.
> Huele a otro sitio, y la brisa
> es casi tibia, aunque es marzo:
> El ojo ve una bahía
> en otra parte, y los barcos
> y otra brisa, que lo inunda
> con su filo de salitre
> con su olor a pan horneado.
> Y de repente uno quiere
> llorar a grito pelado
> porque está lejos, y no existe
> la mentira de un regreso. ("(madrugada)," 24).

[1] *En el imperio de la papa frita* (Santo Domingo: Editorial Colmena, 1989): 7; translation mine.

[2] *Hispanic Immigrant Writers*, Silvio Torres-Saillant, Ed. (New York: Ollantay Press, 1989): 40.

[3] "Alfredo Villanueva Collado: *La voz de la mujer que llevo dentro*," *Extra mares*, Cecilia Bustamante, ed. (forthcoming): 2; translation mine.

Cultural Exile and the Canon: Writing Paris into Contemporary Latin American Narrative

Marcy E. Schwartz

Cultural exile, whether political, periodic or prolonged, leaves traces in the discourses it produces. Paris has become inscribed in Latin American narrative texts, as an ideal space, a projected voyage, a literary Mecca, an esthetic ideal, a place for personal artistic expansion. The City of Light delineates a space where protagonists and their language come up against their Latin American identities and the problematic "place" of European cultural hegemony. Paris appears in the thematic imaginary, captured not only in its own fictionalized spatial projection, but in the signs that come from different worlds, in the tension of sign systems in confrontation.

When Bakhtin describes the historical and cultural conditions under which the novel emerges as the predominant genre in Europe, he also defines an important aspect of the legacy of cultural colonialism in Latin America. Julio Cortázar, Alfredo Bryce Echenique and Juan Carlos Onetti are just a few of the novelists who have inscribed Paris into their texts, realizing the "multi-languaged consciousness [of] international and interlingual contacts and relationships"[1] that Bakhtin notes as an essential element in the formation of the novel.

A long tradition of gazing toward Europe is also reflected in the international literary market, where Paris reforms and in part determines the Latin American narrative canon. The cultural products of this international industry reflect these complex economic and cultural relationships in their discourse. The Latin American gaze on Paris, the formation of the contemporary canon and the resultant place that Paris occupies in Latin American narrative, are pieces of the phenomenon of shifting cultural boundaries in post-colonial discourse.

Julio Cortázar's narrator in "El otro cielo" admits that "los pasajes y las galerías han sido mi patria secreta desde siempre."[2] The protagonist takes refuge in these nineteenth-century arcades, with "ese falso cielo de estucos y claraboyas sucias, ... esa noche artificial que ignoraba la estupidez del día y del sol afuera" (148). Where there was once a street or an alley, now wrought-iron and glass provide a tenuous roof protecting the mosaic-tile floors and the walls' stucco frescoes that host leisurely visitors. These are the passages Benjamín honors in his appraisal of Paris as capital of the nineteenth century.

Here the passages join not only the two adjacent sides of city buildings, but intimate images of Buenos Aires and Paris, superimposing them in that mesh of time and space of which Cortázar is so fond. In fact, the story begins with this idea of melting, enmeshing territory: "Me ocurría a veces que todo se dejaba andar, se ablandaba y cedía terreno, aceptando sin resistencia que se pudiera ir así de una cosa a otra" (147).

In this story the Pasaje Güemes in Buenos Aires "yields its ground" to the Parisian Galerie Vivienne, leading the protagonist through spatial and temporal territories. The elegantly floral, garlanded passages guide him to the object of desire ("el término de un deseo" 164), to the prostitute's garret in the Galerie Vivienne which "empezó a llenarnos los huecos" (151). The discourse further confounds the movement between cultural settings with the temporal overlapping of Paris during the Prussian war, Buenos Aires in the 1920s, and Buenos Aires again during World War II. The narrator/protagonist simultaneously wanders through the Paris of the previous century, with its gas lamps and carriages, and the Buenos Aires of the 1940s where he learns of Hiroshima.

In Cortázar's text, the spaces of different continents slide into one magnificent, illicit otherness. The story focuses on Paris, yet really begins in the Pasage Güemes, where, in his adolescent strolls in Buenos Aires, the protagonist first contemplates prostitutes. Later, he escapes into his secret world in the Galerie Vivienne, with its plaster garlands and its upstairs brothels, harbored from the wind and snow by glass roofs, mounting the stairs by candlelight, as if the Pasaje Güemes had directed him there.

This story not only plays with spatial and temporal zoning, but juxtaposes the ideals, images, and significance of these two "other heavens" in the protagonist's memories. They serve as settings for his rites of passage(s), for his clandestine and privately protected sexual experiences. They protect him from the "otro mundo", that street realm, "el del cielo alto y sin guirnaldas" (150). These floral passageways entangle the narrator in a double life, moving from his daily stock market job, his sedate and predictable fiancée and his mother, into "ese mundo diferente donde no había que pensar en Irma y se podía vivir sin horarios fijos, al azar de los encuentros y de la suerte" (155). In the neighborhood café where he spends time with his chosen Josiane, their group of friends observes a silent South American who also frequents the café, a shadow or mirror image of the narrator observing his own otherness.[3]

Paris and her secret zones attract the narrator but at the same time betray him. The garlands sometimes become morbid lies, the ceiling a false sky, his separate world a deceitful trap. The narrator begins to be invaded by

> el sentimiento indefinible ... que algo estaba amenazando en mí el mundo de las galerías y los pasajes, o todavía peor, que mi felicidad en ese mundo había sido un preludio engañoso, una trampa de flores ... (162).

He begins to feel alienated, a stranger to the very *barrio* that nurtured his dreams and fantasies. He vacillates, still yearning for "mi cielo de estucos y guirnaldas ... [donde] nací otra vez a mi mejor vida tan lejos de la sala de Irma" (166). This heavenly otherness pulls at the discourse as it both attracts and torments the narrator. The story ends with the protagonist sipping *mate* in Argentina with pregnant Irma, contemplating the upcoming elections between Perón and Tamborini; the text leaves us at the end in Buenos Aires, where it adolescently began, but with the reminder that the Pasaje Güemes was conceived in Paris.

The spatial map of this story centers around the Paris arcades, but at significant moments in the narrator's experiences those very passageways, in all of their Parisian, wrought-iron, mythical and elaborate ornamentation, call upon the Pasaje Güemes as this character's initial orientation, his esthetic origin, whose own origin is, of course, Paris. Forming this parabolic ambiguous territory, the story weaves together European and Porteño galleries into a narrative text that carries the mark of Latin Americans who have traversed cultural boundaries, reached Paris as their desired object, and incorporated its world of signs.

The Myth of Paris

In his discussion of the chronotope in folklore, Bakhtin defines the function of local myths as traces of the events that shape them, as legends that attempt "to make sense out of space" (189). The chronotope is that connection between space and time, between characters and their actions within historical and spatial settings. "El otro cielo" is a text that reveals the dialogical relationship between multiple chronotopes:

Chronotopes are mutually inclusive, they co-exist, they may be interwoven with, replace or oppose one another, contradict one another or find themselves in ever more complex interrelationships (252).

Paris's long tradition as a mythologized space in Latin American thought explains its eventual emergence as a text that will be borrowed, cited, voiced and acted in the discourse. The mythification of Paris in Latin American culture reveals an attempt to make sense out of local cultural spaces along with an attempt to grasp for a distant projected image of prestige:

Una Atenas que fuera Citeres ... y algunas veces Lesbos: tal definía París sin pensar que es indefinible. Al cabo de algunos años se le comprende más, lo que equivale a decir que se le quiere mejor. Al confuso entusiasmo de bárbaro, sucede una helena y lúcida devoción.[4]

In Cortázar's story's title, "cielo" simultaneously encompasses rooftops, sky and heaven, that opening yet covered protection, a yearning for otherness and distinction that Paris represents in Latin American esthetic literary tradition. Paris as the Latin American intellectuals' object of desire did not begin with Cortázar in the late 1950s, but has a well recognized history. Notable Peruvian critic and publisher Abelardo Oquendo calls a stay in Paris "the intellectual's obligatory military service."[5] Paris has held a place of prestige and elegance for Latin Americans writing home about their trips and experiences in France, feeding Paris' burgeoning image. The city maintains a phoenix of style and class that its observers and tasters contrast with home: "A ejemplo de tus parques civilizados que obedecen a una oculta geometría, quiero mondar cada mañana el alma bárbara."[6] This twentieth-century laudatory appraisal of Paris echoes Sarmiento's *civilización* versus *barbarie*, and the pervasive *afrancesado* theory of Latin American development. The memoirs of Peruvian, Uruguayan and Argentine statesmen and writers, from the mid-nineteenth century into the 1930s, all stress the sublime, the refinement, the intensity, the voluptuousness of Paris.

Paris is thus purported to be the *cité par excellence* for personal enrichment and expansion, especially for the writer and intellectual. César Vallejo, discussing the phenomenon of young Latin Americans in Europe in the 1930s, states that America "carece de un hogar cultural propio," and dubs Paris the "centro intelectual que consagra, y que fomenta la cultura individual."[7] In the same decade, an Argentine describes the ghosts of Paris:

> Es fácil adivinarlo: cuando llegue a Buenos Aires, este compatriota nues-
> tro será un eco doliente de París. Era en Buenos Aires, antes de su
> viaje, un hombre vulgar y vacío: París ha hecho de él, en sólo dos
> meses, un hombre de espíritu ... tocado por la gracia de la civi-
> lización ... [8]

The wit, spirit, grace and refined intelligence of Paris is to be absorbed by the Latin American "savages," converting them into noble, civilized Europeans.

Sarmiento proclaims that "Pour s'introduire dans le milieu in-
tellectuel de Paris, il faute être auteur ou roi."[9] Paris is adopted by
Latin Americans as the world's literary capital; choosing Madrid or
Barcelona, being Spanish cities, would have directly contradicted
efforts toward political and cultural independence from colonial
power. There is a transference of cultural and ideological standards that adopts Paris in rejecting Spain. Noé Jitrik explains that
Latin Americans, in trying to shake the colonial yoke, were hard-
pressed for cultural self-definition. The Spanish language seemed
to impose a model contradictory to cultural freedom, and thus,
they bought into and believed in France's promise for cultural re-
generation. In the past several decades, writers even justify their
Paris refuge as an affirmation of their own literature:

> ... los escritores latinoamericanos siguen queriendo vivir en Fran-
> cia como si de esa residencia, forzada o voluntaria, fuera a seguir
> surgiendo mágicamente un camino para las literaturas propias.[10]

These travelling and sometimes transplanted intellectuals want
to live out intensely their Latin American identity, searching to embrace their complex heritage, of which European cultural ancestry
is a part. If not to better identify and integrate pieces of a hidden or overlooked European identity, many intellectuals use their
time in Paris to better understand their own Latin Americanness.
Distance, then, becomes a road to the writer's self-awareness, and
travel an opportunity for fulfilling one's authentic cultural identity:

> Prendre de la distance non pour s'évader mais au contraire pour se
> dépouiller de préjugés étriqués et parvenir à mieux se connaître,
> soi et les autres, tel paraît être le propos de l'écrivain-voyageur.[11]

Cortázar, who left Argentina for Paris in 1951 and eventually
became a French citizen, states that it is only after coming to live in
France that he discovered "his true Latin American condition."[12]
He reacts against the "mandatory class attendance" in Latin America as a requirement for considering himself a Latin American

writer (275). His texts propose "a literature whose national and regional roots are expanded by a more open and complete experience" based in Paris (276). Finally, he exposes the metaphysical/esthetic search of his work:

> ... yo siento que también la argentinidad de mi obra ha ganado en vez de perder por esa ósmosis espiritual en la que el escritor no renuncia a nada, no traiciona nada, sino que sitúa su visión en un plano desde donde sus valores originales se insertan en una trama infinitamente más amplia y más rica ... ganan a su vez en amplitud y riqueza, se *recobran* en lo que pueden tener de más hondo y de más valedero (276).

The presence of Paris, then, is much more than the prestigious magnet that draws international intellectuals into its bohemian haven; it pervades the texts themselves, introducing images, sounds and lexicon that create a variegated texture.

Paris in Canon Formation: The Literary Market

Before examining how Paris reveals its pervasive presence in the verbal discourse, it is important to look at the role of Paris *outside* the discourse, in the realm of literary production. For many Latin American writers, Paris is not only the writers' inspirational literary capital, but also the center for cultural legitimation, the required first step toward international recognition, and thus an essential determiner of the canon of "list" of works accepted and included in the hegemony of cultural institutionalism: "Ecrire en espagnol est bien. Etre traduit en français est mieux, puisque cette langue assure à l'oeuvre littéraire une diffusion internationale."[13]

In his discussion on Latin American journalism in Paris in the 1920s and 1930s, Marc Cheymol states that modern Latin American literature is founded in the journalistic fervor of Paris during the "Anées Folles." The Paris journals, such as *Revue de l'Argentine* and *Revue de l'Amerique Latine*, "ont été à la fois le reflet et le monteur de l'évolution des lettres hispanoaméricaines ... une sorte de tribune où cette littérature a pu prendre conscience d'elle-même."[14]

Clearly, Latin American narrative still looks to Paris for recognition in both the intercontinental and inter-American canon. The same sentiment is echoed by a contemporary Uruguayan critic and anthologist in Paris, who calls French the "vehicular language" and Paris the bridge to enable writers to begin publishing, and then to continue publishing in other languages within Europe.[15] The protagonist of a contemporary short story by Uruguayan Cristina Peri-Rossi is a literary critic in Spain writing an article about Raimundo

Arias. When his daughter asks him who this poet is, he answers: "un famosísimo escritor a quien nadie conocía por no haber salido nunca de su país no europeo."[16] Thus, contact with Europe, and preferably Paris, is not only lauded but *recommended* or perhaps even required for literary success.

The "crisis editorial" in Latin America has significantly contributed to this new shift in Paris's attraction for writers. While Spain's restrictions due to censorship under Franco helped create Latin American publishing capitals in Mexico City and Buenos Aires, recent economic crisis has caused these publishers to turn away new propositions, particularly in fiction, leaving writers dependent on how European capitals will judge them, publish them, and thus how the next stage of the literary canon will be constructed. The suffering economy, the paper crisis, and the lack of funds for investing in newer writers, has left Latin American publishers almost completely paralyzed in the past two years. In reviewing the history of publishing over the past four decades in several South American capitals, publishing seems to peak between the late 1950s and 1970. These dates coincide with the "boom" in Latin American fiction, and are reflected in the proportion of books published in literature and the humanities versus science, education and technical studies.[17] After the dictatorships in Uruguay and Argentina, in the late 1970s and early 1980s, publishing resurges in an effort of "reapropiación de los medios de canalización cultural."[18] There are anti-dictatorial newspapers, socio-political studies and economic analyses being published, as well as a proliferation of literary contests and prizes.

However, the recent economic crisis affects both publishing and eventual sales. Many publishers interviewed spoke of sales falling thirty to sixty percent from 1987 to 1989. A variety of alternative marketing strategies are common in all Latin American capitals: book fairs, selling books by mail and through book clubs, starting used book departments in conventional commercial bookstores, and promoting the sale of books in supermarkets and outdoor kiosks. In 1989, a Buenos Aires daily newspaper printed an article entitled, "La cultura Xerox, o el arte de recibirse sin tocar un libro," about the paper and publishing crisis, and students' ever-increasing dependence on photocopying.[19]

Due to the cost of paper and modern technology, the book industry in Latin America has become increasingly dependent on importing. The "editoriales artesanales" (small, family-run or basement presses) are dying out, after a resurgence in the 1970s. In a published interview, Andrés Carbone, president of the Cámara del Libro in Peru and manager of the largest bookstore chain, was asked why not import less and publish more in Peru. In his response, he considers national editions a dream or a utopian solution (Barrig 19).

Thus publishing necessity continues to draw Latin American writers to European literary prizes, universities, conferences and publishing agents. Daniel Moyano, a widely-published Argentine novelist, published his first novel after winning a short story prize in France. After participating in a conference on the Latin American short story at the Sorbonne, he was approached by an influential literary agent from Barcelona. Luisa Futoransky and Alicia Dujovne, both Argentine novelists living in Paris, have published first in French, and only *then* manage to secure a contract for their novels in the original Spanish. The French contact is not only essential for publishing internationally, but also for establishing the writer's reputation at home. The Argentine critic David Lagmanovich spoke at a recent conference in Tucumán, Argentina. He divided Argentina into two distinct countries: Buenos Aires and "el interior" (the provinces); he criticized the control of the capital and of international publishing, saying that "los autores del interior" don't turn into "autores argentinos" until they have published in Europe.[20]

Paris as a literary capital extends not only to Latin Americans looking for literary opportunities. In his introduction to a conference on Paris and the phenomenon of literary capitals, Pierre Brunel begins to define the "tête écrivante" where "l'hégémonie de la parole" is exerted, and not only in French and Spanish.[21] Paris between the two world wars attracts 30,000 South Americans, and is dubbed their "floating capital" (Brunel 7). Yet these *latinos* shared Paris with many other expatriates:

> Toutes les langues du monde se mettent à rugir dans les cafés. De temps en temps, on entend quelques mots de français, bien peu, just ce qu'il faut pour ne pas perdre la notion de la situation géographique.[22]

Paris between the wars attracts international intellectuals because of its "universalité du politique" of culture, forming a vortex that,

> inséparable du traumatisme historique, a pour lieu la ville, qui, parmi les mégalopoles européennes, est extrême-occidentale, cela qui fonctionne comme le centre du vieux monde et l'articulation des autres mondes géographiques.[23]

Paris is, in fact, where many first editions in Spanish were published just after the first world war. Brunel characterizes a literary capital as a city offering the activity of publishing, interviews, meetings; a city with the infrastructure of media and cultural institutions; and a center that supports translations. It is a space that opens itself world-wide:

> ... la capitale littéraire est chef d'un lieu dont les frontières ne sont pas fixes ... Un domaine plus vaste se dessine qui peut même chercher à *s'étendre au monde entier* (Brunel 3, my emphasis).

The transcultural nature of the literary capital turns a vocation of letters into an imperative activity rather than a choice, making the city itself, and the writer's presence there, "une *manière* qui lève les servitudes et les obstacles de l'entreprise littéraire" (Bessière, 185).

The infrastructure of media and intellectual institutions contributes to Paris's "literary imperative." Paris supports a good number of institutions that help determine the formation of the canon: universities, international organizations (UNESCO, for example), museums, and, most importantly, a huge publishing industry that depends on and answers to these very cultural authorities. Television and radio programs, Sunday newspaper supplements, translations and anthologies are produced for a market created by the institutions of the literary capital. Other than anthologies in French, too numerous to list in detail here, of Latin American poetry and short stories, and the conventional academic syllabi and course programs in French universities, several examples follow of recent events and publications that reveal Paris's active role in canon formation:

- 1980: Conference on Latin American short story writers at the Sorbonne; three editions of an anthology followed, published in Montevideo, Barcelona, and Bogotá;

- 1986: *Europe*, a monthly cultural journal published in Paris, dedicates an entire issue to Argentine literature;

- 1987: UNESCO sponsors a conference on French-Uruguayan relations;

- 1988: The Festival du Livre à Nantes dedicates this year to books from Río de la Plata, distributing bibliographies of new translations;

- 1989: "Ex Libris," a literary television talk-show has a special program on Latin American writers;

- 1989: Helena Araújo's study on women writers includes a chapter on "Women Writers Translated into French."[24]

- 1989–1990: The French university system chooses three Latin American novels about exile as the "agrégation" for all Spanish majors. The novels, *Navíos y borrascas* by Daniel Moyano, *El Jardín de al lado* by José Donoso, and *Primavera con una esquina rota* by Mario Benedetti, are all by writers who have lived in Europe. Each of these writers will visit all the major universities in France, giving lectures and readings.

- 1990: Forthcoming publication of a new anthology on stories from Río de la Plata region is edited by Olver Gilberto de León.

This brief reporting includes publicized events and commercial publications, which are covered by the media and which continue to generate, as in the case of the 1980 conference, more publications and events. This list does not include art exhibits, hundreds of published translations and critical studies, and newspaper and magazine articles or interviews appearing regularly in Paris on Latin American writers. (*Magazine Littéraire*, for example, has a number of issues dedicated to Latin American writers throughout the 1970s and 1980s.) The list does, however, give an idea about the variety and number of large community happenings in the Paris literary world focusing on Latin America, aside from what appears in the already widely circulating, general media. Because of this propensity, with its established audience and ready resources in this literary capital, contemporary Latin American writers are as much attracted to a concrete potential for success as they are to the mythical glamour of Paris.

The problematics of cultural independence revealed in the publishing industry goes back to colonial history. In his chapter on publishing policies and the book industry in Mexico, Robert Estivals notes that multinational publishing houses in Mexico published mostly foreign authors, especially Spanish and Argentine. "Ils continuent ainsi à véhiculer au plan littéraire, scientifique et technique la culture ancienne et à maintenir une forme de colonisation culturelle."[25] Then there are the European publishers especially commited to producing Latin American literature. In the early 1900s, the Paul Ollendorff bookstore and publishing house in Paris almost entirely dedicated its business to publishing and distributing Hispanic writers. In his study of Ollendorff's enterprise, Botrel notes the hesitancy of Spanish publishing at the time, and the more enthusiastic yet realistic risk-taking of the French publishers. He calls the Latin American literary market the *enjeu* between the Spanish and the French industries:

> Historiquement il est certain que la conquête du marché latino-américain du livre s'inscrit dans le cadre plus général de la conquête économique de nations sous-devélopées par des nations plus devélopées. Cette conquête s'effectue dans un contexte latino-américaine idéologiquement favorable à l'Europe, à l'éxclusion de l'Espagne contre qui s'est faite l'índépendance. Le marché du livre se trouve, donc, en quelque sorte, être un secteur privilégié, le livre étant à la fois marchandise et véhicule d'idées ou d'idéologie.[26]

This literary colonialism is not confined to between the two world wars. Carlos Barral, the Barcelona publisher who initiated the international 'boom" market of Latin American fiction in the 1960s, admits to the same energetic, agressive approach in his goal of enlarging awareness of Hispanic literature with literary prizes and new collections.[27]

As Sara Castro-Klarén reminds us, "the question of the canon is not only a question of interpretation but also a space of ideological struggle."[28] The Latin American esthetic gaze fixed on Paris is only one side of the canonical coin. Paris as literary capital envelopes Latin American literature, legitimating it, assigning it new value through the city's intellectual and cultural institutions. Paris helps create Latin American narrative as a commodity, marketing and distributing it as an appropriated European good. And the texts that participate in this appropriation, those that agree to a European cultural hegemony controlling their distribution, also reveal the conflict of Latin American identity within a Europeanizing cultural market. If the novel lacks its own generic canon, as Bakhtin tells us and the current debate over canon formation may indicate, then this complicated transnational process of legitimation within the literary market is one more episode in novelistic discourse's struggle between its unofficial, "low" or hierarchically problematic stance and official (and economically recognized) status. Thus we are concerned not only with how literary discourse is created, biographically, by writers living in Paris, but with how that discourse is created, produced, legitimated and distributed in and by society. Latin American literature is a social commodity whose value is attributed, and whose canon is in large part determined, via transnational interactions.[29] The thematic and discursive results of this cross-cultural production of literature will be examined in the next section.

Paris, Text and Otherness

In one of Geertz's well-known essays, he mentions that, "It is in country unfamiliar emotionally or topographically that one needs poems and road maps."[30] Signs, patterns, matrices and maps abound in these narratives that take on encounters between Latin America and Europe. "El otro cielo," our first narrative example, imposes temporal grids over the visual, architectural maps of the galleries in the two juxtaposed cities. The cities, then, lend an ordering, or disordering dimension that the discourse exploits. The narrative chronotopes are the result of "a multitude of routes, roads and paths that have been laid down ... by social consciousness" (Bakhtin 278), as they reappear with all of their linguistic and social dimensions.

A glance at discursive aspects of the transcultural literary experience in two more writers from different generations and regions reveals Paris as not only the motivating magnet but now an essential intertext integrated into an important corpus of recent Latin American narrative. The texts' maps and patterns struggle to encompass all of the cultural and linguistic worlds which often overlap, bombarding or tearing at one another. The interplay of content so evident in these texts meets Julia Kristeva's requirements for intertextuality:

> ... not simply an intersection of two voices ... but the result of the intersection of a number of voices, a number of textual interventions, which are combined in the semantic field but also in the syntactic and phonic fields of the utterance.[31]

The discourse in Spanish meanders in and out of spatial and temporal zones, mixing with French in Onetti and converging lexically and syntactically in Bryce Echenique. The Spanish of these Latin American texts is affected by what Bakhtin calls "interillumination":

> ... each given language—even if its linguistic composition (phonetics, vocabulary, morphology, etc.) were to remain absolutely unchanged—is, as it were, reborn, becoming qualitatively a different thing for the consciousness that creates in it (12).

Paris emerges from these texts, not only spatially and thematically, but also in the sounds and syntax of the discourse itself.

Before Paris can become an intertext, however, it must first become a text. The ideals, history, voices and trajectories about and toward Paris from Latin America congeal into a textual world, one of the "multitude of bounded verbal-ideological and social belief systems ... filled with various semantic and axiological content ... " (Bakhtin 288). The city, once it is a text, is read, interpreted, understood or confused, and eventually cited within the new fiction. It helps produce writing by offering signs: "La ville capitalise la littérature et l'écrit est l'archéologie de la ville; la ville est elle-même une manière d'écrit—ce qui offre signes et language" (Bessière 188). Thus, Paris (and France in general) does not simply serve the text as geographical setting or thematic imagery, but has a much more comprehensive function as an ordering principle, as a structural world of signs and references, as a system of "thèmes inconscients, les archétypes involontaires où les mots, mais aussi les couleurs et les sons, prennent leur sens et leur vie."[32] Paris participates in these novels and short stories as a sort of communicating character, with its own history integrated into Latin American cultural identity. The city becomes another textual author(ity) voiced within the narration.

Juan Carlos Onetti's *La vida breve* is a perfect example of how Paris becomes an intertext in Latin American fiction.[33] Mami is a middle-aged French prostitute living in Onetti's fictitious Santa María in Argentina. She reminisces about home, recalling Paris and her French world in cabaret songs. The title of the novel, in fact, comes from one of those reminiscent songs, "La vie est bréve," quoted in the middle of the novel. Mami is not a major character in the novel, yet she is placed in this corrupt, depressive, alcoholic and murderous Southern Cone story as a reminder of *another* underworld. She spends her days gazing at a map of Paris, continually reinventing her game that plans out routes to and from various places in the city:

> Mami, como una vaca ciega, ... estaría acercando la cabeza teñida de amarillo al plano de la ciudad de París, itinéraire practique de l'étranger ... ella venía de Sacre Coeur por la Rue Championnet y se había detenido (aquel día, junto con el mundo, era suyo) en la esquina de la Avenue de St. Ouen—, dudosa entre tomar el Boulevard Bessières o la Avenue de Clichy para descender ... el saloncito oscuro y mal ventilado que no frecuentaba desde meses, que podía estar ya en los antípodas, en Buenos Aires, fuera del plano en todo caso.[34]

Onetti intersperses the French street names, the word *chanson*, song titles and lyrics, giving the discourse a cadence of reminders from Mami's past. She embodies that ambivalent back and forth journey between Paris and Río de la Plata:

> ... bajo las frases de la vieja *chanson*, Mami revivió a la muchacha que había emigrado de un Paris victorioso, treinta años atrás, para

conocer la lengua y el alma de un pueblo nuevo a través de los clientes melancólicos de Rosario, San Fernando, Mataderos y los cabarets ... (154).

When her lover Stein takes her back to Europe, it is an "agridulce excursión al pasado, tan parecida a ésta que realizaba ahora de pie junto al piano ... mediante la repetición de *chansons* y de posturas ancestrales" (154).

Mami is the Paris of brothels and cabarets; old and wrinkled now, she is also the woman Stein loves as a mother—she is both the maternal figure and the whore, a polarity of attractions transplanted in South America. She is the presence of Paris in both the story (plot, happenings, *récit*) and in the discourse (the linguistic weaving-in of French and of Mami's "world"), juxtaposed with Latin American reality. That alternative, that pull toward "the other side" or another part of one's (or the text's) life, pulls simultaneously at the intricate plot in a well-defined South American setting, and at the verbal texture of the novel. The nostalgic and bittersweet tension between the novel's Southern Cone cities and Paris even parallels metaphorically that continuously shifting movement between fiction and life that Onetti so exploits in this novel.

The Latin American in Paris presents some of the same ambivalence and mixing of cultures in the discourse as we have seen in Onetti's version of the French woman penetrating Latin America. Paris is present on both sides of the Atlantic, in myths and intertext in Latin America, and as architectural labyrinth and demystifying reality on the European side. Thus, these are not just narratives that "take place" in Paris, but rather stories whose discourse reveals the complexity of chronotopes in a transcultural literary phenomenon.

The narratives about the Latin American in Paris delineate complicated identity issues for the Hispanic subject as character, very clearly elaborated in Alfredo Bryce Echenique's novel *La vida exagerada de Martín Romaña*. The textual tension that we are about to examine in the narrative grows out of the illusory myth outlined in the first part of this study and the eventual demystification of real experience with European life. An introduction to a Barcelona edition of *Martín Romaña* calls the novel "un implacable ajuste de cuentas entre su autor y la abnorme ciudad—maravillosa para el visitante y monstruosa para el habitante ... "[35] This novel especially exploits this cultural polarity and ambivalence, this time between Paris and Lima, and the resulting complications of cultural identity and otherness.

This story of Latin American university students in Paris during the May 1968 "revolution" begins and ends with Martín's trajectories to and from Paris. Martín begins to narrate his tale by recounting his false starts and stunted attempts to get to Paris. Although he admits that he was never meant to be a sailor, he finally manages to get to Paris by boat. However, his trip is not without perils and close calls: he decides that his ship will be the first to shipwreck in the Panama Canal. "Me embargó una pena infinita, al imaginar que no sobreviviría para contar la historia en mi café limeño ... "[36] Thus, Martín embarks on his inevitable trip to Paris, after being detained, not having a visa and being sent back, and losing his luggage, already including a projected nostalgic return to Lima. The rest of the novel transpires between Martín's arrival in and departure from Paris. The narration draws this initial and persistent frame around the story it starts to tell.

The last scene of the novel takes place in the Paris airport, a sort of grand finale that regroups the entire story's signs and characters. Martín approached Paris and its illusion, and as he leaves, Paris closes in the distance. Paris contracts and concentrates in the image of the airport and its good-byes, a city and its airport that "las autoridades debieron haber cerrado por triste" (455). As the departure looms larger, Paris fades in the distance:

> ... ciudad que a mí me parecía haber abandonado para siempre, mil años atrás. Curioso. No había logrado creer más en su existencia, desde que Inés empezó a hablar de partir, París se había convertido en una mención literaria, una vaga referencia a la tristeza y al miedo y al amor con demasiadas ilusiones (453).

Thus Paris is an idea, or ideal, in which one believes or loses faith. The airport expands as Paris contracts in this closing scene that envelopes both the illusions and disillusions, the proximity and the distance, of the Parisian narrative chronotope.

The discourse of the novel reflects this confusing ambivalence between Paris and Lima. Signs throughout the discourse cross and overlap not only language boundaries but cultural modes, idiomatic humor and semantic codes. In Paris, *putamadre* becomes a verb ("Putamadreé como loco ... " [21]); in Lima, Marcel Proust becomes an adjective ("... en un loco marcelprousteo ... " [18]). The references to French culture are more than mere allusions; they are Hispanicized, intertextually and gramatically woven into the texture of the narration. Here Bryce exploits what Bakhtin calls hybridization:

> ... a mixture of two social languages within the limits of a single utterance, an encounter, within the arena of an utterance, between

two different linguistic consciousnesses, separated from one another by an epoch, by social differentiation or by some other factor (358).

The narrator appropriates this new world of signs, embedding them into his language, although not without a tension that signals them as *other*, in the same way that he signals himself as *other* in the European episodes of his own story.

In the criss-crossing of intertextual worlds in Bryce Echenique's narrative, there is no consistent coherency. His discourse shifts back and forth, sometimes privileging one realm and sometimes another. The text approaches Paris with a South American or *limeño* group of signs, and then switches to approach recollections of Lima or encounters with *latinos* via European signs: "abandoné las dificultades limeñas para insertarme de cabeza en las de aquel sueño parisino sin dificultades limeñas ... " (19). Paris is understood, then, through the Latin American filters, and subsequently Latin America comes to be comprehended through newly-acquired European filters. These filters are not simply ideological or cultural references and linguistic mishaps, but superimposed textual grids that together map out the discourse.

Bryce Echenique's writing confirms what Bakhtin describes in Rabelais: the writing's new "word-linkages" that challenge the "habitual matrices" of language use (169). Bakhtin delineates seven series of signs that the novelist manipulates in *Pantagruel*: anatomy, clothing, food, drink, sex, death and defecation, and shows how Rabelais crosses borders in a kind of semiotic synaesthesia. Bryce, along with other culturally exiled narrators, sets up especially complicated linguistic territories that go beyond the thematic and the semantic, playing with sounds and syntax, poetically wrenching words and references not only from their habitual geographical and architectural realms, but from their familiar discursive context as well.

The Latin American expatriates' experience in Paris is full of ambivalence and otherness. In trying to consume Paris, Paris consumes them:

> ... l'expérience de la réalité parisienne est à la fois une expérience de la possession—l'expatrié ne cesse de vivre des éléments extérieurs de l'espace parisien—et une expérience du manque d'appropriation. ... ce qui fixe l'altérité et, en même temps, la met à la disposition du sujet (Bessiére 191).

In embracing Paris, the cultural (if not also political) exile experiences both the heritage of European culture (which seems so familiar and reaffirms esthetic ideals so effectively transmitted through the cultural colonialism over several centuries), and the alienation of not belonging. Heteroglot discourse allows these writers "the right to be 'other' in this world" (Bakhtin 159), mediating but also problematizing their otherness. Their characters—Mami's South American companions and Martín in Paris—invite that otherness, participating in and claiming Paris as their own through discourse.

Bakhtin reminds us that "we must deal with the life and behavior of discourse in a contradictory and multi-languaged world" (275). Textualized Paris in Latin American narrative reveals cultural and linguistic categories that overlap in an intertextual discourse that problematizes cultural identity. Paris inserts itself, not only as setting or theme, but as a text with its own language, history, myth and story. It is invited by that magnetic affinity and mystified charm, and then imposes itself as the canon's international institutional site. Paris creeps up on discourse within contemporary Latin American narrative, writing itself polyphonically into the story and into its production. Discursively as well as in the transnational cultural market, identity fragments in a self-reflexive construction of cross-cultural gazes back and forth across the Atlantic. These are linguistic gazes, heard, visualized and textured with the multiplicity of worlds of signs bombarding one another. These gazes resonate from the literary texts that are inspired, produced, marketed, distributed and read by Paris. Their discourse emerges from beneath the cultural exile of their authors, and beyond the literary colonization of their production.

---

[1] Mikhail M. Bakhtin, *The Dialogic Imagination*, trans. Caryl Emerson and Michael Holquist (Austin, TX: University of Texas, 1981): 11.

[2] Julio Cortázar, *Los relatos 3. Pasajes* (Madrid: Alianza, 1976): 147.

[3] Alejandra Pizarnik discusses the fusion of the *sudamericano* with the murderer-at-large, Laurent. According to her, their textual origin is found in the short epigraphs beginning each of the two sections of the story, from Lautréamont's *Les chants de Maldoror*. Lautréamont, of course, is the perfect double figure of the South American (writer) who is also French. See Pizarnik, "Nota sobre un cuento de Cortázar: 'El otro cielo'," *La Vuelta a Cortázar en nueve ensayos*, Noé Jitrik, et al. (Buenos Aires: Pérez, 1969): 55–62.

[4] Ventura García Calderón, *Frivolamente ... (sensaciones parisienses)* (Paris: Garnier, 1908): vi.

[5] Aberlardo Oquendo, personal interview, Lima, Perú, 15 June 1989.

[6] Ventura García Calerón, *Cantilenas* (Paris: América Latina, 1920): 17.

[7] César Vallejo, *Desde Europa: Crónicas y artículos (1923–1938)*, prologue and notes by Jorge Puccinelli (Lima: Fuente de Cultura Peruana,

1987): 324 & 30.

[8]Roberta Gache, *Paris, glosario argentino* (Buenos Aires: Babel, 1928): 27.

[9]Carcano, Miguel Ángel, "Sarmiento et la France," *Revue de l'Argentine* 5.3 (1939): 6.

[10]Noé Jitrik, *Las armas y las razones. Ensayos sobre el peronismo, el exilio, y la literatura. 1975–1989* (Buenos Aires: Sudamericana, 1984): 154. See also David Viñas, "El viaje a Europa," *De Sarmiento a Cortázar. Literatura argentina y realidad política* (Buenos Aires: Siglo Veinte, 1974): 132–202.

[11]Eve-Marie Fell, "Paris et la patrie: Réflections d'un métis péruvien", *Voyages et séjours d'espagnols et d'hispano-américains en France* (Tours, France: Université de Tours, 1982): 164.

[12]Julio Cortázar, "Acerca de la situación del intelectual latinoamericano," *Ultimo round II* (México: Siglo XXI, 1985): 269.

[13]Edmond de Narval, "Notre Programme," introduction to the first issue of *La Revue Argentine* 1.1 (1934): 4.

[14]Marc Cheymol, "Les revues latino-américaines à Paris (1900–1940)," *Revue des revues* 5 (1988).

[15]Olver Gilberto de León, personal interview, Paris, France, 27 December 1989.

[16]Cristina Peri-Rossi, *La tarde del dinosaurio* (Barcelona: Plaza y Janés, 1985): 45–46.

[17]Uruguay published an average of 500 titles per year from 1959 to 1967, half of them in literature and the humanities; by 1976, the country produced only 400 titles per year, and only 60 of them in literature and the humanities. See Alvaro Barros-Lemez, "La larga marcha de lo verosímil. Narrativa uruguaya del siglo XX," in Hernán Vidal, ed., *Fascismo y experiencia literaria: Reflexiones para una recanonización* (Minneapolis: Institute for the Study of Ideologies and Literature, 1985): 469–86.

[10]Mabel Moraña, "Autoritarismo y discurso lírico en el Uruguay," in Vidal 410.

[11]This is not just a phenomenon of the 1980s. A similar article appears in Lima in 1977 in a magazine's special issue on "The Book in Peru": Maruja Barrig, "Testimonios" *Runa* 5 (1977): 16–19.

[20]Daniel Moyano, personal interview, Madrid, 11 Nov. 1989.

[21]Pierre Brunel, "Qu'est-ce qu'une capitale littéraire?," *Paris et le phénomène des capitales littéraires* (Paris: Université de Paris-Sorbonne, 1986): 1–2.

[22]González de Mendoza quoted in Marc Cheymol, *Miguel Angel Asturias dans le Paris des Années Folles* (Grenoble: Presse Universitaire de Grenoble, 1987): 96.

[23]Jean Bessière, "Paris, capitale littéraire transculturelle, 1920–1939," *Paris et le phénomène des capitales littéraires*, 188.

[24]"Traducidas al francés," *La scherezada criolla: ensayos sobre escritura femenina latinoamericana* (Bogotá: Universidad Nacional, 1989): 203–216.

[25]Robert Estivals, *Le livre dans le monde 1971–1981. Introduction à la bibliologie politique internationale* (Paris: Retz, 1983): 351.

[26] Jean-Francois Botrel, *Sociedad de ediciones literarias y artísticas - Librería Paul Ollendorff* (Bordeaux: Institut d'Etudes Ibériques et Ibéro-Américaines de l'Université, 1970).

[27] In his memoirs, Barral mentions "la relación intensa con editores españoles acuñados en la autarquía y vocados principalmente a la prosperidad a toda costa y a *la colonización librera de las Américas*" (my emphasis). Carlos Barral, *Años sin excusa. Memorias II* (Barcelona: Barral, 1978): 263–4.

[28] Sara Castro-Klarén, "By (T)reason of State: The Canon and Marginality in Latin American Literature," *Revista de estudios hispánicos* (March 1990): 3.

[29] See Arjun Appadurai, "Introduction: Commodities and the Politics of Value," in *The Social Life of Things. Commodities in Cultural Perspective* (Cambridge UP, 1988): 3–63.

[30] Clifford Geertz, "Ideology as a Cultural System," *The Interpretation of Cultures; Selected Essays* (New York: Basic Books, 1973): 218.

[31] Margaret Waller, "Interview with Julia Kristeva," trans. Richard Macksey, in *Intertextuality and Contemporary American Fiction*, ed. Patrick O'Donnell and Robert Con Davis (Baltimore: Johns Hopkins UP, 1990): 281.

[32] Gilles Deleuze, *Proust et les signes* (Paris: Presses Universitaires de France, 1986): 60.

[33] This novel, perhaps Onetti's most famous, written *before* his political exile in Madrid in the 1970s, was first published in Buenos Aires in 1950. I searched for any edition of it in Montevideo and Buenos Aires during the summer of 1989, and found no copies. In Madrid, I acquired an expensive, hard-bound edition published by Edhasa, the Spanish branch of (Argentine) Sudamericana, which has had three editions since 1977.

[34] Juan Carlos Onetti, *La vida breve* (Barcelona: Edhasa, 1985): 240.

[35] Bryce Echenique, *La vida exagerada de Martín Romaña*, intro. Fernando Sánchez Dragó (Barcelona: Círculo de Lectores, 1983): ii.

[36] Alfredo Bryce Echenique, *La vida exagerada de Martín Romaña* (Bogotá: Oveja Negra, 1985): 19. All further citations from the novel are from this edition.

The Chilean Exile's Return:
Donoso versus García Márquez

Mary Lusky Friedman

As the December 1989 election brought to an end the 17-year government of Augusto Pinochet, many of those his regime forced into exile were returning to Chile. "Hubo un millón de exiliados," reports Jacobo Timerman in *Chile: El galope muerto* in 1988, "y la mayoría retornó."[1] Despite the categoricalness of Timerman's remark, it is hard to know exactly how many Chileans left their country because of Pinochet, and even harder to know how many have gone back. The official Chilean government figure of 11,000 exiled is "indisputably low."[2] Some 20,000–40,000 Chileans at one time bore passports marked "L" (which stands for the secret "lista nacional"), identifying them as unwelcome in Chile (Brown 88–89). These people had to seek prior authorization to enter Chile, and were routinely denied permission to return even for short stays. The Chilean Commission for Human Rights estimates that 200,000 suffered political exile (Brown 89). Of these, some were banished officially by the government and others fled intimidation or blacklisting, or accompanied a proscribed family member. In a population of 11,000,000 people, this conservative figure represents one person in 55, one of the highest proportions of exiles in the world. Some sources set much higher the number of Chileans living abroad. A July 1988 Americas Watch report estimates that "up to a million Chileans" were then living outside Chile, "for either political or economic reasons."[3]

As for the pace of exodus and return, the years between 1975 and 1979 "saw a flood of Chilean leaders, workers and intellectuals and their families disperse around the globe" (Brown 87). Eighty thousand went to Venezuela; 15,000 to France; 12,000 to Canada; 9,000 to Australia and significant numbers as well settled in Mexico and Spain. (The United States, to its shame, accepted during that time only 2,000–3,000; U.S. immigration laws at that time favored refugees from communist regimes over those fleeing right-wing dictatorships. Only when Senator Edward Kennedy, then chairman of the Senate's refugee subcommittee, sponsored a special program, did the U.S. accept any Chilean applications for asylum (Brown 112–13). Chileans began to return in significant numbers in 1983. In 1982 the Chilean government began issuing lists of people authorized to return from exile, although these lists were maddeningly uncomprehensive. By June 1988 only 555 persons were officially recognized as political exiles (Rickard & Brown, 92), and the *New York Times*, on September 2, 1988, reported the number as 169.[4] Although no one is sure how many Chileans have actually returned home, many did return to campaign and vote in the 1989 plebiscite, and perhaps hundreds of thousands may eventually resettle in Chile.

This is the context in which two books appeared that describe the return of an exile to Chile. *La aventura de Miguel Littín clandestino en Chile*,[5] by Gabriel García Márquez, is a non-fiction account of the foray into Chile of film director Miguel Littín, who re-entered his country illegally for six perilous weeks to make a documentary film about life under Pinochet. Littín collaborated with García Márquez in producing the book; he allowed the writer to debrief him in a weeklong series of tape recorded interviews. García Márquez retells the filmmaker's story, recreating Littín's voice in an invented first person narration. He preserves the factualness of the account, but organizes the tale to enhance its suspense and to throw into relief particular motifs. The other work is a novel, *La desesperanza*,[6] in which José Donoso describes the return to Chile of a fictional folk singer named Mañungo Vera. (Since Donoso himself had just returned to Chile when he wrote the book, he almost certainly records there his own experience as repatriot.)

The works have a lot in common. Not only were both published in 1986, but both describe the return to Chile of an exiled artist at precisely the same moment—January of 1985, just after the death of Pablo Neruda's widow. Possibly their most important point of contact is that each after its fashion lays claim to realism, testimonial realism in one case and novelistic realism in the other. Unlike Isabel Allende's cheerful romances about contemporary Chile and Ariel Dorfman's allegorical and sometimes baroque treatment of Chile's horrors, they aim at giving a plain, true-to-life account of Chile at a particularly dark time when a state of siege remained in effect and no thought of the 1989 elections held out hope. Not surprisingly, the books coincide in describing the poverty of Santiago's *poblaciones* at a time when the economic miracle of the late 1970s had collapsed. Both document the anxiety of the curfew and report the manipulation of the press to purvey misinformation. Both remind the reader that Pablo Neruda, some twelve years after his death, continued to be a presence in people's minds. What is surprising, though, is that these two books create very different impressions of the experience of return, and of Chile itself at that precise historical moment.

Before I examine the ways in which the books differ, let me point out two ideas that the works do share. Both books, although in very different ways, portray the return of an exile as a transformation of self into other. Miguel Littín, who, to enter Chile undetected, posed as a Uruguayan advertising executive on a business trip, recalls: "En realidad, el proceso más difícil para mí fue el de convertirme en otra persona ... Tenía que resignarme a dejar de ser el hombre que había sido siempre, y convertirme en otro muy distinto" (García Márquez 12–13). The change of identity, although temporary, had to be thoroughgoing. Not only did Littín swap his jeans and sheepskin jacket for fine European suits and custom-made shirts. He submitted as well to a distortion of his body—a make-up artist shaved his beard, accentuated his baldness, plucked his eyebrows to make his face seem longer and equipped him with graduated lenses that altered the expression of his gaze. And, with the help of two psychologists, he adopted a Uruguayan accent; learned to gesture with his hands when he talked; and suppressed his own characteristic laugh. What is more, with his new identity Littín acquired a new wife (a member of the Chilean resistance) and—this seems Borgesian to me—assumed an invented past appropriate to a middle-aged upper middle class Montevidean. Of course, he never stopped *being* Miguel Littín, but as he returned from exile he found himself, as García Márquez puts it, "exiliado dentro de mí mismo" (9).

Donoso's protagonist Mañungo Vera, too, returns to Chile with an assumed identity of sorts. For twelve years his European agents have imposed on him the charismatic image of *cantante guerrillero*, and at age thirty-four, Mañungo feels a painful split between his public persona and the man he really is. Mañungo feels guilty for having used Chile's agony to enhance his own fame. What is worse, he feels empty, inauthentic, cut off from other people. Separated from his Parisian wife, he has custody of a seven-year-old French-speaking son who rebuffs his overtures of intimacy.

By returning to Chile, Mañungo hopes to rebuild an authentic self. He hopes, as Donoso puts it, to "transformarse en otro" (13). To do this, he must revisit the sources of his creative power and renew contact with his maternal demons. He must return, at least metaphorically, to the remote Southern island of Chiloé, where a tidal wave killed his mother and where a teacher named Ulda initiated him in music and in love. And he must listen once more to what chilotes call "la voz de la vieja," the breakers on the island's western shore, and reboard the Caleuche, or magic ship of art. According to Donoso's interpretation, this charmed vessel, whose name means "gente transformada," bears witches and artists off to immortality and allows them to change themselves into whatever they desire.

In the first night and day, Mañungo spends wandering Santiago's streets he enacts a symbolic journey to Chiloé—and to hell. He arrives in Chile to find that Matilde Neruda has just died. He attends her wake; escorts a woman friend Judit on a mission of revenge during the curfew hours; and tries to avert the death of an alcoholic named Lopito. By the time the novel ends, he has entered genuinely into the sorrows of Chileans who have stayed at home, and in the final scene he strides toward Fausta, an older female artist (and, at that moment, an incarnation of his bruja/madre), his face "dolorosamente cambiado" (329).

Transformed he is. And Donoso tells us this is so by depicting him, as the book ends, as the father in a family group. Paired with Judit, he carries piggy-back Lopito's orphaned daughter, while his own son and Judit's daughter press around his legs for his attention. Passersbys assume that Fausta is the children's grandmother. Mañungo's initial isolation has given way, at least for the moment, to the sense of belonging and purpose that a family provides. Littín, too, as he re-experiences his homeland, gradually reinserts himself into his family. During his first days back he crosses paths with his mother-in-law and his wife's aunt in the street, and does not dare identify himself to them. But as he regains his bearings, he resumes more and more his identity as "hijo de Hernán y Cristina," and the book's most moving scene describes his surprise visit to his mother. The re-establishment of family, then, figures in both books as the exile's most significant way of engaging with an interrupted past. This is a second point in which the works coincide.

The motif of the returning exile as a false self to be transformed, and that of the family as metaphor for community refound, stand out in both books. One might think that this coincidence is fortuitous. After all, Littín had to disguise himself to avoid being jailed, and Donoso's novels all use metamorphosis as a central theme. As for reunion with family, surely any returnee would try to reknit family ties. Yet both motifs offer cogent metaphors for experiences repatriots must commonly have. Beyond the facile notion that an exiled self is a false self, it must be true that anyone who has made a life outside Chile feels more than logistical dislocation at moving back. The relationships, habits and tastes that help build a self alter sharply when an exile returns home. People act—and *are*—different in different milieux. It is plausible that any Chilean returning to his homeland would feel estrangement from the person he has come to be. The other motif, the portrayal of family remade, refers not just to the exile's literal reunion with relatives, but to his reinvolvement with other people. Exile enforces isolation of many kinds. Not only does it excise a person from his cultural and professional world, but it creates psychological pressures that work against intimacy.

Despite these parallels, the books, as I have said, give different impressions of the experience of return, and of Chile itself at that particular moment. Littín's return is a victory; "Littín vino, filmó y se fue," one subheading reads (122). After all, he managed to film all over Chile, even inside the Moneda Palace, and escape to tell the tale. His story, as García Márquez' title confirms, is an adventure, filled like any spy thriller with justified paranoia, danger narrowly escaped and humor when terror is dispelled. Donoso's novel chronicles failure, not triumph. It exposes the psychological harm done to Chileans, both those who fled and those who stayed at home. Donoso's characters are all in some way monstrous. (One, the proletarian Don César, is literally a half-man, who pushes his legless trunk along on a skateboard.) They lead straitened lives in a world where politics has become the only legitimate area of concern. Prey to guilt and the self-destructiveness it inspires, they fail in human relationships and in their creative lives. Judit, for example, denies herself pleasure out of guilt. A member of an aristocratic family, she has been spared rape at the hands of a jailer, while her friends suffered violation in nearby cells. Bent on avenging herself on some Holofernes of the regime, she breaks curfew to seduce and kill the man who pardoned her, but in the end only shoots a small white bitch beset by male dogs. Her act, a symbolic suicide, only partially expiates her guilt at being a child of privilege. She cannot let herself love or be loved by Mañungo. Lopito, her repulsive, alcoholic friend, fails as poet, husband and father, and engineers his own death at the hands of the carabineri.

As portraits of Chile's internal resistance to Pinochet, the books differ sharply. Littín asserts that a cult of Allende exists among the Chilean lower and lower-middle classes. And he glorifies what he perceives as a unified left. His success in mobilizing, on very short notice, six film crews of Chileans to work clandestinely, must have helped to convince him that his underground contacts formed an efficient network of dissenters. They even secured for him an interview with Fernando Larenas Seguel, leader of the guerrilla movement the Frente Patriótico Manuel Rodríguez. Donoso, in contrast, does not idealize the left. He depicts the petty factionalism of a fragmented resistance, who bicker over the staging of Matilde Neruda's funeral and the disposition of Neruda's papers. His view of Neruda, too, is less one-sidedly favorable than is Littín's; he reminds us that Neruda played an unsavory role in the assassination of Trotsky. Yet Donoso recognizes the poet as a hero of the ludic imagination. Neruda, he tells us, succeeded where the Chileans of *La desesperanza* fail, at nurturing his own private sensibility.

It is the private self that Donoso champions, against ideologies of all stripes. He commends each Chilean, exile and non-exile alike, to his/her own past as a way of repairing a broken individual life. The imagery of his book portrays *social* change as an uncontrolled natural force, an "huracán de olas colosales" (123) that each person weathers as best he can. The best way to breast the wave, he seems to suggest, is by setting sail in the Caleuche, the ship of art. *La desesperanza* brings home Donoso's point, for it is the sheer fictive grace of the book's last scene that redeems the characters and gives the reader a momentary reprieve from the rational. García Márquez, in contrast, although he writes the story of one man, presents Chile as a people waiting to reassert its public will. His book is polemic, meant to inform the reader about Chile and rally him/her to a collective recovery of a national paradise lost. It is this difference—ultimately a difference in political stance between a liberal and a Marxist—that most sets the books apart.

Either book could be accused of giving only a partial view. Donoso sidesteps the need for action in the political realm, while García Márquez idealizes too much Allende's government. Both books, though, are worth reading seriously as portrayals of a Chile that is now in the process of reconstructing itself.

[1] Jacobo Timerman, *Chile: El galope muerto* (Buenos Aires: Planeta, 1988): 29.

[2] Cynthia G. Brown, *Chile Since the Coup: Ten years of Repression* (New York: Americas Watch Committee, 1983): 89.

[3] Stephen Rickard and Cynthia Brown, in consultation with Alfred Stepan, *Chile: Human Rights and the Plebiscite* (New York: Americas Watch Committee, 1988): 92.

[4] Shirley Christian, "Chile Ends Exile of Allende Family," *New York Times* 2 Sept. 1988, national ed.: A1, A4.

[5] Gabriel García Márquez, *La aventura de Miguel Littín clandestino en*

Chile (Buenos Aires: Sudamericana, 1986); page references will be given in the text.

[6]José Donoso, *La desesperanza* (Barcelona: Seix Barral, 1986); page references will be given in text.

A Satiric Perspective on the Experience of Exile in the Short Fiction of Cristina Peri Rossi

Cynthia A. Schmidt

Cristina Peri Rossi's work was already well-known in her native Uruguay when she went into exile in Spain in 1972. Her years in exile have been highly productive. In addition to literary translations and journalistic writing, she has published four volumes of poetry, five collections of short stories and two novels. If we were to single out a common thematic thread unifying her works before and after exile, it could be her criticism of oppressive social structures. CPR explains the sense of continuity in her writings: "Escribo contra la realidad. Empecé a hacerlo porque la realidad que veía a mi alrededor—en mi casa, primero; luego en mi país— no me gustaba. Y sigo escribiendo, me parece, por la misma razón ... En este sentido, poco importa cuál sea la realidad geográfica."[1]

Exile, a reality which CPR has been forced to experience, is a frequent target of her satiric vision of social ills. Two highly imaginative short stories, "La tarde del dinosaurio" and "La influencia de Edgar A. Poe en la poesía de Raimundo Arias" focus on the psychological trauma and social margination of the Uruguayans who were ideologically opposed to the military coup of 1973. The former is about exile within the limits of the country, while the latter tells a tale of extraterritorial exile. Imagination, fantasy, a keen sense of the absurd, irony and humor all come into play in CPR's vision of a reality which is other than the desired. In these stories, as in all of CPR's fiction, allegory serves as a structuring principle, linking the singular case to its abstract, universal meaning.

Both stories recount the events from the perspective of a child, and in both cases the loser of the local "war" is the child's father, represented as a worn-out small-time intellectual. No one escapes the critical vision—both the victors and the defeated are demystified. Far from attempting to detail a sweeping portrait of the Southern Cone diáspora, Peri Rossi's families are at once a microcosm of Uruguayan society and human society. Social catastrophe is interpreted in individual terms—defeat in politics is equated to loss in love, and loss of social esteem is reflected in the lucid uncompromising scrutiny of a young son or daughter.

"La tarde del dinosaurio" encompasses multiple levels of reading. On the literal level it is the story of a child of divorce who lives with his remarried mother and stepfather. The child feels sympathy for his real father, a social misfit, and resents his adoptive father, a highly successful businessman. Within this reading, the child's recurring nightmares of a huge brontosaurus can be interpreted as the result of the anguish and confusion caused by his family situation. On an allegorical level, the story depicts the fissures within Uruguayan society created by repressive military rule. The broken and re-formed family represents Uruguay after the coup of 1973. The natural father and the adoptive father are metaphors for the state, the mother embodies Uruguayan civil society and the child is at once the innocent victim of the fractured country and its future. Within the double articulation of the allegory, the regional situation is a reflection of Peri Rossi's vision of the human condition, permeated with millenary fears brought on by our own irrationality. My analysis will focus on how the story blends historical fact and free imagination to depict the alienating effect of social upheaval in Uruguay.

The narrator provides a brief historical allusion to account for the contrasting lifestyle of his two fathers: "ellos habían tenido ... una guerra pequeña, no de las grandes guerras internacionales, ... una guerra dentro de los límites del país, pero guerra al fin" (84)[2]. This reference undoubtedly corresponds to the period immediately before the coup when the Tupamaros assassinated several government officials, and President Bordaberry responded by declaring "internal war."[3] The narrator tells us the results of the war: "De la guerra había surgido un sentimiento de seguridad para unos y un sentimiento de inseguridad para otros"(84).

The boy's real father, to whom he refers as Father no. 1, is one of those who suffered adverse effects from the internal war. Father no. 1's situation and personal characteristics seem to parallel the liberal faction of the constitutional government in exile. The son's observation: "Le era muy difícil no preocuparse por todos los hombres y mujeres que encontraba en su camino"(98) hints at the socialist concept of a welfare-oriented polity. Father no. 1 lives in a state of internal exile. The child's description of him reveals both the causes and effect of his failure. Besides having lost the custody of his child, he is nearly indigent, and the reader is first introduced to him in terms of lack: "—¿No tendrás un cigarrillo para darme?—le había pedido su padre, el primero, el que no tenía oficina, ni casa en la ciudad, ni otra casa en el mar o en la montaña, ni auto propio, ni tenía televisor ni nevera ni mocasines de piel ni cigarrillos ni nada"(82).

This father is a journalist. One day he decides to show his articles to his son, but he has to look in drawers of unmatched socks and other unlikely places to gather them together. The articles run a gamut of topics from growing roses to sailing to instructions for preparing a delicious rice pudding. The narrator reflects: "Se ve que su padre era un tipo muy capaz. De escribir cualquier cosa"(85). In reality, he had never planted roses, he was afraid to sail and he hated rice. Despite the shortcomings he recognizes in Father no. 1, the child feels genuine sympathy for this tender and inept fellow: "Era más amable y más suave, vivía dando explicaciones de todo. A él le parecía que las explicaciones las usaba para sí mismo, porque le debía resultar muy complicado vivir"(84). Although kind-hearted and well-meaning, Father no. 1 is too weak, too reflective, and too beaten-down by life's problems to try to take control. He prefers to make peace. Thus, Father no. 1 echoes the bankrupt liberal faction which proved itself incapable of overcoming Uruguay's economic crisis and lost the capacity to articulate an alternative political response.[4] Although it produced convincing rhetoric, it could not systematize a program and put its words into action.

Father no. 2, his mother's second husband and a winner of the war, represents the military dictatorship. He is depicted as if he were part of the *Junta de Comandantes*, the self-proclaimed builders of the nation: "Tenía una oficina toda para él. Parece que no se trataba de un empleado cualquiera, sino de un patrón algo así. Daba órdenes por un dictáfono y le mostraba la oficina como si toda fuera suya, como si él mismo, con gran esfuerzo, hubiera colocado piedra sobre piedra, ladrillo sobre ladrillo ... "(82). The most salient characteristic of Father no. 2 is his authoritarianism: "daba órdenes con la aparente seguridad de que sus órdenes respondían íntimamente a los deseos ajenos"(85).

Peri Rossi's satiric picture of the military regime's vision of the future finds its symbol in "la máquina." Father no. 2 insists his son accompany him to the office to admire "el último modelo de calculadora que hemos adquirido"(89), which the father proclaims to be "símbolo del futuro, símbolo de la unidad familiar, símbolo de esfuerzo y del genio del hombre"(94). When the father exhorts the child to think up an appropriate name for the machine, the boy reflects on its meaning: "la máquina parecía ... un soldado que sólo cumplía órdenes, sin discutir, sin pensar, ... un soldado exento de reflexión, pero adoctrinado, programado, útil para servir y para callar. Obediencia." *Obediencia* thus encapsulates Peri Rossi's vision of the regimes' plan for its citizenry. The machine represents its impersonal and alienating rule as well as the sterile and unimaginative future to be created in a country where intellectuals were considered subversives, and the most talented and creative people were censored, imprisoned, tortured and exiled.

Although he has two fathers, the boy continues to have only one mother. The mother resembles Uruguayan civil society, weak and subordinated to a paternalistic state. His mother married young, and later found she was married to "un loco." The way the child refers to her seems to disclose an attitude between resentment and resigned disgust: "su madre. O sea la esposa de su padre, que ya no era su esposa, aunque seguía siendo su madre. ¿Por qué uno no podía divorciarse de las madres, como había hecho su padre?"(83). Even though he disapproves of her fickle behavior he cannot disown his mother, just as one cannot disown the people of one's country. She is the average Uruguayan who initially supported the Left's demands for a restructuring of the economy to later reject them in favor of middle-class security. Turning against the liberal factions and succumbing to the military's gradual take-over, this sector acquiesced to the erosion and destruction of the constitutional government.

The boy is the country's youth who must grow up under the dictatorship and will inherit its legacy. He embodies the tension of living in a country divided by a civil war: he retains a feeling of loyalty to his real father, but he must live with and obey his adoptive father, the man his mother married. The boy's haunting oneiric vision—his recurring dream of a dinosaur emerging from the waters—is a pervasive and enigmatic symbol. When the monster first appears, the boy is afraid of it, but it gradually becomes familiar: "Se acostumbró a verlo aparecer, a nombrarlo, a caminar con él por las calles, a tenerlo por compañero y amigo. ... Dino, monstruo ingenuo, y familiar" (99–100). The boy is aware that one day the dream creature will burst into his waking life and carry out the terrible threat of his dreams. When this happens, he realizes he must mediate between the dinosaur and the other people: "Su tarea consistía en detenerlo. Apaciguarlo. Domesticarlo. Evitar la destrucción. ... También debía impedir que alguien lo matara al descubrirlo"(110).

The story draws to a close as the child witnesses the portentous emergence of the huge brontosaurus from the sea. It walks like a baby trying out its first steps in a fragile, watery territory. It looks toward the house and calls out "¡Papá!" In this final cry for help, for recognition or of warning, we realize the child has fused with his oneiric vision. This dinosaur is a paradoxical creature: he is baby-like but prehistoric, fearful yet familiar. He opposes Father no. 2's vision of the future as a supercomputer—the irruption of this irrational nightmare was not calculated in Father no. 2's meticulous plans for obedience, order and progress.

Explaining her use of nightmarish landscape, Peri Rossi provides important clues for the meaning of this symbol: "[S]omething I have felt most of my life [is] hallucination, the paranoic hallucination of persecution is a way of interpreting and understanding the world. ... For me literature is a vision, a creation of symbols to interpret and understand reality. This reality is nightmarish not only ... because, for instance in Argentina thirty thousand people have disappeared and one out of five Uruguayans have suffered cruel torture and persecution, but also because when it is not the military, the totalitarian regime in power, who persecute us, there often remain our internal phantoms, our own hallucinations."[5]

With the insight afforded by this statement, we can see Dino as an oneiric representation of paranoia of persecution at both a personal and political level. The prehistoric dinosaur represents the repressed horror at the torture and abuse of the regime which had accumulated gradually behind the boy's submissive daytime facade. The dinosaur is the revelation of the future, suggesting an apocalypse when the youth rise up against the absurd and alienating structures of the military dictatorship.

"La influencia de Edgar A. Poe en la poesía de Raimundo Arias" deals with the trials of extraterritorial exile. The story is centered around a father and his young daughter who go into exile after the father is accused of professing "la fe marxista-leninista." The mother had left them previously to join the guerillas. These characters do not correspond to specific political entities as in "La tarde" but rather represent the plight of exile in general.

The story develops through constant shifts between the two spaces created by the experience of exile: the "here and now" as opposed to the "over there and then." The "here and now" is a European country, unnamed, but obviously Spain. The father returns home after a hard day trying to sell *jabones-Maravilla* in the streets of a bustling city. His daughter, Alicia, informs him that they have no money. Continuing what seems to be a daily ritual for the pair, the father studies his address book and admits there is no one they can ask for money. The story ends as Alicia, dressed as a Charrúa Indian, goes out the door to beg for money in the streets.

This story line is constantly interrupted with extended flashbacks relating the experiences of the father and daughter in their country of origin, their ocean voyage and their arrival.

The "over there and then" is their non-European country where there was a revolution. Paradoxically, an element of differentiation between the country of origin and the country of refuge, according to Alicia, is their common language: "Ella comió ... pan con mantequilla y mermelada de melocotón, que era como en este país llamaban a los duraznos. ... las frutillas eran fresas, en el país donde habían decidido ir, por hablar el mismo idioma." (51)

The characters' displacement results in disorientation, humiliation and loss of identity. The humiliation of the father is a leitmotif of the story. Life seems to be nothing but a series of indignities for him, in his own country as well as in the country of refuge, and in his relations with both his wife and his pre-adolescent daughter. In Europe, the humiliation begins at the moment of disembarkment: "nadie les recibió, mas bien fueron mal-recibidos"(48). The narrator provides an endless list of all the documents they were required to present. An absurd situation is created when the Spanish functionary insists the presence of the mother is necessary in order for the girl to enter the country: "—Deberá venir la madre a confirmar que la niña es fruto del matrimonio con usted—... Usted puede ser un delincuente, un raptor, un violador de menores, y esta niña, su rehén"(49–50). They decide to perform a blood test to verify his paternity. Here we see a literal translation of the figurative expression as the Spanish authorities extract blood from the father-daughter couple: "un cuarto de litro de sangre más de lo necesario, como se hacía con los extranjeros, porque eran extranjeros" (50). In exile, the father suffers daily humiliation to survive as he fights his way down the jammed sidewalks, peddling soap.

The indignity he suffers in exile is a variation of that which he experienced in his own country. Through the contrast between the father, a literary critic and would-be novelist, and his revolutionary wife, Peri Rossi satirizes the perceived superfluousness of the academic at a time of political upheaval. The title of the story is a paper the father is writing. He runs into his wife's sister, a screen for a clandestine revolutionary group, in a grocery store. He is attracted to her and would have liked to show her his paper, but he tells himself "ella no tenía tiempo para esas cosas." As if to confirm the father's imagined belittlement in the eyes of his sister-in-law, the reader is given access to her thoughts: "Ella pensó que era una lástima que él fuera un intelectual pequeño-burgués, tal como le había dicho su hermana antes de abandonarlo"(46). He was working on a novel about the revolution at the time his wife joined the guerilla.

Heaped upon his feelings of disparagement as an intellectual, is his sexual emasculation. To cover up when his wife goes underground, they say she went to Czechoslovakia with another man; thus he meekly assumes the public image of a man betrayed by his wife. We note the reversal between the traditional male and female roles—when she becomes a warrior, he must become the caregiver for their daughter. It seems he is ill-equipped for violent tasks: when they are taking his blood for the paternity test in Spain, he faints as he always does when he sees blood. At this moment he recalls his wife's admonition: "Así no se puede hacer la revolución"(50).

Finally, he must endure disapproval from his young daughter. He is expulsed from the country for having written "artículos que eran verdaderos panegíricos a la turba guerrillera que pretendía socavar la patria y el prestigio de las instituciones nacionales. Muy dignamente asió a su hija de la mano—no soy objeto, para que me lleves en brazos, dijo ella—"(47). Precisely in the moment when he wanted desperately to summon up all his self-respect, he is forced to face insubordination from a child. The reader does not fail to see the irony of the dangerous subversive intentions the government attributes to a man who is seen as a useless intellectual by his wife and sister-in-law. At the moment of disembarkment, Alicia observes that no one has come to meet them, to which the father replies, "Bien sabes que no soy un jugador de fútbol." Alicia looks at her father's skinny legs in his only pair of pants, "y reflexionó que como hija no había tenido demasiado suerte"(47–48).

With the repatriation comes a loss of identity. On one hand, the father and daughter feel isolated from and misunderstood by the Europeans, and, on the other, their presence in Europe makes them aware of their lack of knowledge regarding their own cultural heritage. As Alicia dons her Indian costume, the father and daughter realize how little they know about their country's original inhabitants because they were destroyed by the Spaniards and reelaborated by Hollywood. Alicia's disguise is a creative and cynical solution to their economic problems. In order to survive in this hostile land, she exploits the Europeans' ignorance regarding Latin America, projecting a false image of an indigenous population which bears correspondence to neither the reality of her country nor her own cultural identity.

The transition between the home land and the country of refuge —the sea voyage—creates a third space, both in the surface of the narrative and in psychic dimensions. This passage is characterized by loss, symbolized by the loss of time as they sail from west to east. Alicia is incensed by the fact that they have stolen four hours from her. She imagines traffickers in stolen time: "Pensó en barcos … que atravesaban el mar con su carga secreta de tiempo … robado … a involuntarios emigrados, como su padre y ella"(53). Her image creates a metaphor for the exiles' divestment of their inalienable rights. "—Putaquelosparió a los barcos—" Alicia cries out. This emotional outburst expresses her feeling of impotence in the face of cosmic injustice. Her father does not know how to comfort her about the lost time, nor has he any consolation for the even greater injustices of which he has been victim: "le habían robado mucho más de cuatro horas, y no había podido hacer casi nada para cambiar el orden de las cosas"(52).

In the new country, Alicia becomes her father's parent. She assumes control and treats him like a child, and he, in turn, behaves childishly and is submissive to her. The role reversal symbolizes the overwhelming psychological effects of exile. So debilitating is the exile, and so incapable is the father of reconciling himself to it and facing up to the continual humiliation that he experiences infantile regression. The shock of violent times and sudden change has had the opposite effect on Alicia, causing her to mature overnight.

The father attributes his daughter's resilience and ingenuity to the idea that her generation is a new breed: "Esta era otra raza, provista de una singular resistencia … habían asimilado las enseñanzas de íntimas, oscurísimas derrotas … Concebidas en noches amargas"(58–59). However, since Peri Rossi's vision of a disharmonious and fractured world allows for no heroes, Alicia's final words serve to demystify this elevated vision of the country's youth: "—Estoy segura de que lo que piensas acerca de nuestra generación es completamente falso"(59).

In these stories, CPR uses free imagination to dramatize the dehumanizing effects of civil war, the implantation of an authoritarian regime and exile. In addition to her criticism of the practices of the military regime, CPR implicates the reasons why liberal intellectuals—persons like herself—failed to prevent the military take-over and had to go into exile. The self-mockery we glimpse behind the satirization of tired, impotent journalists and literary critics allows no room for self-indulgent pity. The unrelenting and unforgiving child observer will accept no justification or rationalization for this failure. CPR's intuitive creatures, surely first cousins to the child who cried out, "The emperor has no clothes on," do not hesitate to expose the perversity and falsehood which surrounds them. Their creative and unexpected self-transformations serve to both defy and parody the alienating structures of which they are victims. While the ominous dinosaur is a paranoic response to life under the dictatorship, Alicia's Indian disguise calls attention to the humiliation and incomprehension which the Latin American exiles must endure in Europe.

[1]Interview with Ana Basualdo, "Cristina Peri Rossi: Apocalipsis y paraíso," *El Viejo topo* 56 (1981): 48.

[2]Cristina Peri Rossi, *La tarde del dinosauro* (Barcelona: Plaza & Janés, 1985). Page numbers following all quotations from the stories correspond to this edition.

[3]Martin Weinstein, *Uruguay. Democracy at the Crossroads* (Boulder: Westview Press, 1988): 41.

[4]Ibid, 47–49

[5]Psiche Hughes, "Interview with Cristina Peri Rossi," *Unheard Words.* Mineke Schipper, ed. (New York: Allison & Busby, 1984): 267–68.

Women Poets of the Cuban Diaspora: Exile and the Self

María A. Salgado

Exile, both external and internal, is a constant in Cuban poetry. This theme acquired its most salient features during the struggle for Cuban Independence, when José Martí (1853–1895) wrote from the distant asylum provided by other countries in the hemisphere (particularly the US), and Julián del Casal (1863–1893) without leaving Cuba, took refuge in a poetic world of his own making.[1] The historical forces of colonialism that had shaped the destiny of those two poets continued to shape the fate of future generations bringing about an almost uninterrupted succession of exiles, culminating with Fidel Castro's 1959 Revolution. This Revolution resulted in the latest Cuban Diaspora, when it sent into exile the two generations of poets whose works are the topic of this paper.

As it had happened so often in the past, for the Generation of the 1950s (also known as the First Generation of the Cuban Revolution), the tensions inherent in the most recent political upheaval led to a tragic confrontation between politics and poetry. The result was a split in this generation that has caused the exile and nostalgia of those who left and the alignment with the regime (or the escapism) of those who remained behind. A similar break occurred with the members of the "Second Generation," also known as the "Novísimos" or as the "Generation of 1966."[2] In the following pages, I want to examine the poetry written by the women poets of these two generations of the latest Cuban Diaspora, paying special attention to the way the exile experience may have influenced their portrayal of themselves and their surroundings. However, before beginning, I want to make some brief comments about the place of these authors in the general context of Cuban letters.

In the 1950s, Cuban poetry was still dominated by the aesthetic currents of the 1930s, propagated in the island in part through the visits of two masterful Spanish poets: Juan Ramón Jiménez (1881–1958) and Federico García Lorca (1898–1936), two of the main proponents of *poesía pura* and the currents of *vanguardismo* in Hispanic letters. These trends were to predominate in the poetry of some of Cuba's great poets writing from the 30s through the 50s:

Mariano Brull (1891–1956), Dulce María Loynaz (1903), Eugenio Florit (1903), Emilio Ballagas (1908–1954), as well as José Lezama Lima (1910–1976) and the younger "Orígenes" group. However, side by side with these purely aesthetic trends, there was a strong undercurrent of social poetry, both in its *negrista* or afro variety, popularized by Nicolás Guillén (1902-1989), and in its more "revolutionarily" committed aspect, that is, a poetry slanted towards denunciation of imperialism and the exploitation of the proletariat, a trend introduced by Regino Pedroso (1896–1983) and Manuel Navarro Luna (1894–1966).[3] Since Castro's Revolution,[4] socially committed poetry has come to the fore. However, a number of women poets have not forgotten the artistic lessons learned from the great poets of the past.[5]

The type of "elitist" aesthetic tenets most clearly aligned with the metaphysical quests of pure poetry—favored by Juan Ramón Jiménez and the Cuban poets who fell under his influence—are evident in the verses of most women poets of the Cuban Diaspora.[6] The poems of Amelia del Castillo (1925) are representative. They express her anxiety at the lack of answers confronted by modern men and women. In the poem "Sola," the images used to portray the anguish of the poetic persona reveal her alienating disconcertment:

> Sola junto al abismo de mi misma,
> inquieta. (...)
> Sola con mi yo turbio.
> Barca sin rumbos en la herida abierta;
> sendero sin orillas, horizonte sin cielo,
> gusto amargo de fiesta ... [7]

In other poems, however, instead of disconcertment there is a hopeful ontological quest for union with the forces of nature. This sense of pantheistic fulfillment is evident in the poetic persona of "Yo":

> Yo soy la dura piedra de granito
> suave al capricho de la gota de agua;
> Y soy amor y manantial y fragua (...)
> donde se forjan sueños de infinito. (PC 20)

A similar search for reintegration is expressed in the lines of "Tránsito y regreso," a text in which the poetic voice identifies itself with the world of nature and longs to be reborn with it:

> Una paloma, un árbol, un camino;
> alas y mar surcando el horizonte.

> Frescor de valle, plenitud de monte,
> sueño de palma acariciando el pino. (...)
> Y renacer en cada primavera
> como la planta que dormida espera
> un nuevo germinar de su semilla. (PC 21)

It is hardly surprising to find out that this subjective poetry, clearly of metaphysical vein, does not treat the topic of exile through obvious references to the Cuban landscape or to specific circumstances of the 1959 Revolution.[8] Rather, it is presented in the ontological terms of the exile suffered by every human being.[9] Perhaps the poem in which Castillo best captures these feelings is the *romance* "Peregrina." As its title clearly indicates, the poem uses the motif of the pilgrimage—entwined with two other well-known motifs (life is a dream and the labyrinth)—to elaborate the author's growing concerns with the lack of answers to her urgent questions. The poem is a pilgrimage through times past:

> He dormido mis sueños en tu arena
> y se aleja tu arena de mis playas ...
> Voy errante, desnuda de raíces,
> perdida en laberinto de añoranzas. (PC 24)

Castillo does not find an answer in this poem. However, her words suggest that she does not despair. On the contrary, she continues her search; she even intimates that her own poetry is the means of shaping her nostalgia and defining her hopes:

> Dame un punto de luz y de horizonte
> para soñar los sueños que me faltan ...
> Déjame luego hacer con hilos tuyos
> una verde madeja de esperanzas. (PC 24)

Rita Geada (1934) is another poet who writes of the doubts that concern modern humanity, trapped in a world in which the old answers are no longer valid. A world, where, as she says in one of her poems, history is a lie: "Con mentiras se escribe la historia / mientras la verdad es manca."[10] Geada suggests that egotism and misunderstanding have stripped of meaning the old myths—yet the myths are essential for providing hope and security for mankind. The void created by the destruction of those myths has left modern humanity adrift:

> No más paraíso traicionado.
> No más engañoso reflejo en la milenaria caverna.
> No más sombra vana de lo que fue,
> de lo que ha sido,
> de lo que no volverá. (LUPC 385)

An equally hopeless bewilderment (she calls it here "la posible resurrección de la nada en su tronco seco," LUPC 385), appears in "doblemente desterrados." In this poem, a dismayed Geada, speaks of the uselessness of individual efforts to change history ("¿Hasta cuándo dar manotazos inútiles en el aire?," LUPC 386). While in the poem "Esta nueva Babel" she complains of the inefficiency of dialogue; that is, she explains that after centuries of being used for lying, everyday language has been destroyed, thus, "para poder hablar con lenguaje de hermanos" it will be necessary to move to another dimension (LUPC 390).

Rita Geada's idyllic portrayal of the past suggests that her negative vision of the present is due to the traumatic destruction of the world of her childhood and adolescence in Cuba. The poem "Era cuando todo nos llamaba" describes those happy days of internal and external harmony.

> Intacto entonces aquel árbol
> de infinitas respuestas (...)
> Era el verdor, el mar,
> La Isla de mágicos atardeceres.
> El Universo en mí, en mí creciendo.
> Era lo inefable.
> Era el amor en todo (LUPC 387)

The present, however, is only ruins and desolation:

> Los mitos yacentes bajo los escombros
> de esta nueva Babel que nos circunda. (...)
> cuando le queda al hombre
> tan escaso tiempo
> para reafirmar su identidad humana. (LUPC 388–89)

Geada's alienation from the present is a reflection of her own self alienation. "Yo soy" reveals the perplexity of the poetic persona. She describes herself in images such as "La de asombros blancos y mariposas," "Ave extraviada en playas desconocidas," and "interrogante muda / que aún no ha hallado su respuesta," and projects an aimless future for herself, "cuando desterrada de las verdes orillas / y de los vastos mirages / el mundo sea mi ruta de sombras" (PC 30).

Similar feelings are expressed by other members of the First Generation of the Cuban Diaspora. Mercedes Cortázar (1940) speaks of being "extranjera / en este mundo de las formas" (LUPC 503) and of cities where children "tratan de ocultar con sus juegos / la próxima hora de espanto" (LUPC 502); Lourdes Gómez Franca (1933) mourns her past in images of an interior landscape in which "mueren las huellas / de [su] adolescencia."[11] Ana Rosa Núñez (1926) complains that "No hay forma de escapar a la respuesta / o lo que es peor, a la pregunta" (LUPC 169); Yolanda Ortal (1940) portrays her frustration at the contemporary lack of values by saying that "estamos anclados / en un mar de aguas absurdamente inmóviles" (LUPC 454), and that her soul is "Mecánica y absurdamenta insertada / en el engranaje preciso y exacto / de una existencia sin razón, ni por qué ni luz" (LUPC 456); Martha A. Padilla (1934) protests against the present, while rebelling against her own passivity: "Este momento es mísero / No abunda ni el pregón de un níquel dócil / Estoy contra la cal de cien paredes / Estoy arrepentida de ser mansa / De escurrirme entre grietas como un lince" (LUPC 376). Pura del Prado (1931) comforts herself thinking that historical circumstances are transitory and time will restore the old harmony: "La Isla estará invictamenta viva, / aunque faltemos. / Sobrevivirá a los derrumbes históricos" (LUPC 285). Mireya Robles (1936) recognizes her own futility and speaks of being ready to "emprender / [sus] caminos de ausencia," since God has already prepared her "para la nada" (LUPC 354). Teresa María Rojas (1938), whose poems are not totally devoid of hope, also speaks of an uncertain future in which "Gimiendo la eternidad / viene a morirse en el glóbulo / lácteo de mis senos ... " (LUPC 337). Although Nivaria Tejera (1930) has written some poems steeped in Revolutionary fervor,[12] she also echoes the pervasive negativism of her generation when she speaks of a humanity in which "Cada hombre lleva dentro de sí mismo / Un perro solitario que erra y que gime sin detenerse nunca / Un perro que muerde la luna y come estrellas y se nutre de esta nada."[13]

As mentioned at the beginning of this study, the poets of the Second Generation—Belkis Cuza Malé (1942), Dolores Prida (1943) and Isel Rivero (1941)—were faced with the same ideological choices confronted by their predecessors, but their poems project an even more bitter and pessimistic vision of themselves and modern society. However, this pessimistic strain was present in the poems they wrote while in Cuba, a fact that suggests that their dissatisfaction cannot be solely ascribed to the disillusionment brought about by political exile. Rather, it appears to be caused by deep metaphysical anguish. Cuza Malé's cynicism is evident in her attacks on the mechanization rampant in the modern world. In "Están haciendo una muchacha para la época" she describes the mass-production of woman in a consumer society. The new woman, made out of "alambres, cabelleras postizas, / senos de algodón y armazón de madera," is expected to fill "los requisitos de una aeromoza" and "liber[ar] su sexo / sin dar un mal paso con un hombre."[14] Dolores Prida is specific in her references to physical exile and its concomitant alienation. "Verano en Nueva York" speaks of aimless wanderings over the streets of a stifling urban scene:

> Traigo las suelas manchadas
> de pavimento remendado.
> Traigo la risa deshojada
> en un ramo de papeles viejos
> para espantarme las moscas de la cara. (LUPC 536)

Isel Rivero's poems are even more anguished. "Presente" is characteristic. In this poem she describes a world ruled by chance ("Cara o escudo / la moneda da vueltas"), in which death and destruction reign supreme: "Mañana nos ajusticiarán; / Tanta sangre envolverá el pavimento / que tus pies resbalaran si no son muy diestros" (PC 83). And in "Subyugación de la palabra" she suggests the impotence of communication with potent images:

> Claveteo mi lengua sobre el escritorio:
> dos gotas de esperma (...)
> Al bajar la dulce cortina
> estoy muerta sobre el piso.
> Mañana es ya de noche. (PC 84)

To conclude, alienation of self is one of the major themes of the poetry of the women writers of the Cuban Diaspora. The alienation and anguish that permeates their poems is, to a large extent, the result of the trauma of physical and metaphysical exile. These poets are aware that they have ceased to be part of Cuban history and that their poems, written in a foreign culture, are no longer part of Cuban literature. They know, that at present, they are only an anomalous curiosity: one among the several marginal and marginated Hispanic groups living and writing in the US. However, their circumstances may not be as isolated as it may first appear: Hispanic literature in the US is growing rapidly and, additionally, these poets' alienation from themselves and their surroundings may be seen as metaphoric of the plight of modern humanity— isolated and lost in a world whose purpose few seem to understand. From this perspective, the situation of the writers of the Cuban Diaspora (whether male or female) is symptomatic of the human condition. Their poetry has come to address today's universal malaise in terms that can be understood by all, thus widening the thematic and formal boundaries of contemporary Hispanic letters.

[1]I speak here of the physical condition of exile. By and large, Martí and the many other poets whose ideology forced them to live away from Cuba, have written poems addressing their political beliefs while creating nostalgic, idealized internal images of their homeland. On the other hand, Casal and most of the poets who remained in Cuba, while at odds with the regime, have escaped into imaginative poetic worlds and have avoided any references to their historical or political circumstances.

[2]I base my definition of the First and Second Generations of the Cuban Revolution on Eduardo López Morales' prologue to *La generación de los años 50*. [Eds. Luis Suardíaz and David Chericián (La Habana: Letras Cubanas, 1989)]. For him, the members of the First (the "Generation of the 50s" of the title) were born between 1924 and 1940, and those of the Second, between 1941 and 1955. Other critics use the same dates, but differ in the names by which they identify the Second Generation: Giuseppe Bellini [*Historia de la literatura hispanoamericana* (Madrid: Castalia, 1985)] calls them "los Novísimos," 489, and Julio E. Miranda [*Nueva literatura cubana* (Madrid: Taurus 1971)] "Generación del 66," 53.

[3]José Antonio Pontuondo, *El contenido social de la literatura cubana* (México, DF: El Colegio de México): 76–78

[4]In order to better define the "Generation of 1950," López Morales resorts to renaming it "primera promoción poética de la Revolución" (7), basing the new name on the fact that what characterizes this group is its subordination of subjectivism and aesthetism to civic concerns. López Morales also explains that within Cuba every writer has confronted and accepted the Marxist-Leninist reality of their historical circumstances (36).

[5]In two studies of the women poets of these two generations, who have remained in Cuba, I have verified their adherence to traditional poetic trends. The verses of the four women members of the Generation of the 50s prove conclusively that they favor aestheticism over civic concerns. (See my article "En torno a la expresión poética femenina de la Generación de los años 50 en Cuba," *Confluencia* 3.1 [Fall,1987]: 13–21). The six members of the Generation of the 60s whose poems I examined, although far more concerned with social and political topics, also appear to be aware of the importance of basing their works on the great models of the past. (See "La poesía tradicional y el compromiso ideológico en la expresión poética femenina de la Segunda Promoción de la Revolución Cubana," *La historia en la literatura iberoamericana*. Memorias del XXVI Congreso del Instituto Internacional de Literatura Iberoamericana. Edición, compilación y prólogo de Raquel Chang-Rodríguez y Gabriella de Beer (New York: Ediciones del Norte, 1989): 179-87.

[6]Due to the difficulty of finding the complete works of these contemporary and little-known poets, I have limited this study (as well as the other two previously mentioned) to the poems collected in a variety of anthologies. I must clarify also that, due to the lack of bibliographies and general information with regard to these poets, I have been unable to establish the exact dates of composition of most of their poems.

[7]*Poesía Compartida. Ocho poetas cubanos*, Roberto Cazorla, et al. (Miami: n.p., 1980): 19; henceforth PC.

[8]Obviously some images used by these poetas, do respond to this more limited vision and may be interpreted within the narrow context of the

Cuban Revolution.

[9]The refusal to write about immediate experiences is a lesson implicit in the pure poems of Juan Ramón Jiménez. He was not only the standard-bearer of pure poetry in the Hispanic world, but also a poet who suffered political exile at the end of the Spanish Civil War. In his poems, however, exile is always metaphysical. His opposition to writing circumstantial poems was legendary and he defended it in the following words: "Yo no creo que el poeta (como tanto se dice y más con esta nueva y más verdadera guerra del mundo [la guerra civil española]) deba nunca acomodar su poesía a las circunstancias; ahora, por ejemplo, a las de la guerra. No, no creo, ni he creído ni creeré nunca en la poesía de ocasión, ni en la guerra ni en la paz," *Guerra en España (1936–1953)* (Barcelona: Seix-Barral, 1985): 33.

[10]*La última poesía cubana. Antología reunida (1959–1973)*, Orlando Rodríguez Sardinas, Ed. (Madrid: Hispanonova, 1973): 385; henceforth LUPC

[11]*Poesía en Éxodo. El exilio cubano en la poesía (1959–1969)*. Ana Rosa Núñez, Ed. (Miami: Ediciones Universal, 1970): 82.

[12]See, for example, those included in the anthology *ISLAS*, Revista de la Universidad Central de Las Villas 9.4 (1987).

[13]*Poesía joven de Cuba*, Roberto Fernández Retamar & Fayad Jamis, Eds. (La Habana: Segundo Festival del Libro Cubano, ca. 1959): 85.

[14]*Antología de la poesía cubana*, José Miguel Oviedo, Ed. (Lima: Ediciones Paradiso, 1968): 147.

Paul Sierra

A la deriva

(1990: oil on canvas, 60" × 50")

Paul Sierra

Although I grew up in Cuba, life began for me when I enrolled in the Art Institute of Chicago. A visit to Puerto Rico in 1975 gave momentum and direction to my work as a painter. On that trip I rediscovered the imagery of the Caribbean I had left behind when my family emigrated to the American Midwest. It was the catalyst that helped me begin putting it all together as a painter— the imagery, the colors, and the personal statement.

Since 1985 my work has focused on the exploration of simultaneous realities within a single set of images. This trend began with a series of paintings depicting the rites and symbols of Afro-Cuban mysticism represented by Cuban *santería*. In these pieces the apparent realities were African mysticism counterbalanced by Spanish Catholicism, while the fundamental realities were the tangible world contrasted with the intangibility of the spiritual world.

In my recent pieces a landscape and an interior struggle to dominate the canvas. Landscape invades interior; interior reaches out to landscape; landscape overtakes interior. It is an uneasy relationship between two realities. Sometimes the relationship is one of open conflict; at other times the two realities coexist in uneasy détente.

The juxtaposition of interior and exterior has continued in the series on which I am currently at work. Here multiple realities occur as paintings within a landscape or interior within a painting. These pieces have helped me clarify in my own mind the motivations behind my desire to explore contrasting realities. It stems from the contrasting realities in my own life—my multiple identities as Cuban and American; as artist and everyday person; as man and boy; as dreamer and realist.

Paul Sierra

In My Garden the Hero Sleeps

1990: oil on canvas, 48" × 79"

Courtesy Opus Galleries, Miami

Contributors

Marjorie Agosin, born in Chile, is the author of five books of poetry, including *Zones of Pain* (White Pine Press, 1989) and *Bonfires* (Bilingual Review Press, 1990). She is also a literary critic and Associate Professor of Spanish at Wellesley College.

Luis Cruz Azaceta, born in La Habana, Cuba, resides in New York City. One of the USA's major artists, he has had numerous group and individual exhibitions at such galleries as the Frumkin/Adams Gallery, Lisa Sette Gallery, Opus Gallery and the Chicago International Art Exposition. His art was included in the international touring exhibition, *Hispanic Art in the United States: Thirty Contemporary Painters and Sculptors.*

Jesús J. Barquet, Ph.D. from Tulane University and Licenciatura from the University of Havana, teaches at Loyola University, New Orleans. He is the author of *Sagradas herejías* (Miami: Sibi, 1985) and *El Libro de las Estaciones* (New Orleans: Di Amatori, 1991); and received the Essay Prize in *V Letras de Oro 1990–91* for "Las peculiaridades del grupo *Orígenes* en el proceso cultural cubano."

Juan Armando Epple, Ph.D. Harvard, 1979, came to the USA in 1974 as an exile from Chile. His short stories have appeared in several anthologies, including *Chilean Writers in Exile* (1982). He was recently awarded the Grand Prize in a Chilean short story contest organized by *La Época*. He is an Associate Professor of Romance Languages at the University of Oregon.

Oliva Espín is Professor of Women's Studies at San Diego State University. She is a psychologist who specializes in therapy, research and training concerning issues of importance to Latina women.

Mary Lusky Friedman is Associate Professor of Spanish at Wake Forest University. Author of *The Emperor's Kites: A Morphology of Borges' Tales*, she is writing a book on José Donoso.

Ismael Frigerio, born in Chile and residing in New York City, has had various solo exhibitions in such galleries as Scott Alan Gallery, Intar Gallery, Galería Botello and the Museum of Contemporary Hispanic Art. His art was included in the international touring exhibition, *Hispanic Art in the United States: Thirty Contemporary Painters and Sculptors.*

Alina Galliano, from Cuba, was an Honorable Mention in the *Premio Letras de Oro* for her poetry collection *Entre el párpado y la mejilla*. Her poetry has appeared in various reviews and anthologies, including *Linden Lane Magazine, Poesía cubana contemporánea, Poetas hispanoamericanas contemporáneas.*

Alfredo Gómez Gil, born in Alicante, Spain, belongs to the group of "semi-exiled" poets who have followed those of the "Generación del 27" established in the USA. He is Professor of Spanish and Latin American Studies at Hartford College for Women.

Flora González Mandri, born in Cuba, teaches Spanish and Latin American Literature at Emerson College, Boston, "El regreso" is from a memoir titled *Una casa que rueda*, about the Cuban exile experience in the USA. She is writing a book on José Donoso.

Carolina Hospital, Cuban American writer and literary critic, resides in Miami, where she teaches English at Miami Dade Community College. She is the Editor of *Cuban American Writers: Los Atrevidos* (Linden Lane, 1988). Her poetry was also featured in *The Americas Review* 17.1 (1989).

A. Pablo Iannone, from Argentina, teaches philosophy at Central Connecticut State University. His publications include a poetry book, *Astérida* (1973), and various articles and books on philosophy. "South" is part of *Expatriate Memories*, which he began writing after coming to the USA.

Teresa Justicia, born and raised in Puerto Rico, has taught English at the University of Puerto Rico and New York University. She is presently an Assistant Professor of English at Hostos Community Collége, CUNY.

Pablo La Rosa, born in Cuba, is Assistant Professor of Spanish at Baker University. A collection of his stories, *Uvas, caletas y otros trópicos*, was a finalist in the 1988 *Letras de Oro* competition.

Adelaida López, born in Colombia, is the co-author of *Las dos caras de la escritura* and author of a children's novel, *Magia de tierra y agua*. Winner of the First Prize in the Linden Lane Poetry Contest, she teaches Spanish and Latin American Literature at Occidental College.

Edgar O'Hara, born in Lima, Perú, has published a book of poetry *Lengua en pena* (México: Fondo de Cultura Económica, 1982). He teaches Latin American Literature at the University of Washington.

José Paredes, born in Chile, is the author of five books of short fiction and poetry. His play, *Todas esas vidas*, was produced in Santiago, Chile, in 1985. He is Editor of the Editorial Sinfronteras.

José Quiroga, born in La Habana, Cuba, is Co-Editor of *Aldebarán, Revista de Literatura* (San Juan, P.R.). He recently completed a book of poetry, *Carne de papel*, and lives in Washington, D.C.

Guillermo Reyes, born in Chile, recently received his MFA in Theater from the University of California, San Diego. A play version of "Patroklos" called *Farewell to Hollywood* has been included in the Cleveland Public Theater's Festival of New Plays. His stories have been published in various journals, including *The Americas Review*, *Puerto del Sol*, and *Christopher Street*.

Louis Marcus Rodríguez, born in Santiago, Chile, is a graduate of the State Conservatory of Music of Trossingen (Germany). In the USA fulfilling a musical engagement at the time of the Chilean military coup, he decided to remain here. He has published books in various literary genres.

Eliana Rivero, born in Cuba, is Professor of Spanish at The University of Arizona. Her publications in the last five years reflect a growing interest in U.S. Hispanic Literatures. Her book *Infinite Divisions: An Anthology of Chicana Literature* (with Tey Diana Rebolledo) is forthcoming from The University of Arizona Press.

Freddy Rodríguez, born in the Dominican Republic, moved to New York City at age 18. He studied at the Art Students' League and the New School for Social Research, and received a degree in textile design from the Fashion Institute of Technology. His work has been exhibited at the Museum of Contemporary Hispanic Art, Scott Alan Gallery, the Queens Museum, and the Bronx Museum.

María A. Salgado, born in Tenerife (Canary Islands), is a Professor at the University of North Carolina at Chapel Hill. She has published numerous articles on Spanish and Spanish American literature with emphasis on Modernism and contemporary poetry. Her books include *El arte polifacético de las caricaturas líricas juanramonianas* and *Rafael Arévalo Martínez*.

Cynthia Schmidt is an Associate Professor of Spanish at the University of San Diego. Her studies focus on contemporary Latin American narrative, women writers and Latin American writers exiled in Spain.

Marcy E. Schwartz will receive her Ph.D. in 1991 from the Johns Hopkins University, where she teaches French and Spanish. Her translations will be included in the forthcoming anthology *Women Writing in Latin America*. She is an Assistant Professor of Spanish at Rutgers University.

Donald L. Shaw is Brown Forman Professor of Spanish American Literature at the University of Virginia. His publications include *Borges: Ficciones* (London: Grant & Cutler, 1976); *Nueva narrativa hispanoamericana* (Madrid: Cátedra, 1985), and *Alejo Carpentier* (Boston: Hall, 1985).

Paul Sierra, born in La Habana, Cuba, emigrated to the USA in 1961. He studied at the Art Institute of Chicago and the American Academy of Art. He is represented by Scott Alan Gallery (New York), Gwenda Jay Gallery (Chicago), Louis Newman Galleries (Beverly Hills) and Opus Gallery (Miami). His art was included in the international touring exhibition, *Hispanic Art in the United States: Thirty Contemporary Painters and Sculptors*.

Enrique Valdés, a Chilean author and musician, is the author of the novels *Ventanas al sur* (1975), *Trapananda* (1984) and *El trino del diablo* (1985). He is presently working on his Ph.D. in Spanish American Literature at the University of Illinois, Urbana-Champaign.